D1758817

MEDIEVAL WOMEN

Joachin
cleophe
salome
Jen suis contente
Jen suis contente

MEDIEVAL WOMEN

Deirdre Jackson

The British Library

For Kurt and Charlotte Weinberg

First published in 2015 by
The British Library
96 Euston Road
London NW1 2DB

ISBN 978 0 7123 5865 1

Designed by Maggi Smith, Sixism
Printed in Malta by Gutenberg Press

ACKNOWLEDGEMENTS

I am indebted to Lara Speicher and David Way for encouraging me to write this book and to Robert Davies for seeing it through to completion with patience and kindness. I am grateful to Sally Nicholls who obtained the images, and to Maggi Smith for her elegant design. I benefited from the advice of Monica Green, Margaret Howell, Henrietta Leyser, Katherine Smith, Anne Stanton and Alison Stones. Comments received from Kathryn Rudy and Barry Taylor, readers for the press, were clever and witty in equal measure. Anne Cobby, Judith Collard, Daniel Lacy, Deborah Latham, Nigel Morgan and Suzanne Paul read drafts of chapters and offered valuable suggestions. I am grateful to all of them. I also thank Sarah Biggs, Rebecca Bridgman, Diana Caulfield, Ilya Dines, Sibel Ergener, Garnet and Gayle Jackson, Hillary Ratna, Kristine Rose-Beers, Lucy Freeman Sandler, Patricia Stirnemann, Marina Voikhanskaya, Kurt and Charlotte Weinberg, and Catherine Yvard. For practical help, insight and good cheer, I relied on Amy Marquis. I owe a great debt to Nigel Morgan whose knowledge of medieval manuscripts has few parallels and whose willingness to share it is exemplary. I could not have persevered without the support of Stella Panayotova, Keeper of Manuscripts and Printed Books at the Fitzwilliam Museum; her dedication to research and visionary thinking are an inspiration. I am also obliged to other curators and keepers who permitted me to examine manuscripts in their collections, particularly members of staff at the British Library, Cambridge University Library and Cambridge colleges.

CONTENTS

INTRODUCTION

ONCE IGNORED or relegated to the periphery, women are no longer absent from studies of the life and culture of the Middle Ages, a period extending roughly from the fifth to the fifteenth century. The list of publications at the end of this book reflects the industry of scholars from a wide range of disciplines who have investigated women's contributions to Western European history and thought. Medieval society gave priority and privilege to men, but despite their shared subordinate status, women's experiences varied considerably from one individual to another. Shaped by geographical, political, legal and religious factors, a woman's life was further defined by her family background, marital status, number or lack of children, age, health, wealth and class. *Medieval Women* explores these issues, focusing specifically on the evidence provided by manuscripts. As outlined in the following pages, these objects offer us unparalleled insights into the values, beliefs and aspirations of the individuals who created them and the patrons for whom they were made.

The word 'manuscript' comes from the Latin noun *manus*, meaning hand, and the verb *scribere*, which means to write. Printing with moveable type was invented in Germany around 1455, but in the preceding centuries, every book was copied by hand on to carefully prepared animal skins with a pen made from a feather (*penna* in Latin). After scribes had completed their tasks, artists were often called upon to supply decorated initials and images, using precious metals and pigments derived, for the most part, from plants and minerals. Many of these paintings seem as vibrant today as the moment they were conceived. Because paintings in manuscripts survive in greater numbers and, generally, in better condition than those on walls and panels, they are the richest single source of medieval pictorial art that has been preserved.

Contrary to popular belief, although monasteries functioned as centres of learning and book production throughout the Middle Ages, not all manuscripts were made by monks. By the thirteenth century, commercial workshops made up of secular professionals had been established in university towns and urban centres, including Cambridge, Oxford, Paris, Bologna and London. Significant numbers of women worked alongside men in the book trade, helping to meet the growing

Christine de Pizan (*c.* 1364–1431), one of the first medieval women to earn her living as a writer. This manuscript of her collected works was made under her supervision. In 1414, she presented the volume to Isabeau of Bavaria, Queen of France.
Christine de Pizan, Collected Works, France, Paris, *c.* 1410–14.
Harley 4431, f. 4r

demand for manuscripts. In Paris in the mid-fourteenth century, for example, the illuminator Bourgot and her father, Jean le Noir, illustrated books for such illustrious patrons as John the Good, King of France, and his son and successor, Charles V. Impressed by their work, John the Good persuaded Bourgot and Jean to leave the service of their previous patron, Yolande of Flanders, Countess of Bar, and to focus instead on illuminating books for him. A deed of 1358 records that Charles V, acting as regent for his father, gave them a house in Paris that had been confiscated from a traitor. The property was in lieu of payments owed by the king to Bourgot and Jean, which must have been a considerable sum.[1] Making manuscripts was a thriving industry and one in which women participated as both craftspeople and patrons.

Christian, Jewish and Islamic manuscripts exhibit common features, but surviving copies of Hebrew and Arabic texts, made in medieval Europe, form a body of material that lies outside the scope of the present book.[2] It is worth noting, however, that Christians derived from Arabic authorities many of the medical remedies and beauty tips mentioned in the following pages, including a cure for halitosis and a balm designed for women whose lips had been chafed by their lover's kisses. Jewish scholars played a crucial role in the transmission of philosophical, scientific and medical knowledge to the West, and the Hebrew Tanakh (Christian Old Testament) was central to medieval theology and influenced people's conceptions of women. No book had a greater impact on medieval thought than the Bible, whose opening chapters describe the creation of Eve from Adam's side and her temptation by the serpent and enticement of Adam. Because Eve was perceived as a paradigm of women in general, this story was used to justify women's subordinate status and to illustrate their alleged weakness, cunning and sensuality.

The idea that the Church dominated all forms of artistic and literary production before the dawn of the Renaissance is, however, erroneous. Ample evidence contradicts the assertion that during the Middle Ages 'most art, music, and drama had religious themes and was displayed or performed in church buildings' and that 'the majority of literature was written and copied by clerics and concerned religious topics.'[3] Medieval writers challenge many of our assumptions, and even a cursory survey of medieval art and literature shows how futile it is for us to try to impose our own values and distinctions on the past. Categories such as religious and secular were defined in different ways, and the boundaries were often blurred. A detailed description of sexual intercourse occurs, for example, in the work of the twelfth-century German nun, Hildegard of Bingen. She acknowledged that women, as well as men, derive pleasure from the act, and described it from a woman's point of view. 'When a woman is making love with a man', wrote Hildegard, 'a sense of heat in her brain, which brings with it sensual delight, communicates the taste of that delight during the act … and soon the woman's sexual organs contract … in the same way as a strong man can hold something enclosed in his fist.'[4] By contrast, the 'secular' author Christine de Pizan (*c.* 1364–1431), one of the first medieval women to make a living as a writer, encouraged women to be modest, chaste, sober and pious, and to love and fear God. She also advised them to be cheerful to their husbands at all times and to ensure that dinner was ready to be served when they came home from work.[5]

To convey the contradictions, ambiguities and rich interplay between the sacred and profane, women are discussed under general themes in this book, rather than rigid categories. Medieval perceptions of gender and sexuality are considered in the first chapter, since these issues were germane to all women, including those who had taken vows of chastity. Moving from the universal to the particular, the next two chapters consider how individual women dealt with marriage and raised their children in a patriarchal society. Chapters four and five concern education and devotional practices, and chapter six, on literary patronage, shows how many women, though barred from universities, made major contributions to intellectual life. Although other chapters have a wide chronological span and geographical range, chapter six focuses on the multicultural environment of England from the twelfth century to the end of the thirteenth, because it was there that writers composed some of the very first works ever written in a modern European language. The final chapter, devoted to occupations, highlights the varied jobs accomplished by women, from shearing sheep to casting bells.

Throughout this book, images, a vital component of many medieval manuscripts, are analysed alongside texts. Just as different types of texts, from poems to tax records, reveal different facets of medieval life, pictures have their own language and deserve equal scrutiny. Traditionally, scholars in the discipline of art history have focused on problems relating to style and workshop practices, and they have attempted to distinguish the hands of different painters responsible for specific images or cycles of pictures and to detect collaborations between craftspeople. While fundamental to a full understanding of medieval images, these issues are not the focus of this book, which instead considers pictures in manuscripts as critical evidence of the ways people thought about and responded to women.

Artists who illustrated manuscripts frequently copied motifs from completed volumes, pattern books and other visual sources, and worked from preparatory sketches and written instructions rather than live models. Their depictions of women were, however, also shaped by their own observations. Endlessly inventive, artists recycled motifs to suit their purposes and devised new compositions that often surpassed their prototypes. Many images of women are idealised, but it was standard practice for medieval artists to represent women in contemporary guise. Consequently, images reflect general perceptions of female beauty as well as specific changes in fashion, down to minute details of hairstyles, accessories and sleeve lengths.

Far more manuscripts owned by royal and aristocratic women have been preserved than books made for less elevated patrons. For much of the Middle Ages, only the highest-born women had the financial means to commission manuscripts, the requisite education to read them and the time and privacy to do so. Deluxe books, gleaming with gold, retained their appeal and were passed down from one generation to the next, which also accounts for their survival. Gradually, however, women who were not born into privilege joined the ranks of readers. An eloquent witness to this development is an inscription written in a fifteenth-century prayer book by Jeanne Hervez, the wife of a Parisian grocer. Jeanne not only inserted her name in the book, but also added that if she happened to lose it, she would give 'a reward of beans and swiss chard to the person who returned it.'[6] The inscription is dated 1547, by which time both female literacy and the ownership of books in both manuscript and printed forms were widespread. Jeanne's book was made in the 1490s, over fifty years before she added her *ex libris*; she was evidently not the original owner of the manuscript, but had inherited it or purchased it second-hand.

In addition to the thousands of manuscripts that have survived, written records attest to the importance that women assigned to reading. The household accounts of Eleanor of Castile, Queen of England (1241–90), for example, show that she employed two scribes and an illuminator to make manuscripts for her. She valued their services so highly that she supplied their necessities, including their shoes, and they often travelled with the royal household. That Eleanor had her own scribal workshop was unparalleled – there is no evidence of a similar workshop at any other northern European court at this time.[7]

Records kept for Mahaut, Countess of Artois, another bibliophile, are delightfully detailed. These disclose, among other things, that Mahaut, who commissioned thirty books between 1300 and 1330 alone, was so concerned for her comfort while reading that she ordered a costly desk to be constructed for the purpose, and that in 1312 she paid a woman named Maroie, a female scribe, twenty-five sous for copying a devotional book for her.[8] Archival evidence also reveals that Isabeau of Bavaria, Queen of France and patron of Christine de Pizan, owned thirty-nine volumes which were entrusted to the care of her librarian Catherine de Villiers, who had previously been employed in a similar capacity by Jeanne de Bourbon, queen of Charles V.[9] Like Eleanor of Castile and numerous other royal and aristocratic women, Isabeau of Bavaria (1371–1435) took her books with her when she travelled, and documents show that in 1387 she had a trunk made for that purpose.[10] She also commissioned prayer books for her young daughters, so that they could learn to read.[11] Not surprisingly, women who owned books were the most likely to provide manuscripts for their children and to pass on their own habits of literacy, a topic covered in the chapter on learning.

Latin, the *lingua franca* of Europe used by the male elite, was both the language of higher education and the language of the Church. Some nuns were prodigiously learned, but relatively few women received an extensive education in Latin grammar. Nevertheless, more Latin prayer books have survived than any other single type of book owned by women, which strongly suggests that many learned to read the language. Some probably recited the prayers and psalms by rote, others would have attained a fuller comprehension of the texts, and still others would have achieved fluency. Oral tradition played a significant part in the devotional lives of medieval women, and many who had never seen let alone owned a prayer book, would have memorised the basic prayers (Our Father and Hail Mary) and the Creed, central to Christian belief. Joan of Arc, whose family was neither wealthy nor titled and who had a rudimentary education, certainly mastered her prayers, and, judging from the testimony of her contemporaries, her religious fervour surpassed that of many learned clerics.

By the twelfth century, when entertainers regaled courtly audiences with tales of adventure and romance, they used vernacular (everyday) languages that could be understood by the full range of people assembled, even those who had no formal education. As explained in the chapter on literary patronage, women who did not possess the requisite education to engage meaningfully with the Latin texts of the male clerical and academic elite were among the most active patrons of literature in the vernacular. They encouraged and rewarded writers and commissioned translations from Latin sources into the major languages spoken in Western Europe today. Works in the vernacular commissioned by women, or dedicated to them, include the earliest known treatise on healthcare in any modern European language, the earliest known historical chronicle, the earliest known military treatise, and the earliest known bestiary (book of beast lore). The period also saw the rise of the first female authors writing in the vernacular, literary pioneers, like Clemence of Barking and Marie de France, who forged a place for themselves in a field dominated by men.

Manuscripts made centuries ago in different parts of Europe form part of an immensely rich literary and artistic heritage. Most of the volumes discussed in *Medieval Women* are held by the British Library in London, which possesses one of the finest and most comprehensive collections of manuscripts in the world. Over two hundred of the most remarkable are on permanent public display at the British Library, and a significant number have been fully digitised and can be viewed on its website: http://www.bl.uk/manuscripts. It is important to consider illustrations in relation to the texts that they help to articulate and to see them in their original contexts. Readers who wish to do so will find many of the manuscripts examined in *Medieval Women* on the website. Thousands of images from other manuscripts may be viewed on the British Library's Digital Catalogue of Illuminated Manuscripts: http://www.bl.uk/catalogues/illuminatedmanuscripts/welcome.htm.

CHAPTER ONE

SEXUALITY

IMAGES OF WOMEN, reflecting ideas about femininity, sensuality and love, occur in a wide variety of medieval manuscripts and illustrate diverse texts, from devotional books to historical chronicles and tales of romance and adventure. In these works, women are variously presented as objects of desire, powerful seductresses, or independent individuals shaping the course of their own lives. Particular attributes of feminine beauty associated with youth – pale complexions, long fair hair, tiny waists and small breasts – were especially admired from the twelfth to the sixteenth century. These ideals were firmly linked to class. It is no coincidence that the highest-born women represented in medieval manuscripts have the smallest waists, the lightest complexions and the blondest hair.

Both medieval texts and images inform us about socially constructed roles for women, female sexuality, and codes of behaviour, as well as how feet were shod, breasts concealed, waists laced and hair arranged. Surviving beauty tips, including recipes for hair dye and cosmetics, and detailed descriptions of clothing demonstrate that medieval women with sufficient wealth and leisure made considerable efforts to enhance their appearance. Critical comments made by men who perceived women to be obsessed with fashion suggest that upper-class women wanted to appear attractive and to keep up with the latest trends. One father, writing *c.* 1371, warned his daughters of the foolishness of such behaviour: 'God have mercy on us this day after some [women] have heard of any new fashion or novelty of gown or array [and] shall never rest until they have a copy of it, and they say to their husband or lord every day: "Such a thing and such would become me well and it is very fair, I pray you that I may have it."'[1] His assumption that a woman would need the permission of a man to make a purchase reveals the underlying imbalance in power governing relations between the sexes in the late fourteenth century, but his description of a woman wanting a new dress or accessory is convincing. Gowns in vibrant hues and a multiplicity of styles, fur-lined cloaks and elaborate headdresses are among the details that attract our interest when we view images of women in illuminated manuscripts today.[2] Whether or not we agree with Oscar Wilde's assertion that 'life imitates art far more than art imitates life', it is probable

Allegorical illustration showing a lover addressing three fashionably dressed women outside the Castle of Love.
Charles of Orléans, Poems and other works.
S. Netherlands, Bruges, *c.* 1483, and *c.* 1490.
Royal 16 F. ii, f. 188r

that these details of costume and coiffure also appealed to the women who owned and perused these volumes and who may well have drawn inspiration from the ideals of feminine beauty presented in their books.

Ironically, images of one of the most desirable women depicted in medieval manuscripts, the beautiful Bathsheba, appear in devotional books designed to promote pious behaviour. According to the biblical narrative, King David saw Bathsheba bathing while he was walking on the roof of his palace. Although she was the wife of one of his soldiers, Uriah the Hittite, he summoned and slept with her, and she became pregnant. To conceal his sin David recalled her husband from battle, expecting that he would have sexual intercourse with Bathsheba and that David's affair and the paternity of the child would remain a secret. When Uriah did not sleep with his wife, David adopted a more drastic course of action, sending him back to war with a message instructing his commander to place him in the front lines, where he was killed.[3]

The story is depicted in a series of tinted drawings of Old Testament narratives in an English psalter, possibly commissioned by King Edward II or his consort, Isabella of France, *c.* 1310–20. Worthy of the noblest patron, it is an extraordinary book with an unrivalled pictorial programme, comprising 223 prefatory images, 24 calendar scenes, 104 half- or full-page paintings, 23 decorated initials and 464 drawings in the margins. Unlike many medieval manuscripts, which contain images by several artists, a single artist of exceptional talent who worked closely with one main scribe was responsible for the bulk of the illustrations. The first tinted drawing

King David on the ramparts of his castle, conversing with Bathsheba, wife of Uriah the Hittite. This Psalter was possibly commissioned by Isabella of France (1295–1358), consort of King Edward II of England. It derives its name from Queen Mary Tudor, who owned it in the sixteenth century.
The Queen Mary Psalter, England, probably London, *c.* 1310–20.
Royal 2 B. vii, f. 56v

King David commits adultery with Bathsheba, wife of Uriah the Hittite. The Queen Mary Psalter, England, probably London, *c.* 1310–20. Royal 2 B. vii, f. 57r

illustrating the affair between David and Bathsheba shows the king on the ramparts of his castle, gesturing to Bathsheba who stands in an adjacent tower. His intentions are revealed in the caption beneath, which reads: '*Coment david mountaunt soun chastel vist Bersabee la femme urye e la priast de fornicacion e ele consenti*' ('How David ascending his castle saw Bathsheba, the wife of Uriah, and asked her to have sex with him, and she consented'). Curiously, the object of David's desires is shown fully clothed rather than in the act of bathing. The idea that David spied on Bathsheba from the vantage point of the palace roof has also been misunderstood or rejected by the artist, who instead has them greeting each other from nearby buildings like genial neighbours. Exceptionally blunt, the caption alone conveys the message that this is a scene of seduction. Without the caption, which is written in Anglo-Norman French, the language employed by the English nobility at the time the book was made, we could mistakenly think that the elegant figures are chatting about the weather.

The next scene shows the king in bed with Bathsheba, who drapes her arm over him as if to suggest that she is a willing partner. A less sensuous interpretation of the lovers' tryst would be hard to imagine; both individuals gaze into the middle distance as if consumed by boredom, and bedclothes conceal their bodies. Subsequent panels include David handing Uriah the message that is effectively his

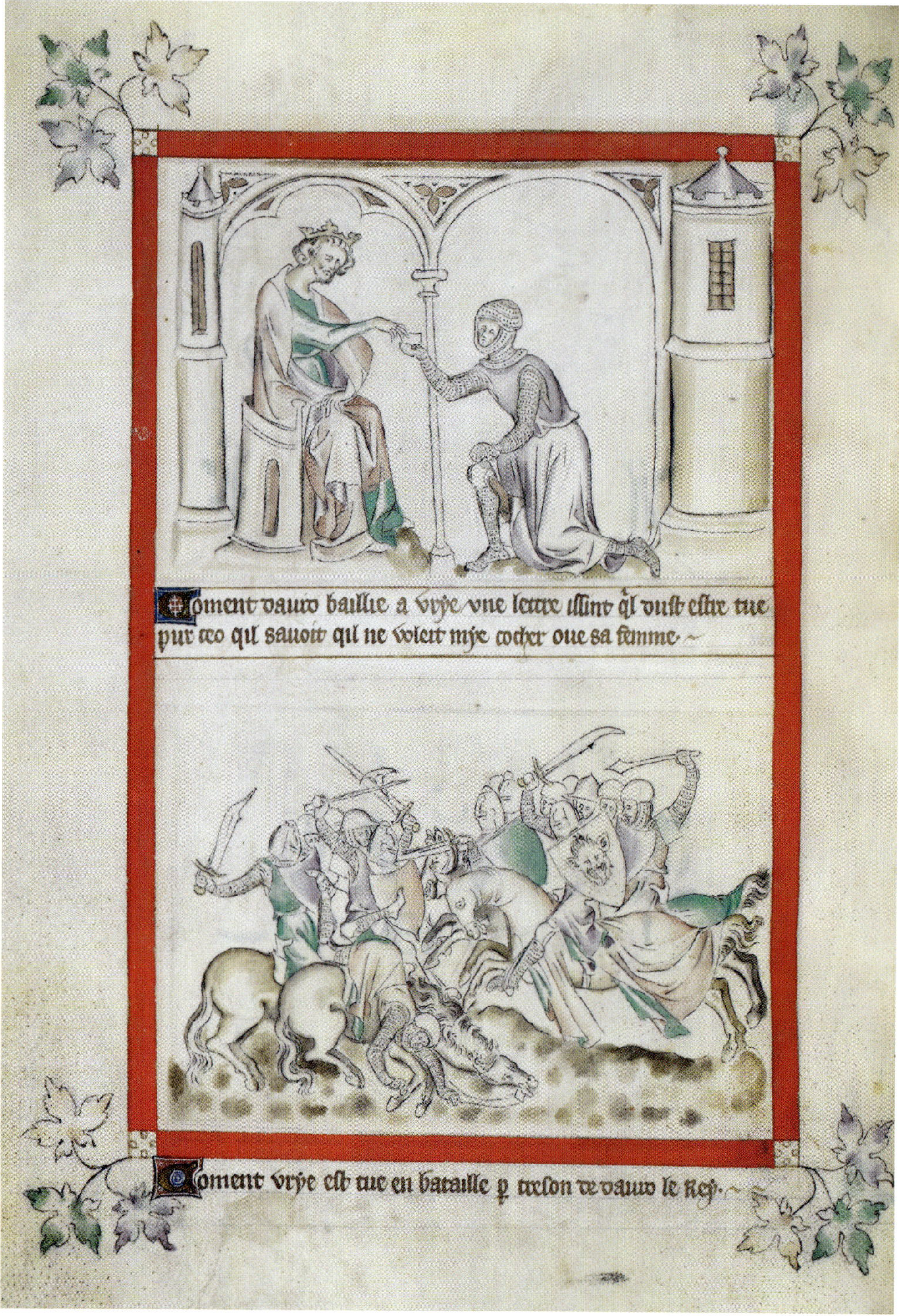

King David sending Uriah into battle; Uriah slain. The Queen Mary Psalter, England, probably London, *c.* 1310–20. Royal 2 B. vii, f. 57v death warrant, and the latter toppling from his horse, having received a fatal blow. The final caption, 'How Uriah is killed in battle by the treachery of David the king', is a harsh but accurate indictment of the king. The figures are shown in fourteenth-century guise, which would have made the ancient story seem up-to-date to its courtly audience. Uriah, encased in chain mail, is a faithful knight and vassal, never flinching from duty to his king, while David, instead of honouring his feudal obligations, is exposed as an adulterer and murderer. Although she complies with David's request, Bathsheba is not characterised as a seductress in this cycle of images, and her body is hardly exposed.

Although artists had previously created narrative scenes showing Bathsheba in the nude,[4] a new way of telling the story emerged in France *c.* 1460; artists wanting to explore the possibilities offered by the naked female form focused specifically on Bathsheba, delineating in explicit detail the physical attributes of the woman who inspired the king's lust.[5] In illustrations of this type, David is a figure in late middle age, often running to fat, and is generally shown in the distance, usually at a window or balcony. With the king relegated to the background, the beautiful young Bathsheba serves not only to stimulate David's illicit thoughts, but also, potentially, those of viewers of the paintings, who are privileged to share the object of the king's gaze and desire. Painters often used framing devices to enhance the impression that Bathsheba was within arm's reach. A stone surround, for example, frames the image of Bathsheba in a book of hours, made for an unknown patron in western France (perhaps Angoulême or Cognac), *c.* 1500, creating an aperture through which the viewer is invited to look (p. 18). The Latin inscription, incised on the sill, reads: '*Domine ne in furore tuo arguas me*' ('Lord, rebuke me not in thy indignation'), the opening words of the first penitential psalm (Psalm 6). But the allusion to God's anger at David's adulterous affair with Bathsheba, an event that has yet to take place at the moment captured in the painting, does little to distract our gaze from the woman immersed in the fountain.[6]

As represented in the image, Bathsheba, with her golden hair and small breasts, epitomises medieval ideals of female beauty that were espoused for centuries. In a sermon on the Song of Songs, the twelfth-century cleric Hugh of Fouilloy digressed from his theological musings to disclose his appreciation of small breasts: 'beautiful indeed are breasts that protrude but little and are moderately full … restrained, but not compressed, gently bound so that they are not free to jounce about.'[7] Heroines of medieval literature also exemplify prevailing concepts of female beauty. For example, Nicolette, the heroine of the anonymous romance *Aucassin and Nicolette*, composed *c.* 1200, is described as follows: 'she had fair and tightly curling hair, laughing grey eyes, a straight nose set in an oval face, and red lips, brighter than any cherry or rose in June; her teeth were small and white, and her small, firm breasts

Bathsheba bathing.
Book of Hours, France,
perhaps Angoulême or Cognac,
c. 1500. King's 7, f. 54r

lifted the bodice of her dress as they might have been two walnuts, while her waist was so tiny that you could have ringed it with your two hands.'[8] As shown on the facing page, Bathsheba's hair is fair, and her breasts, though larger than walnuts, are sufficiently small to adhere to medieval standards of feminine beauty. Her right breast is about to be pierced by a dart released from the bow of the stone *Amor* (Cupid) adorning the fountain. The presence of Cupid, and of the personification of Abundance (an allusion to fecundity) directly opposite, adds another dimension to the tale. Although nowhere stated in the Bible, in which Bathsheba's feelings towards David go unrecorded, the inclusion of Cupid in the miniature strongly suggests that Bathsheba will respond positively to the king's overtures.

Female personification of lust (*Luxure*). The male goat on which she rides is a symbol of sexual potency. In the background, King David spies on Bathsheba.
The Dunois Hours, France, Paris, *c.* 1440–50 (after 1436).
Yates Thompson 3, f. 172v

The story of David and Bathsheba showed that unchecked lust could lead to adultery, murder and, ultimately, hell. Reciting the seven penitential psalms, attributed to the repentant David, was believed to be one of the best ways to resist the seven deadly sins: pride, idleness, anger, gluttony, avarice, envy and lust. In a remarkable book of hours painted *c.* 1430 by one of the most active artists in Paris, each of the seven penitential psalms (6, 31, 37, 50, 101, 129, 142) is matched with an allegorical illustration of one of the seven deadly sins. Lust (*Luxure*), at Psalm 129, is shown as an alluring woman dressed in a golden gown with fur-lined sleeves and a fashionable horned headdress known as a temple or *hennin*. Enchanted by her own appearance, she gazes into a mirror, a symbol of vanity. Reminiscent of those wielded by Eros, the two arrows she clutches in her right hand allude to her seductive powers, while the male goat on which she rides is a symbol of sexual potency ('horniness'). Numerous medieval authors described the animal as libidinous. 'The he-goat (*hircus*) is a lascivious animal, butting and always eager to mate; his eyes look sideways on account of wantonness', wrote Isidore of Seville in his seventh-century *Etymologies*, a vast encyclopedia consulted throughout the Middle Ages that was widely disseminated and served as inspiration for writers of the bestiaries.[9]

While Lust canters through a garden, a traditional setting for amorous adventures in medieval illustrations, David and Bathsheba are portrayed in the background. The king stands at the left with his mouth agape, seemingly stupefied by Bathsheba's beauty, and the latter, with lily-white

Jean, Comte de Dunois adoring the Virgin and Child. Although women certainly commissioned and read books of hours, many beautifully decorated copies, like this one, were made for male patrons. The Dunois Hours, France, Paris, *c.* 1440–50 (after 1436). Yates Thompson 3, f. 22v skin, appears on the right, immersed in a wooden bathtub. Although she is bathing, Bathsheba retains her own elaborate horned headdress, which echoes the one worn by Lust and creates a visual parallel between the two women, both of whom exemplify the dangers of erotic desire. High-status women in other contemporary images are frequently depicted with headdresses like these but without negative connotations. In the context of this particular painting, however, the prongs protruding from the women's heads mimic the horns of the goat on which Lust is mounted, underscoring the sexual message of the composition.

The arms in the border are those of Jean de Dunois (1402–68), who commissioned the manuscript and whose portrait is incorporated in three illustrations, including a depiction of him kneeling before the Virgin Mary. A professional soldier and supporter of Joan of Arc, he was one of the key commanders to drive the English from France and played a decisive role in the capture of Paris. Known as the Bastard of Orléans, Jean himself was the issue of an adulterous union between Louis of France (the brother of King Charles VI) and Mariette d'Enghien, wife of the Picard knight, Aubert de Cany.

Of the seven deadly sins pictured in Jean's book of hours, only Lust and Envy are women, while Pride, Idleness, Anger, Gluttony and Avarice are male. Lust is often represented as a woman in medieval art, but there are notable exceptions. In a book of hours painted in Poitiers *c.* 1475 by Robinet Testard, for example, Lust is shown as a young man riding a goat and stroking one of its horns while men and women, encouraged by a demon, embrace each other in the lower border.[10]

As portrayed in the biblical narrative, Bathsheba elicits our sympathy. She has little choice when she is summoned by David and mourns the death of her husband Uriah, cynically masterminded by her new, powerful lover. Another cause for grief is the death, a few days after its birth, of the child she conceives with David. In the Bible, the blame is assigned to the king alone: 'this thing which David had done, was displeasing to the Lord' (II Samuel 11:27), and it is David, rather than Bathsheba, who is rebuked by the prophet Nathan.

Misogynistic interpretations of the story of David and Bathsheba were, however, common among medieval theologians. Placing the blame for David's sin on Bathsheba, they characterised her as an archetypal seductress whose beauty was the catalyst for the king's moral and spiritual failure, and whose behaviour was typical of women in general. This unsympathetic view was entrenched centuries before the development of titillating images of Bathsheba. Hildebert of Lavardin (1055–1133), for instance, who represents one extreme, wrote, 'A frail thing is woman, constant only in crime. Never on her own does she desist from harm … Consuming all things, she is consumed by every vice. And preying on men, she makes herself the prey. A woman deprived Paris of his sense and Uriah of his life,

David of his virtue, Solomon of his faith.'[11] Not surprisingly, given this negative image, Bathsheba was included in the canon of women reputed by medieval writers to have used their physical charms to gain mastery over men, something that all women allegedly had the potential to do.[12]

In a treatise on proper conduct for women, written for his daughters in 1371–2, Geoffroy de la Tour Landry portrays Bathsheba as a seductress and implies that she staged the encounter with David:

> She [Bathsheba] washed and combed her hair [standing] before a window where the king could see her clearly; she had very beautiful and blonde hair. And as a result the king was tempted by this and sent for her …. And so King David sinned doubly by lust and by murder …. And all his sinfulness came from her combing her beautiful hair and her pride in it. Every woman should cover herself, and should not take pride in herself, nor display herself so as to please the world with her beautiful hair, nor her neck, nor her bosom, nor anything that should be kept covered.[13]

While he does not mention Bathsheba's other physical attributes that may well have caught David's attention, Geoffrey imparts to his daughters the message that public grooming, especially if one has long blonde hair, can lead directly to adultery and homicide. This is not as preposterous as it first sounds. Many surviving ivory combs and mirrors feature scenes of lovers and amorous inscriptions, and Geoffrey's original readers would have recognised that because these items frequently were given as love tokens, and because women often combed their hair just before they went to bed, the activity was associated with sensual pleasures.[14] Geoffrey's description of Bathsheba owes nothing to the original biblical narrative, which simply states that she was 'very beautiful'. Geoffrey's remarks on hair in general and blondeness in particular reflect medieval preferences and preoccupations.

One of the most histrionic reactions to blonde hair is that of Lancelot, the rescuer and lover of Guinevere, wife of King Arthur, as recounted by Chrétien de Troyes in his poem, *Le Chevalier de la Charrette* (*The Knight of the Cart*) written *c.* 1176–82 for Countess Marie de Champagne, eldest daughter of King Louis VII of France and Eleanor of Aquitaine. Literary dedications were intended to flatter patrons and are often extravagant in their claims, but it is worth noting that in the prologue, Chrétien states that the poem's '*matiere et san*' (subject matter and meaning) were supplied by the countess, whose court was a hub of literary creativity. Lancelot's adoration of Guinevere is constant throughout. A comb, lost by the queen and found by chance by one of his companions, evokes such strong emotions that he almost falls off his horse. It is not the comb itself he values (he gives it away), but strands of Guinevere's hair, 'so bright, so clear, so brilliant', which he carefully extracts from it, first 'touching them a hundred thousand times, caressing [them] with his eyes, his lips, his forehead, his face' and then slipping them between 'his shirt and his heart', a treasure more precious to the lovelorn knight than holy relics or 'a wagon-load of emeralds or diamonds.'[15] How blonde was Guinevere? Chrétien, the only writer of French medieval romance to characterise her as such,[16] resorts to a cumbersome metaphor to do her hair justice. He writes, 'let me tell you that gold refined a hundred times, and then again, would have seemed to him, if you set that gold against a single strand of hair, darker than night compared to a summer's day.'[17]

Surviving recipes for blond hair dye, including one advocating washing the hair with a cleanser made from the ashes and bark of ivy wood two or three times a day for three months,[18] suggest that some women resorted to laborious methods

A woman offers her companion a jar of ointment. This illuminated initial, from a health treatise, written for Beatrice of Savoy (*c.* 1207–66), Countess of Provence, marks the opening of the chapter on the care of the face. Aldobrandino of Siena, *Le Régime du corps*, N. France, Cambrai or Thérouanne/St-Omer, *c.* 1265–70. Sloane 2435, f. 37r to achieve tresses that sparkled like a medieval heroine's. Ointments were used to promote a pale complexion, another key attribute of feminine beauty. Keeping lips supple and soft was imperative, and balms, including one made from lilies, were designed for women suffering from cracked lips 'on account of the excessive embraces' and kisses of their lovers.[19] An additional trait considered desirable for woman was sweet breath, something that was difficult to achieve before the advent of modern dental hygiene. A medical text based on a treatise from Salerno, south of Naples, where both men and women practised medicine in the eleventh and twelfth centuries, offers a cure for halitosis, derived from a 'Saracen [i.e. Muslim] woman':

> She took several laurel leaves, a little musk, and ordered the women to hold it under their tongues so as to render the heaviness of their breath unnoticeable. I also recommend this: the woman should hold this remedy under her tongue day and night, especially when she has to carry out the sexual act with someone.[20]

Understandably, the close proximity demanded by sexual intercourse made fresh breath desirable, but it was also important for less intimate social encounters. In his *Chastoiement des Dames* (*The Ladies' Instruction*), a poem on the conduct of women, composed *c.* 1250, Robert de Blois counselled those with bad breath to hold it while exchanging the kiss of peace during Mass and to chew anise, fennel and cumin in the morning.[21]

Lancelot with Guinevere, King Arthur's queen (below left); Lancelot and Guinevere commit adultery (below right). Containing 437 images, this manuscript forms part of a multi-volume set with a total of 748 illustrations.
Lancelot, N. France, Saint-Omer, Tournai or Ghent, *c.* 1320.
Additional 10293, f. 199r, left; f. 312v, right

Desire for a woman, whether she had sweet breath or not, could be all-consuming. From his first encounter with Guinevere, King Arthur's queen, Lancelot is transformed by love. His passion for her motivates all of his actions, every battle fought, humiliation endured and triumph celebrated, causing him to tolerate her aloofness, reciprocate her embraces and become the finest knight. As Lori J. Walters has observed, 'Lancelot's perfection as knight is made possible only because of his total and unquestioning devotion to his lady … Lancelot becomes Arthur's most resourceful knight precisely *because* of his adulterous love for Arthur's wife.'[22] As portrayed by Chrétien, Lancelot is obsessed by feelings for a noble woman who is married and unattainable. Apparently not that unattainable, however, for instead of deflecting Lancelot's desires, Guinevere responds by expressing her own. The queen 'emerges as a female figure who fulfils her own needs and desires; away from the confining atmosphere of Arthur's court, Guinevere shows herself to be … intelligent, level-headed, and determined.'[23]

Chrétien, telling how Lancelot, having ripped the bars away from her window, gains access to her bedchamber, stresses Guinevere's active role in the affair: 'the queen reached out her arms and drew him down, holding him tight against her breast, making the knight as welcome in her bed, and as happy, as she possibly could, impelled by the power of love, and her own heart … And the knight had what he wanted, for the queen willingly gave him all the pleasures of herself, held him in her arms as he was holding her.'[24]

In a later anonymous account of their affair, known as the prose *Lancelot* written *c.* 1230, Guinevere takes the initiative at the moment of their first kiss, seizing Lancelot by the chin and giving him a prolonged kiss on the lips when she realises that he is too overcome with emotion to react. A depiction of the first kiss, and three scenes of Lancelot and Guinevere making love,[25] are included in a copiously illustrated copy of the prose *Lancelot*, made in northeastern France or Flanders (St Omer, Tournai or Ghent), *c.* 1320. A censorious reader, at some unknown date, mutilated one of the lovemaking scenes, but the pair can be seen in the other images, kissing and frolicking in bed. Not all readers were disapproving. A scribe who left a note in a different manuscript tells us that he was asked by his female patron to skip several knightly adventures in order to arrive more quickly at the heart of the story, in which the romance between Lancelot and Guinevere is described.[26]

The frank portrayal of erotic desire, expressed in the story of Lancelot and Guinevere, also occurs in other medieval texts such as the *Roman de la Rose* (*Romance of the Rose*), one of the most popular and widely read medieval poems, which survives in over 300 manuscripts and sustained its popularity from the late thirteenth to the early sixteenth century. In this allegorical work devoted to the theme of love, begun by Guillaume de Lorris *c.* 1230 and completed by Jean de Meun about forty years later, we find, for example, the myth of the adulterous affair between Venus, goddess of love, and Mars, god of war, a retelling of the incident recorded by Ovid in his *Metamorphoses*. Repelled by her husband Vulcan, who was filthy from working at his forge, Venus took as her lover the handsome Mars. Wishing to disgrace the pair, jealous Vulcan took his revenge. Catching the lovers in bed, he bound them together, with bonds of his own devising, and called the other gods to witness their discomfort. To his chagrin, the plan backfired spectacularly. Instead of sympathising with Vulcan, the other gods mocked him, envying Mars his good fortune and wishing that they could take his place. More galling still to Vulcan, from that time forth Venus and Mars pursued their pleasure openly, since they had nothing left to hide. An exceptionally beautiful copy of the poem, made in Bruges *c.* 1490–1500, contains an image of a self-satisfied young Mars in bed, with his arm draped possessively around Venus, looking not in the least perturbed by his predicament. The *Roman* appends no moralising message to the story. On the contrary, the anecdote is told by a caricatured old woman in a satirical speech encouraging young women to be promiscuous.

Vulcan discovers his wife Venus in bed with Mars.
Guillaume de Lorris and Jean de Meun, *Roman de la Rose*, S. Netherlands, Bruges, *c.* 1490–1500. Harley 4425, f. 122v

Styling herself a professor of love, the 'crone' offers a series of practical beauty tips. In order to attract lovers (and why devote yourself to one?) a woman should use hair extensions if her own hair is sparse; adorn her head with towering horns, rivalling those of a buck, stag or unicorn; wear low-cut dresses; bind her breasts if they are large, in order to dance more enjoyably; and keep her 'Venus chamber' clean. Recourse to hair dye and ointments to enhance the complexion, as well as more advice on what to do about bad breath, are also incorporated in her monologue.[27] While offering similar recommendations to those found in advice manuals for young women, the old woman's speech subverts the genre. Her intention is not to improve a girl's moral and social standing, but to ensure that she acquires as many lovers as possible.

Recounted near the end of the *Roman de la Rose*, the myth of Pygmalion, another narrative derived from Ovid's *Metamorphoses,* also centres on the fulfilment of sexual desire. Pygmalion, aptly described by Michael Camille as 'an artist who made his own girlfriend', fell madly in love with a female figure he created.[28] The sculpture at first failed to respond to him, staying as 'rigid as a stake' even though he kissed her cold mouth, clothed her in fur-lined dresses, slid rings on to her icy fingers and, after placing her on his bed, strove 'to rouse some warmth' in her as she lay in his arms.[29] Only after Pygmalion had prayed at the temple of Venus,

The sculptor Pygmalion dresses his statue (above); Pygmalion embraces the statue, trying to coax it into life (above right). This manuscript was illuminated by Robinet Testard for Charles d'Orléans, Comte d'Angoulême, and his wife Louise de Savoy (1476–1531), mother of Francis I, King of France. Guillaume de Lorris and Jean de Meun, *Roman de la Rose*, France, late fifteenth century (1487–95). Oxford, Bodleian MS Douce 195, f. 150r and f. 151r

begging the goddess to animate the statue, did his beloved come alive. His prayer to Venus is a parody of Christian morality; instead of beseeching Christ and the saints to guard him from fornication, Pygmalion vowed that he would never be chaste again if Venus answered his plea, and he made good on his promise by impregnating the statue after she/it had sprung to life.

Detailed descriptions of the various pieces of clothing and love tokens offered to the statue by Pygmalion, including flowers, earrings, a belt and a little purse, in which he placed golden coins and five little stones worn smooth by the sea 'such as maids for a game of marbles use', reflect actual garments worn by courtly women when the work was composed and gifts that they could expect to receive from their suitors, but the sculpture is the ultimate male fantasy, a customised object of desire.

Pygmalion attempted to heat up his statue by embracing it. In the Middle Ages, as today, the metaphor of heat was commonly used to signify sexual arousal. Various medieval writers acknowledged that caressing a woman's breasts was a good way to kindle her fire. In his poem of *c.* 1250, the *Chastoiement des dames* (*The Ladies' Instruction*), Robert de Blois states:

> For this reason were the breasts enclosed: that no other man should place his hand there … a woman who allows her bare breasts to be touched, and her flesh to be touched underneath and on top, does not object to the rest of it [i.e. sexual intercourse]. What better way to heat up him and her, but by touching? And by the heat that is thus made, she agrees just as soon to the rest.[30]

Although it is Robert's intention to discourage men's wandering hands and a compliant attitude in women, he acknowledges that both sexes can 'heat up', and that breasts are erogenous zones for women, not only objects of male desire. Some other medieval authors described in positive terms caressing a woman's breasts as a prelude to sexual intercourse. More direct remarks on the subject are included in Arabic treatises on health and sexuality. 'If you want to arouse the girl, play with her breasts and you will witness a marvel', advises at-Tîâfâshî (1184–1253); 'the woman is drawn to sexual commerce, when one plays with her breasts, and, especially when she is older, do not deprive her of this pleasure.'[31] Avicenna, the eleventh-century Persian polymath whose *Canon* was a standard university textbook consulted, for example, by the students at the famous medical faculty in Montpellier, likewise alluded to stroking a woman's breasts during foreplay, but his remarks on this particular subject elicited little comment from Western scholars.[32]

A man strokes his lover's breasts.
Guillaume de Lorris and Jean de Meun,
Roman de la Rose,
France, possibly Paris,
c. 1380. Egerton 881, f. 126r

Among the natural phenomena described in certain medieval bestiaries are *lapides igniferi* (fire stones), some feminine, others masculine, found on a certain mountain in the East. According to the text, 'when they are at a distance from one another no fire is kindled between them. When, however, the female should happen to approach the male, at once fire is kindled, so that everything around the mountain is ablaze.' An illustration of the subject shows, in the lower half, a couple engulfed in flames, and above, the pair banging the two stones together. The anonymous author, primarily addressing a monastic audience, spells out the moral: 'Men of God, who value that life of yours, distance yourself from women, lest, when you approach one another, the fire be kindled in you both.'[33] He then cites specific biblical figures who refrained from or committed sexual sins and concludes that the love inspired by women, which began to rage at the beginning of time, continues to burn. Distance is crucial. Touching inflames desire and sets the mountain ablaze.

In his vast work on natural history, *De animalibus* (*On Animals*), which includes such wide-ranging topics as 'the greater cleverness of the small animals' and 'the skill required to control bees', the Dominican scholar Albertus Magnus (d. 1280) asserts that adolescent girls are particularly susceptible to feelings of lust.[34] He states, 'certain girls, at about the age of fourteen, cannot have their fill of intercourse. If they have no male at this time, they nevertheless busy their mind[s] with intercourse with a male and they often imagine their penises. They might often rub themselves with their fingers or other instruments until their pathways are loosened by the heat of the rubbing or intercourse … Also at this time the menstrual flow occurs, and defilements, both in dreams and while awake, are multiplied. They then press their legs together, crossing one over the other so that one part of the vulva rubs the other since from this there arises pleasure and defilement.'[35] Since Albertus Magnus does not cite his source, it is impossible to determine the origin of his

Kindling a blaze with *lapides igniferi* (fire stones). In the Middle Ages, as today, the metaphor of heat was commonly used to signify sexual arousal. Bestiary from Holy Trinity Priory, York. The priory's ownership inscription appears at the bottom of the page, England, York, *c.* 1220. Oxford, St John's College, MS 61, f. 103v information. Elsewhere he claims that 'a lustful woman' confided in him that she liked to expose her private parts 'and took great pleasure in catching up wind in her uterus,'[36] but whether his discussion of the solitary pleasures experienced by young women is based on oral testimony or a written authority is uncertain.

The idea that pubescent girls are particularly susceptible to sexual feelings is also conveyed in the illustration for the entry 'Adolescence' in a fourteenth-century encyclopaedia, the *Omne bonum*, compiled by the London clerk James le Palmer (b. *c.* 1327), who worked in the Royal Exchequer. Ambitious and idiosyncratic, the text, based on many different sources, survives in a single copy written in James' own hand.[37] The image, which shows a young man and woman standing next to each other, incorporates allusions to sexual desire. Holding a mirror in one hand and raising her skirt with the other, the young woman looks directly at her male companion as if soliciting his attention, while he touches the pommel of the sword that hangs suggestively between his legs. Neither the text nor the image is explicit, but the underlying message 'is that adolescence is an age of heat that needs to be restrained'.[38]

Adolescence, the age of sexual awakening, as depicted in an initial 'A' for *Adolescens/ Adolescencia* in an encyclopedia written by the London clerk, James le Palmer. James gleaned information from a wide variety of sources and arranged it in alphabetical order. His vast encyclopedia contains over 2000 pages of text and 800 illustrations. James le Palmer, *Omne Bonum*, England, London, *c.* 1360–75. Royal 6 E. vi, f. 58v

Fires can be kindled in different ways. It is, of course, possible for a woman to have erotic feelings for another woman and for those feelings to be reciprocated. References to women experiencing same-sex desire are scarce in medieval sources from Western Europe. Furthermore, the majority of texts that do allude to sexual relations between women were written by men. Guides for priests assigning penances for sins committed, for example, sometimes allude to vices committed by women with women and to the fashioning of 'diabolical instruments', but these do not generally describe the specific activities involved.[39] A rare image of female lovers, found in a thirteenth-century Parisian picture Bible, probably commissioned by Queen Blanche of France in the early 1220s, is just as oblique in its allusion to sexual relations between women. It shows two fully clothed young women embracing, one of whom reaches up to stroke her lover's cheek, a standard gesture of seduction. The leg of the woman on the right, which is positioned between her lover's thighs, is also suggestive. The action in the foreground, however, which illustrates the sin of sodomy, is much less ambiguous. There, a man with his breeches undone, who is clearly anticipating more than a chaste kiss, lies on top of his male companion. Devils poised nearby in readiness strongly suggest that both couples are bound for hell.

Relatively few male authors, who had limited understanding of such things, attempted to articulate precisely what women did when they made love together.

Same-sex couples. The specialized picture bible in which this image occurs was probably commissioned by Queen Blanche of Castile, Queen of France (1188–1252). *Bible moralisée*, France, Paris, early 1220s. Vienna, Österreiches Nationalbibliothek, MS 2554, f. 2r

A substitute for the male member was probably employed, thought Hincmar of Reims, who stated, 'They do not put flesh to flesh in the sense of the genital organ of one within the body of the other, since nature precludes this, but they do transform the use of the member in question into an unnatural one, in that they are reported to use certain instruments of diabolical operation to excite desire.'[40] The anonymous author of a late thirteenth-century treatise called the *Breviarium practice*, wrongly attributed to Arnaud of Villanova, also alludes to sex between women and their recourse to mechanical aids. According to this source, the wives of some Italian merchants, keen for sex but not wanting to risk falling pregnant by male lovers when their husbands were away on business, engaged in sexual relations with each other and made use of such devices.[41] For an author who was writing within the confines of a Cistercian monastery, he seems remarkably well informed.

A lengthier description of sex between women occurs in the *Livre des manières* of Étienne de Fougères, Bishop of Rennes (1168–78), who clearly finds the idea absurd and piles metaphor on metaphor to ensure that his readers will do likewise. 'These ladies have made up a game,' he writes, 'with two bits of nonsense they make nothing; they bang coffin against coffin, without a poker stir up their fire. They don't play at "poke in the paunch", but join shield to shield without a lance. They have no concern for a beam in their scales, nor a handle in their mold. Out of water they fish for turbot and they have no need for a rod. They don't bother with a pestle in their mortar nor a fulcrum for their see-saw.'[42] He notes that sex between women cannot result in offspring, but his many veiled references to the penis show that his main fixation is the absence of the male member (or a substitute) and its apparent irrelevance to the ladies playing the 'game'.

The German abbess Hildegard of Bingen (1098–1179), one of the few medieval women whose views on the topic have survived, likewise stressed the transgressive nature of same-sex desire. In her most famous work, *Scivias*, she writes, 'a woman who appropriates for herself these devilish arts, in that she simulates intercourse, taking the part of a man, with another women, appears most vile in my sight … since she who should feel shame about her desire has impudently taken another law unto herself. And since such people have transformed themselves into a different mode they are contemptible to [God].'[43] For Hildegard, a woman who had sex with another woman usurped a man's place.

Thousands of declarations of love, often couched in poetic and courtly language, celebrate emotional bonds between men and women, but almost no Western

European medieval texts allude to romantic love between women. In a manuscript from Tegernsee, southern Germany, however, we find two poems, dating from the late twelfth or early thirteenth century, which express the feelings of one woman for another. These go well beyond affection. Written by a woman separated from her lover, one of the poems expresses her longing to be reunited. 'When I remember the kisses you gave, and with what words of joy you caressed my little breasts, I want to die', she writes, '... for in the world there is no woman born so lovable, so dear, one who loves me without feigning, with such deep love.' Holding fast to her memories of their happy union, the poet ends with a promise and a plea: 'While the world lasts you'll never be effaced from the centre of my heart. Why say more? Return, sweet love! Do not delay your journey longer.'[44]

Statements expressing pleasure in the physical act of love, remarkable for their frankness, are also found in the surviving letters written by Heloise (d. *c.* 1163) to her one-time lover and husband, Peter Abelard. While Heloise was still a young woman living in Paris, Abelard, intrigued by her intellectual precocity, devised a plan to seduce her, offering to be her tutor in order to spend time with her in private. Abelard set the affair in motion, but Heloise soon fell in love. Long after the couple had been separated by tragic circumstances and she had taken religious vows at Abelard's insistence and become an abbess, Heloise recalled, without guilt, shame or remorse, the sexual passion they had experienced. In a letter to Abelard, she writes:

> In my case, the pleasures of lovers which we shared have been too sweet – they can never displease me, and can scarcely be banished from my thoughts. Wherever I turn they are always there before my eyes, bringing with them awakened longings and fantasies which will not even let me sleep. Even during the celebration of the Mass, when our prayers should be purer, lewd visions of those pleasures take such a hold upon my unhappy soul that my thoughts are on their wantonness instead of on prayers. I should be groaning over the sins I have committed, but I can only sigh for what I have lost. Everything we did and also the times and places are stamped on my heart along with your image, so that I live through it all again with you.[45]

Heloise's honest assessment of her feelings, including her admission that at the most sacred moment of the Mass she sometimes thought of sex, is truly extraordinary coming from a twelfth-century woman, educated at a convent as a young girl and committed to the religious life. Reading her personal correspondence to Abelard, even centuries after the fact, seems like a voyeuristic intrusion. Her statements challenge anyone inclined to think of the Middle Ages as a time when people were so bound by moral strictures that they shunned the subject of sex. More importantly, perhaps, Heloise exemplifies the conflict between the secular and the religious, two areas of her life that she struggled to reconcile.

For people committed to the religious life, erotic desires posed problems. Clerical celibacy was imposed on priests by decree of the First Lateran Council of 1123, and monks, friars and nuns of all orders were sworn to a life of perpetual chastity. The anonymous author of the late thirteenth-century *Breviarium practice*, seeking to explain the lust felt by monks, attributed it to their diet, stating, 'In different monasteries and religious places one comes across numerous men who, sworn to chastity, are often tempted by the Devil; the principal cause is that every day they eat food that leads to flatulence. This increases their desire for coitus and stiffens their member: that is why this passion is called satyriasis [from satyr].'[46] Needless to say, nuns did not suffer from the same affliction, although they might have felt similar stirrings of desire.

A remedy to alleviate the suffering of widows and nuns who longed to fulfil their sexual urges, but could not do so, is found in a popular ensemble of medical texts, compiled in the mid-thirteenth century, which was based on earlier medical treatises written in the southern Italian city of Salerno. The relevant section reads: 'these women, when they have desire to copulate and do not do so, incur grave illness/suffering [*grauem incurrunt egritudinem*]. For such women, therefore, let there be made this remedy. Take some cotton and musk or penny-royal oil and anoint it and put it in the vagina. And if you do not have such an oil, take *trifera magna* [a compound medicine] and dissolve it in a little warm wine, and with cotton or damp wool place it in the vagina. This both dissipates the desire and dulls the pain.'[47] A more straightforward acknowledgement of the psychological and physical challenges associated with abstinence would be difficult to discover.

Because nuns lived together in close proximity, some church authorities considered them to be at particular risk of forming 'unsuitable' attachments to each other. Writing in the seventh century, the monastic reformer, Donatus (d. 624), Bishop of Besançon, stipulated that nuns should sleep fully clothed in separate beds with a lamp burning all night. He also forbade them to 'take the hand of another for affection, whether they are standing or walking around or sitting together', or to call each other 'little girl'.[48] Similar strictures regarding sleeping arrangements for women who had taken religious vows were reiterated at later Church councils.[49]

Nuns were generally confined to their convents and contact with men was kept to a minimum. Thick walls, strong gates and a lack of privacy reduced their risk of having affairs with members of the opposite sex, but degrees of control varied from convent to convent. The idea that religious women were susceptible to amorous feelings found expression in numerous stories about nuns who had broken their vows of chastity. Among the richest sources of such tales are collections of miracles attributed

Nuns attending mass and singing in procession.
La Sainte Abbaïe,
France, *c.* 1290–1300.
Yates Thompson 11, f. 6v

to the Virgin Mary, which began to be compiled in large volumes in the twelfth century and reached a very broad audience. These narratives were disseminated throughout Europe in a variety of languages, ranging from Icelandic to Spanish.[50] One of the most popular tales was the story of an abbess who became pregnant and was reported to the bishop by the disgruntled nuns in her charge. Oppressed by her strict rules, they were only too happy to witness her downfall. When the abbess prayed to the Virgin Mary, she miraculously delivered her baby boy with the help of two angels and then gave him to a hermit to be raised. By the time the bishop summoned the abbess for an audience, he could find no fault with her.

Key moments of the story are illustrated in a sequence of pictures decorating the lower margins of the pages of the Taymouth Hours, probably made in London. The original female owner of the manuscript is portrayed several times in the volume, but her identity has long been the source of scholarly speculation. Kathryn Smith has posited that she was Edward III's sister, Eleanor of Woodstock (1318–55), and that her sister-in-law and guardian, Queen Philippa of Hainault, Edward III's consort, gave the book to her on the occasion of Eleanor's engagement to Reinald II of Guelders in 1331. At the time, she would have been thirteen years old.[51]

A kneeling couple, almost certainly the original owners of this book of hours, receives the blessing of the Holy Spirit. The Taymouth Hours, England, probably London, *c.* 1325–35. Yates Thompson 13, f. 18r

A pregnant abbess falls asleep at an altar while praying for aid to the Virgin Mary. The Virgin hears her prayers, delivers her child and entrusts it to an angel (page on left). The angel gives the baby to a hermit who agrees to take care of it (page on right). The Taymouth Hours, England, probably London, *c.* 1325–35. Yates Thompson 13, ff. 156v–157r

The book was definitely made for a royal woman who would have seen, when she opened her manuscript, the story of the pregnant abbess unfolding in four consecutive images in the margins. The first scene shows the repentant abbess, exhausted by her prayers for mercy, sleeping in front of an altar. Evidently, the Virgin has heard her pleas, for she has come to her aid, delivered her son and entrusted him to an angel. The second image depicts the angel giving the strapping child to a hermit whose cell is so small that it seems doubtful that it will happily accommodate the pair of them. The third shows the abbess undergoing a physical examination by the bishop in order to verify whether or not she is pregnant. To ascertain whether her breasts are full of milk, the bishop gives one of them a firm squeeze. To the dismay of the nuns who have brought the accusation against her, no milk is emitted because

Disgruntled nuns report the abbess to the bishop, but when he examines her, he finds no sign of pregnancy or lactation (page on left). The Virgin Mary nurses the child at the hermit's hut (page on right). The Taymouth Hours, England, probably London, *c.* 1325–35. Yates Thompson 13, ff. 157v–158r

the Virgin has effaced all traces of her pregnancy. The final image shows the Virgin returning to the hermitage to suckle the newborn child, since the hermit, although kindly disposed, is obviously unable to do so himself.

Captions in red ink, written in Anglo-Norman French, the language spoken by the English nobility at the time, summarise the action pictured in the images. In translation, they read: 'Here Our Lady heals the pregnant abbess', 'Here the angel takes the infant of the abbess to a holy hermit', 'Here, the bishop, because of the accusation, touches the breasts to see if he can find milk' and finally, 'Here Our Lady nurses the infant at the hermitage'. These forthright captions and those supplied for other images in the margins of the manuscript seem tailored for a young reader. We do not know how well-versed the original owner was in Latin, the language she would have needed to fully understand the prayers and psalms forming the main text of the volume, but she certainly could have grasped the action shown in the lower borders of the pages, supplied with French captions.[52] It is clear that the captions were written after the images were painted because the scribe was forced to fit them into the space available, and sometimes resorted to writing parts of them alongside the pictures. This suggests that the idea to insert them beside and beneath the images was taken at a relatively late stage in the making of the book. The vernacular language employed in the captions and their grammatical simplicity and concision suggest that they were intended to appeal, specifically, to the young, royal woman for whom the manuscript was made.

When she viewed these images she could take comfort in the assurance that any sin, sexual or otherwise, could be forgiven, and that all who called on the Virgin Mary could be redeemed.[53] It was believed that the Virgin, as Christ's mother, shared a special bond with him. No saint was more efficacious than the Virgin because she could intercede on behalf of sinners with Christ, her son, and persuade him to forgive any repentant sinner. Presenting the abbess succumbing to lust and going unpunished, the story underscores both human frailty and the Virgin Mary's mercy. Lenient in tone, it is a tale of uncontrolled desire without hellish consequences.

Despite the raft of regulations designed to restrict nuns' actions, ribald images in the margins of many manuscripts depict nuns engaging in all kinds of inappropriate activities. While seeming to subvert social norms, it has been argued that satirical images of this type actually 'affirm political, religious, and sexual … hierarchies' and boundaries.[54] By calling attention to the illicit, they define the licit. Examples include a nun playing chess with a friar who reaches forward to fondle her breast, a nun picking penises that sprout from a tree, and a nun nursing a monkey – an image that parodies depictions of the Virgin Mary suckling the Christ Child.[55]

Less outrageous, at first glance, is a nun who does a little jig in the margins of a book of hours, probably made in Liège or Tournai, *c.* 1310–20. The manuscript is small enough to cradle in the palm of the hand, but big enough to accommodate the jousting knights, ferocious battles and madcap antics of monkeys depicted in the margins of virtually every page. The dancing nun's companion, a Franciscan friar, seems to provide the musical accompaniment, but if we look closely we can see that instead of a bow he wields a distaff used for spinning wool and flax, and in place of a stringed instrument, a pair of bellows, tools that almost certainly allude to male and female sexual organs respectively. Although he and the nun are not touching, her raised skirt suggests that she might not be averse to the idea.

We can gain a better understanding of the image of the dancing nun and her male companion if we consider the textual context in which it appears. Written in a clear Gothic script, the text is an excerpt from the Song of Solomon, attributed to

Dancing nun with a Franciscan friar.
Book of Hours, Use of Liège,
S. Netherlands, Liège or Tournai,
c. 1310–20.
Stowe 17, f. 38r.

ecclesie. Ecce tu pulcer
es dilecte mi: et decor'
lectulus noster florid'.
tigna domorum nostra
rum cedrina: laquea
ria nostra cypressina.
Tu autem domine mi
serere nri. Deo gras. R
Sicut cedrus exaltata
sum in lybano et sicut cy
pressus in monte syon q
si mirra electa dedi suaui
tate odoris. Et sicut

the biblical king, which celebrates the passion of two lovers. The opening lines on the page read, '*Ecce tu pulcher es dilecte mi et decorus lectulus noster floridus*' ('Behold thou art fair, my beloved, and comely. Our bed is flourishing'), which suggests that the nun and the friar may have shared more than a moment of religious ecstasy. We do not know the name of the aristocratic woman who originally owned the devotional book in which this image occurs, but she is represented five times in the manuscript in postures of prayer and repentance.[56] Humour and religious convictions are not mutually exclusive; it seems likely that the frolicking nun and the friar who makes music with his distaff were intended to amuse the female patron. While the image can be interpreted as a critique of lax monastic celibacy, it is a jocular jibe, acknowledging that people from all walks of life experienced feelings of desire.

CHAPTER TWO

MARRIAGE

WITH THEIR RIGHT hands clasped and left hands raised, an adolescent girl and boy exchange marriage vows. A woman, positioned behind the girl, places her hand on the latter's sleeve, a gesture of encouragement and assent echoed by the male witness located behind the boy. At the centre of the composition stands the priest, raising his left hand in blessing. Many medieval couples were married by priests in the presence of witnesses in the kind of ceremony reflected in this image, but marriage did not have to be conducted in a church or involve any kind of religious rituals to be valid.[1] A woman and her partner who simply exchanged the words, 'I, X, marry you, Y', formed an 'indissoluble union' that was recognised by the Church, the institution that had jurisdiction over marriage. What if they employed the future tense, saying, instead, 'I, X, will marry you, Y'? As long as they acted on the verbal agreement by having sexual intercourse, that also qualified as marriage.[2]

'Clandestine' marriages of this type could, of course, lead to confusion, particularly if a person made multiple promises under the influence of alcohol or otherwise. This was one of the reasons that ecclesiastics and canon (church) lawyers disapproved of them and that Pope Innocent III, at the Lateran Council of 1215, insisted that a public reading of the banns (the pledge between the couple) was necessary for marriage. Advertising the banns meant that the intention of the betrothed could be made clear to all and any objections to the union could be raised in advance.[3] It was not, however, until the Council of Trent in the mid-sixteenth century that church authorities dictated that a formal nuptial ceremony conducted by a priest and witnessed by two or three individuals was absolutely necessary for a marriage to be valid.[4]

One of the primary purposes of marriage was engendering children, but attitudes to sex were ambivalent. Many ecclesiastics considered sex to be a necessary but undesirable way of maintaining the species. Perpetual virginity was the ideal. If people insisted on having sex, there was only one proper outlet – marriage – and only one good reason – having children. In theory, the only licit sexual activity for a medieval woman was procreative sex with her husband. Ecclesiastical regulations,

Initial showing a young couple united in marriage, at the beginning of Book 4, *De sponsalibus et matrimoniis*.
Gregory IX, *Decretals*,
England, first quarter of the fourteenth century.
Royal 10 E. ix, f. 195r

A cleric lectures a couple on religious regulations concerning sexual intercourse. The scene is set within the initial 'C' for *Cognoscere uxorem* (Conjugal intercourse), the opening words of the text.
James le Palmer, *Omne Bonum*, England, London, *c.* 1360–75.
Royal 6 E. vi, f. 323r

taking account of feast and fast days in the liturgical calendar, restricted the days on which married couples could have sex. Intercourse was not permitted on Wednesdays, Fridays, many holidays, and during Advent and Lent. Long-standing ideas relating to purification led to additional constraints; women were discouraged from having sex when they were menstruating, pregnant or nursing their children.[5] Prohibitions of this type were, of course, impossible to regulate. In practice, it was up to each individual to follow his or her conscience. In the vast twelfth-century compilation of canon laws, the *Decretum*, attributed to Gratian, a textbook used in the universities, the decision of whether or not to have sex on a holy day is left to the couple to decide.[6]

The male clerical elite also denounced creativity in the bedchamber. We would search in vain for a medieval Western European equivalent to the *Kama Sutra* and must wait until the sixteenth century for works such as Pietro Aretino's

Couple making love (above). Aldobrandino of Siena, *Le Régime du corps*, N. France, Cambrai or Thérouanne/St-Omer, *c.* 1265–70. Sloane 2435, f. 9v

Pregnant woman with a physician (above right). This initial introduces a discussion of the care of women in pregnancy and childbirth. Aldobrandino of Siena, *Le Régime du corps*, N. France, Cambrai or Thérouanne/St-Omer, *c.* 1265–70. Sloane 2435, f. 27v

Sixteen Positions.[7] Texts written by medieval canon lawyers and theologians generally prescribe the 'missionary position' to the exclusion of any other.[8] Certainly, in medieval illustrations of couples making love, the man is invariably shown on top of his female partner, as if to stress male dominance in every sphere of life.

A married couple, for example, are depicted having sexual intercourse in a fine copy of the *Régime du corps*, the first known treatise on health and diet written in a vernacular language. It was composed in 1256 by the physician Aldobrandino of Siena, and its originality lies not in its contents, which are derived from standard medical texts written centuries earlier, but in the fact that it is in French rather than Latin, the language customarily employed for books of a medical or scientific nature. The image of the copulating couple occurs at the beginning of a chapter dedicated to sex that starts, 'he who has sense and discernment should devote his understanding and all of his efforts to learning how one should cohabit with a woman, for it is a principal means of maintaining one's health.'[9] It is curious that Aldobrandino addresses his remarks to a male reader, because in the dedicatory preface of most surviving copies of the work, he states that he wrote the treatise at the request of Beatrice of Savoy, Countess of Provence, who was about to visit her four daughters and wished to take it with her. Aldobrandino, who claims to have been a favourite of the countess, tells us that instead of accompanying her on the journey, he composed the book because she had asked him to stay behind to see to other affairs.[10] Since he could not impart his knowledge to her daughters in person, he committed it to writing, a practical alternative. Although Aldobrandino of Siena's name suggests that he was a native of that Italian city, he wrote his medical treatise in French, the language of his patroness, Beatrice of Savoy.

The politically astute Beatrice of Savoy (*c.* 1207–66), who was renowned for her beauty, had every reason to be proud since all four of her daughters, who had inherited her good looks, made auspicious marriages. In 1234 the eldest, Marguerite, married King Louis IX of France. Two years later Eleanor, the second eldest, married Henry III, having been dispatched to England at the age of twelve to exchange nuptial vows with a man she had never met and to reign as queen over a country she had never seen. In 1243 her sister Sanchia likewise settled in England, having married Henry III's brother, the wealthy magnate Richard of Cornwall, whom the German electoral princes later decreed 'King of the Romans'. The youngest sister, Beatrice, named after her mother, married Count Charles of Anjou, who was subsequently crowned King of Naples.

Presumably, Beatrice of Savoy asked Aldobrandino to write the *Régime du corps* in 1256 so that both she and her illustrious daughters could acquaint themselves with helpful tips on health, hygiene and diet, including discussions of bathing, pregnancy, childbirth and childcare. His advice on how to cope with a sea voyage may also have proved welcome, since royal women travelled frequently. Several images in the historical chronicles of the English monk Matthew Paris show, for example, Eleanor of Provence and Henry III travelling by ship.

King Henry III (r. 1216–72) and Queen Eleanor of Provence (*c.* 1223–91) returning to England from Gascony. Matthew Paris, *Historia Anglorum*, England, St Albans, *c.* 1250. Royal 14 C. vii, f. 134v

The handsome copy of Aldobrandino of Siena's *Régime du corps* preserved in the British Library is not Beatrice's original volume, but a later manuscript, made in northern France, probably Cambrai or Thérouanne/St Omer, around 1265–70.[11] A note in gold letters at the beginning of the volume states that it was made at Aldobrandino's behest for a certain Benoit of Florence, possibly an Italian merchant. Over seventy copies of the text survive, but none other contains a note mentioning Benoit of Florence, and it is important to bear in mind that Beatrice of Savoy, who is mentioned in the preface, was the original dedicatee.[12] It is not wholly surprising that Aldobrandino wrote his treatise in French. Women at the time, informally educated and barred from attending university, had limited means of acquiring academic Latin, and they commissioned numerous works and translations in vernacular languages.

Nonetheless, as we have seen, the focus of the chapter on sex in the *Régime du corps* is the welfare of the male partner, whom the author addresses directly in the opening lines quoted above.[13] For Aldobrandino, sex is vital to a man's wellbeing. Stressing the best time for a man to impregnate his wife, he also underscores the point that sex is primarily for procreation.

Regardless of how and when medieval women did it, sex frequently resulted in pregnancy. Consequently, marriage was a different prospect for medieval women than for men. Unless a young man had taken religious vows precluding marriage, once he had reached the age of majority and had forged a career or gained an inheritance, he was expected to marry and establish his own household. For a woman, however, marriage did not hold out similar hopes of independence. With the notable exception of women who had a religious vocation, women were not only expected to marry and to come under the authority of their husbands, but also to bear children, an idea inculcated in them from an early age.[14]

A handbook, written *c.* 1392 by a wealthy Parisian burgher for his fifteen-year-old bride, a woman from the lesser nobility, provides insight into her responsibilities as a wife.[15] It begins with a description of the couple in conversation. Both acknowledge her inexperience in household management and he counsels her to seek advice from other women. He also resolves to give her additional guidance himself, hence the handbook. He is the master and she the mistress, but his tone is indulgent and respectful rather than overbearing. His recommendations are not totally self-serving; he is older and may predecease her. She may marry again. As he states at the outset, he writes with an eye to the future, to prepare her for this possibility and so that she can pass on her knowledge to her daughters and friends. Few details of her life are provided, but her husband reveals that she comes from another country and has long been separated from her parents and relatives, people who would usually have given young wives direction and support. By composing the handbook, he intends to fill this gap. The catalogue of tasks that he expects her to undertake with the help of servants makes fascinating reading. It is not a list of dos and don'ts, but a bespoke travel guide for her to consult as she journeys through a new terrain. Several different ways of getting rid of fleas are recommended, for example, and detailed advice is given on preventing food from sticking to the bottom of a pot (pease porridge is notorious). His idealised vision of domestic bliss consists of coming home from work to find a fire, fresh clothing, clean bed linens, and a welcoming wife. 'Dear sister', he writes, 'I beseech you that, to keep yourself in the love and good favor of your husband, you be unto him gentle, and amiable, and good-tempered … and let him rest well and be well covered by your breasts, and thus bewitch him.'[16] As both woman and wife she is constrained by her subordinate place in a patriarchal society, but the life that her husband describes is not without appeal. Affluence and class offer some compensation. She must supervise the servants, but they will see to the most onerous tasks as she tends roses, orders casks of wine and plans dinner menus.

People in different parts of Western Europe followed different marriage customs, but in many cases, even a woman of modest means was expected to have a dowry. Traditionally a woman's father entrusted the dowry, in the form of money, property or both, to his daughter's husband when she married. If the marriage

Girls from wealthy families who became nuns often gave their dowries to their convents.
Psalter of Henry VI, France, Paris, 1405–10; added miniatures, France, Paris or Rouen, c. 1430.
Cotton Domitian A. xvii, f. 74v

Saint Elizabeth of Hungary (1207–31), daughter of King Andrew II of Hungary, who died at age twenty-four after devoting her life to caring for lepers, the sick and the poor. Two men and a woman, clutching an infant, seek Elizabeth's aid.
London Hours of William Lord Hastings, S. Netherlands, Ghent, before 1483.
Additional 54782, f. 64v

was dissolved or her husband died, the dowry reverted to her. For some women, widowhood brought greater financial independence than any previous stage of their lives. Women whose families were too poor to supply a dowry sometimes worked as servants or in other menial jobs until they had saved sufficient funds to marry. Generally, making a religious vow was not a solution because, by the twelfth century, nuns were often required to use their dowries to enrich their convents when they took the veil. An option for a limited number of women was to become a beguine, part of a movement that originated in present-day Belgium and the Netherlands in the early thirteenth century. Beguines did not take monastic vows, but they were celibate. Among other activities, they dedicated themselves to prayer, attending church services, teaching children, nursing, needlework, gardening and performing charitable acts.[17] Many lived together in tight-knit communities, but they were not cloistered and no dowry was required to join a beguinage, a fact to which the preacher Jacques de Vitry drew attention when he defended this new way of living, stating that many women were prevented from becoming nuns in approved orders because they did not have a dowry or sufficient material resources.[18] Known for her charitable works, Saint Elizabeth of Hungary, canonised in 1235, was venerated by the beguines, and beguinages in Bruges and Ghent were dedicated to her (p. 47). Charitable societies, including those established in Italian city-states, frequently provided dowries for impoverished but 'virtuous' virgins.[19] Wealthy benefactors could also give dowries to poor girls, and an exemplary role model existed for this practice in the form of Saint Nicholas.

Saint Nicholas gives a purse filled with gold to his impoverished neighbour in order to provide dowries for the man's three daughters. Desiring to remain anonymous, Nicholas performed his act of charity in secret.
Queen Mary Psalter,
England, probably London, *c.* 1310–20.
Royal 2 B. vii, f. 316r

Today Saint Nicholas, Bishop of Myra, who ultimately inspired the legendary jolly fat man with a sleigh and a penchant for red clothing, is celebrated as a gift-giver. Nicholas enjoyed the same reputation in the Middle Ages, due to an act of generosity he was said to have performed in his youth. Hearing that a man, who was too poor to provide for his three daughters, intended to hire them out as prostitutes to raise funds, Nicholas surreptitiously lobbed sacks full of gold coins through the window of the man's house, enough to cover the cost of dowries for all three girls. Two episodes from Nicholas' life were most frequently represented in medieval art – his giving of the gold to the poor man, and his miraculous resuscitation of three boys who had been murdered, dismembered and pickled in a vat

King Richard II of England taking as his second wife the seven-year-old Isabella, daughter of Charles VI of France and Isabeau of Bavaria. Jean Froissart, *Chroniques*, S. Netherlands, Bruges, *c.* 1480–94. Royal 14 D. vi, f. 268v

of brine. Resurrecting children was not within the remit of ordinary people, but anyone with sufficient financial resources could imitate Nicholas' charitable actions.

In a treatise on morals and modes of behaviour dedicated to Margaret of Burgundy, who in 1404, at age eleven, married Louis de Guyenne, the heir apparent to the French throne, Christine de Pizan (*c.* 1364–1431) encouraged the 'good princess' to cultivate 'habits of pious charity'. Among other practical suggestions, Christine advised her to emulate Saint Nicholas by secretly sending gifts to 'poor gentlemen or poor gentlewomen sick or fallen on hard times, poor widows, needy householders, poor maidens waiting to marry, women in childbed, students, and poverty-stricken priests or members of religious orders.'[20]

Transfers of wealth concomitant with marriage were not just an issue for the parties with vested interests in a given union, but had an impact on society as a whole. Susan Mosher Stuard explains:

> Dowry, the *dos* of Roman origin, which was given at marriage, formed a major instrument for the transfer of family wealth in medieval times. Today we postpone such transfers of wealth until the death of a senior generation, prompting some economists to bewail the loss in opportunities from capital tied up in the estates of fiscally conservative elders. Medieval people relied on a distribution of wealth more advantageous to youth that encouraged economic growth.[21]

Who, when and why a young girl married was determined above all by her social position. No single factor was more influential than class. Royal and aristocratic girls, whose marriages were generally arranged in order to forge favourable political alliances and accrue property, wealth and status, generally married earlier than women of less privileged classes, who tended to wait until they were in their twenties.[22] In addition, there was often a greater disparity in age between highborn spouses. On 31 October 1396, when he was twenty-nine years old, King Richard II of England took as his second wife the seven-year-old Isabella, daughter of Charles VI of France and Isabeau of Bavaria, in a union intended to seal a twenty-eight-year truce between England and France, kingdoms that had been at war over rights to

Opening page of a psalter made to celebrate the union between the ten-year-old Prince Alphonso of England and his bride-to-be, Margaret, daughter of Florent V, Count of Holland and Zeeland. Manuscripts, especially devotional books, were often commissioned to commemorate marriages. Alphonso Psalter, England, London, *c.* 1284. Additional 24686, f. 11r

Mermaid suckling her baby daughter.
Alphonso Psalter,
England, London, *c.* 1284.
Additional 24686, f. 13r

the succession of the French crown. An illustration in a multi-volume set of Jean Froissart's *Chroniques*, made in Bruges, *c.* 1480–94, shows the diminutive bride being presented by her father to Richard II, who bends down to embrace her (p. 49). Sandwiched between her father and husband, Isabella illustrates the point that for a woman, marriage marked her transfer from her father's household to that of her spouse. The tiny princess is unaccompanied by female relatives, ladies-in-waiting, or a governess. The absence of women underscores the political nature of the transaction, witnessed exclusively by male aristocrats and statesmen.

Books were often ordered by aristocratic and royal couples to celebrate their marriages and they were also given as wedding presents. A prime example is a psalter commissioned by Edward I of England and his consort, Eleanor of Castile, to celebrate the planned union of their first born son and heir apparent, Alphonso, who was to wed Margaret, daughter of Florent V, Count of Holland and Zeeland, in a marriage arranged when the prince was still a child. The opening pages of the psalter, begun *c.* 1284, are emblazoned with the arms of the young prince and his bride-to-be. Positioned between the arms is a seagull, an unusual motif that is perhaps an additional allusion to Holland or Zeeland (land of the sea). While coats of arms were to become standard marks of ownership in manuscripts throughout Western Europe, these are among the earliest to appear in an English devotional book.[23]

The psalter contains, among other images, several scenes alluding to fecundity, including a nesting woodpigeon, a mermaid suckling her daughter, and a doe nursing her fawn, apt subjects for the heir to the throne and his prospective bride, who were expected to perpetuate the royal line. Sadly, on 19 August 1284, just months before the wedding was scheduled to take place, the ten-year-old prince died. Left incomplete, the manuscript was set aside, but it was not forgotten. Work

John Talbot, 1st Earl of Shrewsbury (d. 1453), presenting a magnificent manuscript to Margaret, daughter of René, Duke of Anjou, on the occasion of her marriage to Henry VI of England. Talbot had been instrumental in negotiating the union, and he escorted the princess to England in 1445.
The Shrewsbury Book,
France, Rouen, 1444–45.
Royal 15 E. vi, fol. 2v

on the precious volume resumed *c.* 1297, when it was recycled to mark the dynastic union of Alphonso's sister Elizabeth to none other than John I of Holland and Zeeland, the brother of Margaret, Alphonso's intended bride.[24]

A later volume designed as a wedding gift is a large and profusely illustrated manuscript made in Rouen and presented by the military commander John Talbot, 1st Earl of Shrewsbury (d. 1453), to Margaret, daughter of René, Duke of Anjou, on the occasion of her marriage to Henry VI of England.[25] Talbot had been instrumental in negotiating the marriage, and he escorted the princess to England in 1445. Designed with Margaret in mind, the combination of texts in the manuscript – tales of adventure as well as chivalric treatises – is unique. The frontispiece, stretching over two pages, comprises a genealogical table underscoring Henry VI's right to rule both England and France (then held by the English) and a full-page image showing Talbot on bended knee, presenting the book to Margaret. Although the verses of dedication refer to Margaret as Henry VI's fiancée, she is shown in the painting as his queen, wearing a crown and wielding a sceptre.[26] The enthroned king appears alongside her and their hands are clasped, an evocation of the gesture made to seal nuptial vows. A little white dog, tongue sticking out, nonchalantly treads on Talbot's resplendent robes, which are decorated with emblems of the prestigious Order of the Garter. Dogs in medieval art often symbolise fidelity, but here the animal also alludes to the Earl, for the term 'talbot' was applied to a particular breed of hound used for hunting.[27] A clear division between the sexes pertains; male courtiers and functionaries jostle for space in the chamber to the king's right while the queen's entourage consists solely of two aristocratic women shown to her left, a less prestigious position.[28]

The custom of commissioning a book to commemorate a marriage continued well into the late medieval period and beyond. A notable example is a book of hours made in Florence for Laudomia, daughter of Lorenzo de' Medici, *c.* 1502, in which she is depicted with her husband Francesco Salviati, kneeling on either side of the enthroned Virgin and Child (p. 54). The artist Giovanni Boccardi painted this image, but others in the volume are the work of Attavante degli Attavanti. These include a depiction of the Virgin Mary, pregnant with Jesus Christ, visiting her cousin Elizabeth who is expecting John the Baptist. It is of particular interest because it shows the two women embracing, not in the Holy Land, but in the centre of Florence. Both the Medici palace and the façade of the adjacent church are decorated with the family's arms.[29] Designed specifically for Laudomia's devotional book, this image celebrates both motherhood and the Medici dynasty.

Although medieval aristocratic and particularly royal marriages can be compared to business mergers of today – transactions between big corporations involving protracted negotiations, vast sums of money, competing factions, restructuring,

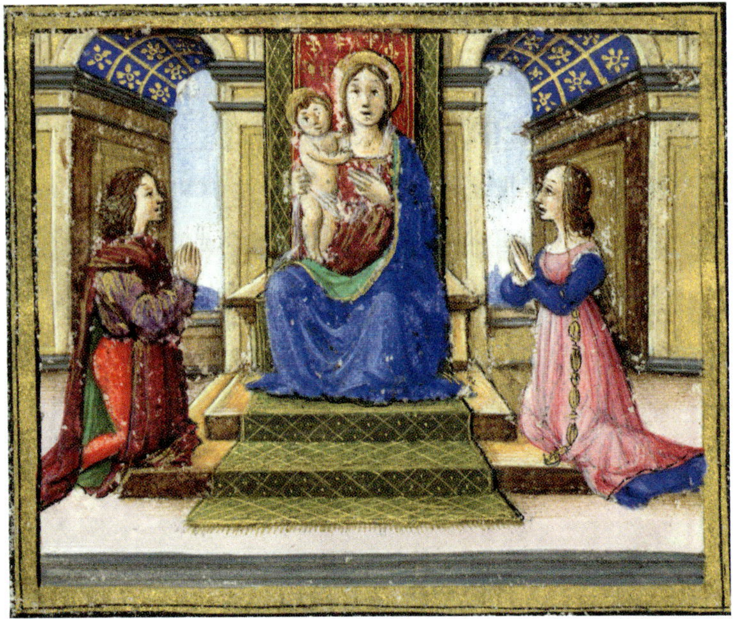

Francesco Salviati and Laudomia de' Medici adore the Virgin and Child (left). The Hours of Laudomia de' Medici, Italy, Florence, *c.* 1502. Yates Thompson 30, f. 30v

Visitation set in Florence with the Medici Palace on the right (below). The Hours of Laudomia de' Medici, Italy, Florence, *c.* 1502. Yates Thompson 30, f. 20v

An imaginative depiction of one of the monumental crosses erected by King Edward I in memory of his wife Eleanor of Castile. The Luttrell Psalter, England, Lincolnshire, *c.* 1320–40. Additional 42130, f. 159v

power politics and little personal feeling – some matches between elite men and women were successful and presumably happy. From the time they were married in the autumn of 1254, Edward I of England (crowned in 1274) and his Spanish wife, Eleanor of Castile, were rarely apart.[30] She frequently travelled with him on military campaigns, even on crusade to the Holy Land, where she gave birth to their daughter Joan of Acre. In thirty-six years of marriage Eleanor bore sixteen children, six of whom survived her.

When the forty-nine-year-old queen died at Harby, near Lincoln, in 1290, her bereaved husband accompanied her body back to London and later erected in her memory a series of twelve stone crosses adorned with multiple portraits of the queen. A cross marked every place that her funeral cortege had stopped on the journey. The final cross, erected near the present location of Charing Cross station, was demolished in 1647 and the rubble used as paving stones, but three others survive.[31] A monument resembling the surviving Eleanor crosses is depicted in the margins of a psalter made *c.* 1320–40 for the English lord Geoffrey Luttrell, who served under Edward I. Poised on one foot like a ballerina *en pointe*, a man holds the monument aloft above his head, seemingly oblivious to its ponderous weight and to the presence of a child seated at the base of the structure. Evidently the king, who once described Eleanor as the woman 'whom living we dearly cherished, and whom dead we cannot cease to love', wished to express his devotion to her in a singular way. No comparable series of funerary monuments have ever been constructed for an English king or queen.[32]

Edward I also paid tribute to his wife by commissioning the master goldsmith William Torel to create two magnificent gilt-bronze effigies for her tombs in Lincoln and London. The tomb in Lincoln Cathedral, containing her viscera, was demolished in the 1640s, but the one preserved in Westminster Abbey, encasing her body, shows the elegant queen, with her thick, long hair cascading down her back, resting in peace with two lions at her feet. A detailed account of expenses relating to Eleanor's death and interment, dated 1293, lists payments made to the masons responsible for the crosses and the tombs, and many other costs, including a payment of 8s, 6d made to a certain Juliana la Potere (the potter), for supplying 300 pitchers on the anniversary of Eleanor's death.[33] Whether these were given away as gifts or served some other purpose is unknown. The payment to Juliana reminds us that elite and royal cultural patronage was not restricted to grand enterprises, but could be expressed in more modest forms, including earthenware jugs manufactured by a working woman to commemorate a queen.

Medieval texts on the subject of marriage comprise a vast and varied body of writings, ranging from codes of canon and civil law and theological pronouncements to popular literature. Advice for married couples can be found in unexpected

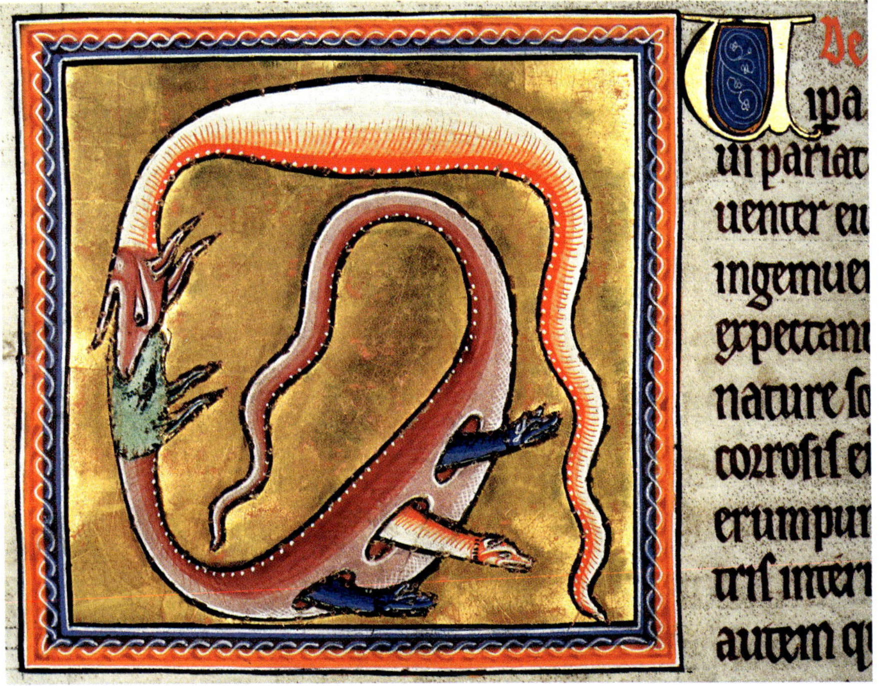

Vipers mating. The young conceived gnaw their way out of their mother's womb, killing her in the process. According to the text, male vipers were also accustomed to mate with female lampreys.
Aberdeen Bestiary,
England, possibly N. Midlands, *c.* 1200.
Aberdeen University Library, MS 24, f. 66v

places. In one bestiary (book of beasts), the anonymous author uses the example of the legendary mating rituals of vipers to shed light on marital relations. After describing how the male viper inserts his head into the female's mouth and discharges his poisonous semen, prompting her to go 'mad with lust' and bite off his head, he segues into advice for married couples, stressing the importance of tolerating the behaviour of one's spouse. Women are counselled to endure their husband's 'harsh, deceitful, uncouth, unreliable [and] drunken' behaviour, just as the female withstands the poison emitted by the male viper during sexual intercourse. 'She is not found wanting', but 'embraces the slimy snake with sincere affection.' Men are also admonished to treat their wives decently. 'You are not her master but her husband', states the author. 'You have gained not a maidservant but a wife. God wished you to govern the weaker sex, not rule it absolutely. Return her care with attention; return her love with grace. The viper pours out its poison; can you not get rid of your harsh attitude?'[34] It was standard practice for authors of bestiaries to incorporate moral messages into their descriptions of animals, and indeed, that was the primary aim of the books, but the focus here on marital relations and the comment that men should not be domineering is unusual.

Many poems and stories have only one message to impart to men contemplating marriage: don't do it. The familiar antifeminist trope, that wives curtail men's liberty, is expressed repeatedly: 'any man who enjoys youth and the joys and delights of the world and who, of his own free will and impulse and without compulsion finds a narrow and sorrowful prison cell, full of tears, anguish, and lamenting, and throws himself into it, has lost his mind.'[35] Literature advocating the single life for men, including the excerpt just quoted, was often written in a humorous vein, but it is undeniably misogynistic, and it undoubtedly shaped men's perceptions of women. An instructive example is the Latin poem *De coniuge non ducenda* (*Against Marrying*). Composed by an anonymous author in northern France or England *c.* 1225–50, the short poem (240 lines) consists of advice intended to dissuade a young man from getting married. The following excerpts, taken from different points in the poem, convey its content and tone and show how the same themes are repeated throughout:

A woman's silly, never staid,
By many longings stirred and swayed.
If husband can't her needs supply,
Adultery's the way she'll try.

Her lustful loins are never stilled:
By just one man she's unfulfilled.
She'll spread her legs to all the men
But, ever hungry, won't say 'When.'

Thus bitter grief and shame begin –
The child that's been conceived in sin.
Its mother knows its bastard line,
The foolish husband says: 'It's mine'

'Whose wife is good is blest' it's said.
But 'good wife' tales are rarely read.
She'll either nag or fornicate –
His lordship she'll not tolerate.[36]

At the conclusion of the poem, discouraged by the prospect of marrying an inane, nagging, sex-crazed, duplicitous wife who may well give birth to bastards that he would be forced to support, the young man opts to stay single. The anonymous author of the poem claims that tales about 'good wives' are rarely read, implying that so few women are virtuous that little has been written on the subject. Certainly, more misogynistic texts survive than works written in praise of women. In an

A jealous husband beats his wife.
Guillaume de Lorris and Jean de Meun, *Roman de la Rose*,
S. Netherlands, Bruges, *c.* 1490–1500.
Harley 4425, f. 85r

anthology of medieval antifeminist texts, and writings countering this tradition, compiled by Alcuin Blamires in 1992 but still requisite reading, seven chapters are devoted to the former and two to the latter.[37] Among the most important works cited by Blamires in the body of antifeminist polemic is another poem, the *Roman de la Rose* (*Romance of the Rose*), begun by Guillaume de Lorris *c.* 1230 and completed by Jean de Meun about forty years later.

Unlike the poem *De coniuge non ducenda* (*Against Marriage*), many copies of the *Roman de la Rose* are illustrated. Of the estimated 310 copies still preserved, 230 contain pictures or spaces that were intended for them.[38] Illustrations in manuscripts of the *Roman de la Rose* generally reflect the actions of the characters described in the text. A copy produced in Bruges *c.* 1500, for example, contains a stark image of domestic violence. The image occurs in a section of the poem in which an allegorical figure, known simply as the 'Friend', explains to the 'Lover', the protagonist of the poem, that it is not possible to establish a good relationship with a woman by being abusive and controlling. In order to illustrate his point, the Friend describes a jealous husband, an extreme misogynist, who vents his rage in a long speech against his wife. Worthy women, he claims, are 'fewer than phoenixes' – no, they are 'fewer than white crows, however beautiful their bodies may be'.[39] Incensed that his wife wastes his money on pretty clothes to attract the attention of her lovers, he is driven to paroxysms of anger. 'It is through you, lady slut, and through your wild ways, that I am given over to shame, you riotous, filthy, vile, stinking bitch.'[40] As shown in the illustration, his tirade ends only when he assaults his wife, pummelling her until her cries alert the neighbours who intervene.

In both the poem *De coniuge non ducenda* (*Against Marriage*) and in the description of the jealous husband incorporated in the *Roman de la Rose*, the key issue for the man is control. He does not want to sacrifice his freedom and be constricted by an overbearing wife, and yet he seeks to regulate her actions, particularly her sexual behaviour. As we have seen, the fictional characters portrayed in these verse narratives state directly that women are endowed with insatiable sexual appetites, and that they will act on these at any opportunity if unconstrained, using cunning schemes to hide their infidelity. This does not mean, of course, that the authors of these poems thought that women were morally bankrupt or that marriage should be abolished. However, the underlying anxiety that a married woman could attract the attention of a rival and become pregnant by him does seem to reflect actual concerns. While a man could father children outside wedlock without risking censure, he did not want to be cuckolded by his adulterous wife and left unable to determine whether the children she bore were his own.

Readers who find the vocabulary and behaviour of the jealous husband disconcerting are not alone. Christine de Pizan (*c.* 1364–1431), the most prominent female author of her day, whose primary patrons were drawn from the French court where she was raised, emphatically rejected what she perceived to be the attack on women incorporated by Jean de Meun in the final and by far the longest section of the *Roman de la Rose*. In 1401 Christine took a stand against the Provost of Lille, Jean de Montreuil, who championed the book and viewed it as an amusing piece of satire and a literary and intellectual *tour de force*. Christine circulated copies of her letters containing her rebuttals of Jean and other learned men who praised the poem, soliciting the support of the French queen, Isabeau of Bavaria, and attracting the attention of Jean Gerson, Chancellor of the University of Paris, who agreed that the book was unedifying. Christine took issue with the obscene language of the

Roman de la Rose, its stereotypical and harsh depiction of women, and the fact that naïve or inattentive readers might take literally the negative caricatures and sentiments voiced by the fictional characters in the text.[41]

After the debate Christine continued to ponder the implications of the negative portrayals of women by male authors and, in 1405, wrote in defence of women one of the books for which she is best known today, *Le Livre de la cité des dames* (The *Book of the City of Ladies*), presenting as positive role models various women drawn from mythology and history as well as her own royal patron, Isabeau of Bavaria, Queen of France.

Christine de Pizan in her study.
Christine de Pizan, Collected Works, France, Paris, *c.* 1410–14.
Harley 4431, f. 4r

The negative portrayal of marriage in the *Roman de la Rose*, exemplified by the fictional jealous husband, could not have been further from Christine de Pizan's own experience. Married in Paris at the age of fifteen and widowed ten years later, she composed poems that express both her memories of her happy union and her grief at losing her husband, Etienne du Castel. A royal secretary, he died unexpectedly in 1390 while away on business, leaving Christine to cope with her widowed mother and dependent children. In one poem, for example, she tells how on their wedding night Etienne, who was nine years her senior, did not force himself upon her, but instead, mindful of her youth and inexperience, put her at ease. 'Marriage is a sweet thing', she writes, 'I can prove it by my own example. God indeed gave to me a good and sensible husband.... The first night of our marriage, I could already feel his great goodness, for he never did to me any outrage which would have harmed me, but, before it was time to get up, he kissed me, I think, one hundred times, without asking for any other base reward.'[42]

After her bereavement Christine, who resolved not to remarry, struggled to mask her grief. Later, on reflection, she felt that the death of her husband had at least one positive outcome. In one of her final works, entitled *Le livre de l'advision Christine* (*Book of the Vision of Christine*), the female allegorical figure 'Philosophy' reminds Christine that if her husband had lived, she could not have pursued her intellectual interests. She states: 'By your account there is no doubt that, if your husband were still alive, you could not be as dedicated to study as you are, because your domestic duties would not allow it.... Thus you should not consider yourself unfortunate that you have among other goods one of the things in the world that it most delights you to possess, namely, the sweet taste of learning.'[43]

Given the patriarchal society in which she lived and the attendant expectations placed on wives and mothers, it seems that Christine could not picture a world in which a woman could happily combine familial obligations and a professional career. Far from rejecting marriage and motherhood, she esteemed both. 'Every man', she once wrote, 'should feel affection in his heart for woman, who is mother to each and every one of them.... From his birth, through life to death, women help and succour him, providing compassion, sweetness and support.'[44] She did not consider this work inferior. She did, however, acknowledge that women who wished to achieve different goals in a society that privileged men had to move outside accepted roles for women. In effect, they had to adopt the male gender themselves.[45] Christine's stable childhood and happy marriage were not the catalysts for her writing. The loss of her beloved husband was what inspired her to 'forge pleasant things'.[46]

Medieval writers present disparate views on marriage and a woman's role within it. Believed to have been ordained by God, who created Eve as a partner for Adam, marriage was one of the seven sacraments of the Church, one of the rites thought to confer grace on humanity. Despite its theological legitimacy, many writers held that marriage was second best to clerical celibacy, and others stressed that it curtailed men's liberties. Numerous male authors claimed that women were more sexually voracious than men, so they could not be trusted to be faithful to their husbands. This idea provided both pretext and justification for controlling women's behaviour and was the source of countless satirical works.

Christine de Pizan acknowledged that the demands of a spouse and raising children impinged on a woman's ability to pursue her intellectual interests.[47] Nevertheless, as exemplified by Eleanor of Castile, arranged marriages imposed on young women of high birth could result in long-lasting, satisfying unions. Couples who ran family businesses also enjoyed benefits: 'The married couple was the foundation of the craft workshop, and a fundamental unit of the urban economy. In some cities in Europe, a man could not establish a shop if he was not married.'[48] As outlined in the final chapter of this book, it was common for husbands and wives to work side by side in the same trades, sharing not only a table and a bed, but also aspirations and skills that they could pass on to their children.

CHAPTER THREE

MOTHERS

IMAGES OF CHILDBIRTH in medieval manuscripts present an idealised picture of the process. Mothers recline on well-made beds fitted with downy pillows and rich textiles, and bedchambers are represented as intimate spaces, just large enough to contain these imposing pieces of furniture and a few solicitous women who either attend to the mother or her newborn child. Although a male servant fetches water for the baby's bath in the image reproduced here, men are rarely shown within the confines of the cosy microcosm, a womb-like sanctuary, fitted with curtains to shut out the bustle of the world at large.

Male physicians sometimes gave advice to pregnant women and assisted at the births of royal or aristocratic children, but the absence of men from the bedchamber in most medieval images reflects reality: giving birth was literally women's labour and they were usually aided by other women.[1] The domestic settings represented are, however, highly stylised. Owners of the expensive manuscripts in which such images appear would have enjoyed a high standard of living and, as we know from wills and inventories, many slept under fur-lined coverlets, but the majority of medieval women would not have experienced the same privileges or privacy.

Pictures of this type shed little light on our understanding of childbirth as experienced by women of low economic status, those who never enjoyed the attentions of servants and who gave birth lying on straw pallets, or squatting on dirt floors. Did these women, in particular, take comfort from the belief that the Virgin Mary gave birth to Jesus Christ in the modest surroundings of a stable? Certainly the Virgin Mary was upheld as a model of motherhood and was evoked in prayers by men and women of all social classes.

In medieval images the moment of birth is rarely represented.[2] Bedclothes usually obscure the mother's body from the waist down, lending secrecy to the mechanics of the physical process. More often than not, her placid expression suggests that she has just woken up from an enjoyable dream. There is no evidence of bodily effluvia, nothing to indicate protracted pain, let alone a placenta. The only evidence of birth is a clean, swaddled infant. Medieval artists, who painted innumerable images of the crucified Christ and of martyred saints, were not reluctant

Birth of the Virgin Mary. Men are rarely depicted in scenes of childbirth. The face of the male servant who fetches water is strategically hidden by the door frame. Breviary of John the Fearless and Margaret of Bavaria, France, Paris, *c.* 1410–19. Harley 2897, f. 385r

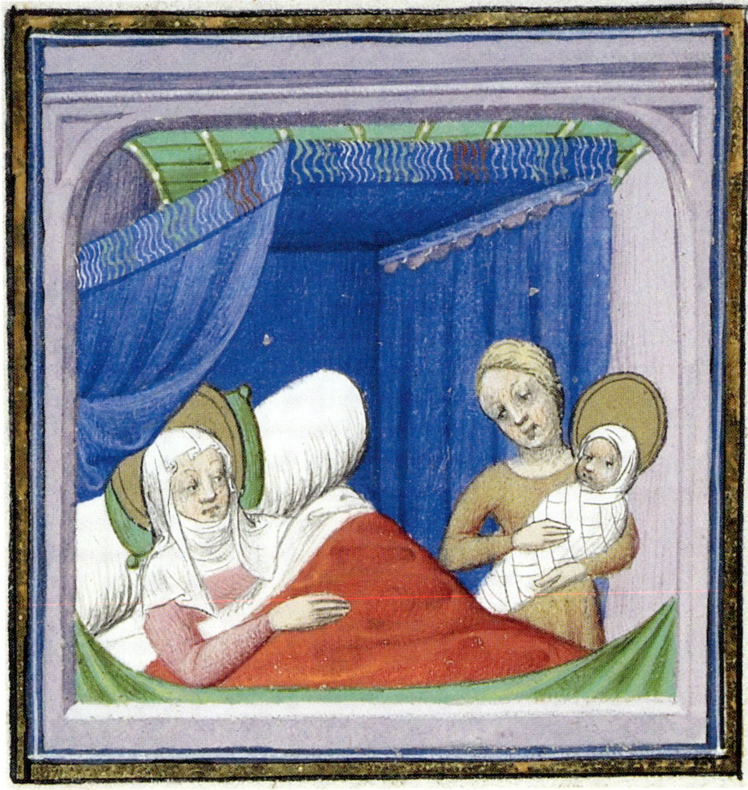

Birth of the Virgin Mary.
Hours of René d'Anjou, France, Paris, *c.* 1405–10, with additions made in Provence, *c.* 1440.
Egerton 1070, f. 101v

to portray the human body in states of nudity and mutilation. Why, then, did they invariably represent childbirth in such a serene and sanitised way?

Christian theologians asserted that because Adam and Eve had disobeyed God, men were consigned to a life of manual labour and women were destined to experience painful childbirth. According to Genesis 3:16, after their fall from grace God punished Eve – and, by extension, all women – by making her suffer severe labour pains. However, as outlined above, most women shown in childbirth in medieval illustrations appear at ease. Once artistic formulas had been established for depicting women in this manner, they were employed for centuries. If medieval artists had adopted a more realistic approach they would have been obliged to depict half-naked women in distress, hardly the ideal focus of pictures of the Virgin Mary, Saint Anne, or a queen giving birth to an heir to the throne.

When artists did depart from artistic norms, it was often because they were inspired by the extraordinary events described in the texts they were called upon to illustrate, including births by caesarean section. For example, an image of the birth of Julius Caesar in a copy of an anonymous French compilation of Roman history,

Birth of Julius Caesar. *Histoire ancienne jusqu'à César* and *Faits des romains*, France, Paris, last quarter of the fourteenth century. Royal 16 G. vii, f. 219r

Les Faits des Romains, made in Paris in the last quarter of the fourteenth century, shows his lifeless mother lying naked on a bed. From the sizable yet precise hole that has been cut in her abdomen, a midwife extracts an improbably large Julius, while an open-mouthed maid, seemingly unnerved by the operation, prepares to bathe him in an adjacent tub. Details of Julius Caesar's unusual birth, including his emergence from the womb with a full head of hair, are recounted briefly in the accompanying text, which the artist has reflected accurately.[3]

In reality, many medieval women, without recourse to antiseptics or drugs to ease their suffering, experienced painful labour and died of complications in childbirth or infections afterwards. Archaeological remains include skeletons of premature infants and of women with foetuses in situ.[4] Authors of medical texts described the various problems that could occur during labour if, for instance, the mother had narrow hips or the baby had a large head or was awkwardly positioned in the womb. 'The science of midwifery demands great experience', wrote Albertus Magnus, 'for both mother and child are easily put in danger during birth if great care is not taken for them both. The prudent and experienced midwife can both lighten and assist in lightening the burden of birth.'[5] Midwives and other helpers were advised to bathe the pregnant woman in water infused with plants, to offer her massages, and to lead her 'at a slow pace throughout the house', sensible recommendations advocated by midwives to this day, although the practice of placing frankincense in the nostrils of the mother-to-be to provoke sneezing is no longer endorsed.[6]

Devotional books containing prayers, acknowledging the perils of childbirth and asking for deliverance, remind us that medieval women also turned to God and the saints for solace.[7] Among the main female saints evoked during labour was the Virgin Mary who, according to the Gospels, had miraculously conceived of God's own son without losing her virginity. Although she was believed to have been exempt from the so-called 'curse of Eve' and to have given birth to Jesus Christ without suffering pain, medieval Christians saw Mary as an empathetic and compassionate ally.[8]

Some women who experienced difficulties in childbirth and called on the saints for aid vowed to dedicate their children to the religious life if their petitions were answered. In his autobiography, written around 1115, Guibert, Abbot of Nogent, describes how his mother, 'racked with continuous pain', prayed to the Virgin Mary for the safe birth of her child, vowing to give the infant to God, a promise she fulfilled after her pitifully small baby came of age.[9] Women who had not necessarily experienced difficult births, but wanted their offspring to become monks or nuns, often made similar vows.

One of the autobiographical stories included in the collection of miracles composed in Galician-Portuguese by King Alfonso X, of Castile-León (r. 1252–84), concerns his younger sister Berenguela (b. 1228), whom his parents, Queen Beatriz and King Fernando III, dedicated to the Virgin Mary, intending for her to be raised at the Cistercian convent of Las Huelgas at Burgos. The nuns of this prestigious institution maintained close ties with the royal family of Castile and it was the site of many events of personal significance to Alfonso.

His account of Berenguela's entry into the religious life is depicted in a full-page painting divided into six consecutive panels. The vow is illustrated in the first panel, which shows Queen Beatriz on her knees, holding the tiny princess aloft in front of a statue of the Virgin and Child. As shown in the next two scenes, the infant suddenly took ill and died. The distraught queen placed her lifeless baby in front of a statue of the Virgin that was enshrined on an altar in the palace of the royal chapel in Toledo.[10] After everyone had been ordered out of the chapel and the doors had been bolted, the Queen kept vigil at the threshold, praying fervently to the Virgin for the resurrection of her child. Her faith was rewarded, for she soon heard the cries of the baby girl. The fifth image shows the queen and princess, borne aloft in a litter, on their way to the convent of Las Huelgas, and the final scene depicts Berenguela, dressed in a Cistercian habit, offered, once again, by her mother to the Virgin.

By placing her dead child in front of the image of the Virgin in the palace chapel in the hope of invoking divine aid, Queen Beatriz was following widespread custom. It was common practice for sickly and stillborn babies to be deposited by their parents in front of images on altars or saints' tombs. The parents would then keep prayerful vigil and/or have masses said by a priest.[11]

Berenguela would not have actually entered orders as a novice until she came of age, and it would have been at this time that she would have worn a habit as her everyday attire. Berenguela was the only daughter of Fernando III and Beatriz to live to adulthood and she did, in fact, assume the veil at the age of fifteen on 2 September 1243.[12] Although her mother Beatriz was long since dead, her father Fernando III and her eldest brother, Alfonso X, were present on the occasion.[13] Berenguela never served as abbess at Las Huelgas, but she exercised authority and is referred to by Alfonso X, who claims to have witnessed the miracle of her resurrection, as the '*Señora*' of the foundation in which she was ultimately buried in 1288.[14]

Alfonso X, *Cantigas de Santa Maria* (*Songs of Holy Mary*), *Cantiga* 122. King Alfonso X of Castile–León (r. 1252–84) commissioned the largest medieval collection of the miracles of the Virgin Mary. Each tale, written in Galician-Portuguese verse, is set to music and illustrated. Several stories concern Alfonso X and members of his family. These images (reading from left to right and top to bottom), tells the story of his baby sister Berenguela who died and was restored to life by the Virgin Mary. She later became a nun at the royal convent of Las Huelgas in Burgos, which had been founded in 1187 by her great-grandmother. She is shown in a Cistercian habit in the final panel. Alfonso X, *Cantigas de Santa Maria*, El Escorial, Real Monasterio de San Lorenzo, MS T.I.1, Ms T.I.1, f. 173r

Some aristocratic and royal women had privileged access to Marian relics that were reputed to ease childbirth. A girdle (belt) enshrined at Westminster Abbey, alleged to have been made and worn by the Virgin Mary and given to the abbey by Saint Edward the Confessor, was customarily loaned to English royal women when they went into labour. The first recorded instance of the relic being employed for this purpose was in 1242 when it was sent to Gascony to Eleanor of Provence, queen of Henry III, who delivered a healthy girl. Eleanor's granddaughter Elizabeth (1282–1316), Countess of Hereford, likewise made use of the relic when she went into labour with a son at Knaresborough Castle, Yorkshire in 1304. Two monks, Robert de Bures and Guy de Asshewell, were dispatched from Westminster and brought the girdle to her, and her household accounts show that she paid them the handsome fee of 40 shillings for their trouble on 15 September. Payments to the king's minstrels on 11 October reflect the joy inspired by the child's arrival, but sadly the records also include expenses relating to Humphrey's funeral, which was held at Westminster Abbey less than a month later on 8 November.[15]

Women in childbirth also prayed to Saint Margaret of Antioch, a feisty fourth-century virgin of dubious authenticity, whose legend dates back to the ninth century. After she had rejected the advances of the Roman prefect Olibrius, who was entranced with her beauty and lusted after her, she was imprisoned and experienced two encounters with the devil: he attacked her, appearing first in the form

Saint Margaret bursting out of the dragon that attacked and swallowed her. The hem of her dress is caught in the beast's jaws. *La Légende dorée* (Jacobus de Voragine, *Legenda aurea*, translated into French by Jean de Vignay), France, Paris, 1382. Royal 19 B. xvii, f. 167v

of a dragon and then as a man. Although Margaret eventually fought off her evil assailants, she was subsequently beheaded at Olibrius' command.

Margaret's association with pregnant women was based on two aspects of her legend. First, as she fought with the dragon, the creature swallowed her alive, but she escaped by making the sign of the cross and bursting out of its belly. Second, just before she was beheaded she is alleged to have prayed for all women experiencing difficult labour, asking God to give them healthy children. The motif of Margaret emerging intact from the dragon came to symbolise successful childbirth, despite the fact that Jacobus de Voragine, whose thirteenth-century account of the saint's life was among the most popular, stated that the episode was 'apocryphal and not to be taken seriously.'[16] Margaret proved to be quite a mouthful, and many images show the hem of her dress protruding from the dragon's mouth as the creature attempts to gulp her down.

Medieval saints are generally depicted with attributes that enable viewers to identify them. In the case of martyrs, these are usually the implements with which they were tortured or killed: a grill for Saint Lawrence, for example, a sword for Saint Paul, a wheel for Saint Catherine. The fact that the dragon came to be Margaret's chief attribute, although the beast was not instrumental to her torture or responsible for her death, demonstrates the importance assigned to this facet of her legend by medieval Christians.

A midwife holds a newborn baby as the mother sits up in bed. This manuscript of the Life of Saint Margaret, shows significant signs of wear, and was possibly placed on the bodies of women in labour like a charm or talisman.
N. Italy, possibly Padua, third quarter of the fourteenth century.
Egerton 877 f. 12r

It was customary for women in childbirth to have Margaret's story read to them, and sometimes copies of it were placed on their bodies. The practice is mentioned specifically in one French version of the Life of the saint, '*Après la Sainte Passion*', in which Margaret claims, 'whatever woman is in childbirth if a sign shall be made over her with the book in which is my life, and she shall have looked at it, and the book shall be placed upon her, God will deliver her without peril.'[17] A fourteenth-century copy of Margaret's story made in northern Italy, possibly Padua, was probably used for this very purpose (p. 69). Recounting the dragon episode, the anonymous author states that Margaret 'came forth from its womb unharmed and without any pain', making explicit the connection between Margaret's ordeal and childbirth. The final image in the manuscript is badly damaged, almost certainly from frequent use. It shows a joyful woman sitting up in bed, having just given birth, and a midwife holding a tightly swaddled, newborn child. No other manuscript of Margaret's life discovered to date contains a similar image.[18]

The accompanying prayer, however, in which Christ himself addresses the baby, beseeching the infant to emerge from its mother's womb, has a long history. The prayer is found, in different versions, in over sixty manuscripts, made in different parts of Europe and dating from the eleventh century onwards. Every version, including the one inscribed in the Italian manuscript mentioned above, contains references to biblical mothers who successfully conceived of children or delivered babies in extraordinary circumstances, including the Virgin Mary (despite her virginity) and her mother Anne and cousin Elizabeth (despite their advanced age). Occasionally there are references to Lazarus, whom Christ is said to have called forth from his tomb and brought back to life. The analogy between Lazarus (encased in the tomb) and the baby (encased in the womb), who is likewise commanded by Christ to emerge, is apposite.[19]

In some manuscripts, the prayer is prefaced by the specific instruction to say it to the woman in labour.[20] Other customs are also mentioned, including the admonition to write down the words and attach them to her body. The writing of the prayer and its oral recitation would not have been mutually exclusive. Once the words had been bound or placed on the parturient woman, midwives, female friends and relatives attending her could have recited it from memory. Mothers-to-be were sometimes advised to ingest the prayer after it had been inscribed on a piece of bread, butter, cheese or other edible substance, as if to increase its efficacy by literally internalising the words.[21]

Margaret's popularity never waned, and her story was retold countless times. Around 1426 John Lydgate, a Benedictine monk of Bury St Edmunds, Suffolk, wrote a version of Saint Margaret's life in English for Ann Mortimer, Countess March. Lydgate, who described Margaret as 'a paragon of meekness', omitted the detail of her being swallowed by the dragon, saying simply that she fought off the creature and it split open. He did, however, stress her conquest of a decidedly chauvinistic devil, stating that when he appeared to her in the form of a man, she 'seized him by the head and threw him to her feet'. 'Your innocence has brought me down', the devil cried, 'a young maiden has crushed me with her slender limbs! I could accept being vanquished by a man, who at least has power and strength. But now, alas, against everything that's right and proper, an innocent virgin, a pure maiden, has overthrown me in my malice.'[22] Margaret, one of the most dynamic female saints despite her 'slender limbs', provided medieval women with a pugnacious paradigm. Though she ultimately suffered a martyr's death, she had nevertheless thrashed the devil.

Pressure on women to conceive and produce male heirs was intense, and this was felt especially by royal and aristocratic women. The subject is addressed in an illustration from a historical chronicle, *Les Grandes chroniques de France*, made in Paris *c.* 1332–40, which shows King Louis VII of France (r. 1137–80) praying to Christ for a son, and his third wife, Adele of Champagne, reclining in bed having just given birth. Since his previous two wives, Eleanor of Aquitaine and Constance of Castile, had given birth to daughters, Louis VII was desperate for a male heir. Fortunately his prayers were answered, and the swaddled infant depicted in the image became the future king, Philip Augustus.

In the illustration there is a clear demarcation between the antechamber in which King Louis VII is pictured and the female sphere of the bedchamber occupied by Adele of Champagne. The queen has bared her breast in readiness to suckle

Queen Adele of Champagne (*c.* 1140–1206) gives birth to the heir to the throne, Philip Augustus. She married King Louis VII five weeks after Constance of Castile, his previous wife, died in childbirth. *Les Grandes chroniques de France*, France, Paris, *c.* 1332–40. Royal 16 G. vi, f. 329v

the newborn, but, implausibly, she retains her crown, a detail included by the illuminator to emphasise her regal status. Genealogical rolls of royal families, many illuminated in gold and precious pigments, further attest to one of the most important roles assigned to women in the Middle Ages: to provide heirs and guarantee the future of the family line.

In a society centred on the family as an economic unit, the absence of an heir also had an impact on people of lower social rank, as explained by Fiona Harris-Stoertz, who writes:

> While lesser persons were not faced with the problems of infertile kings, the production of an heir was still vital to most. In England and some parts of France by the thirteenth century, men could not get freehold of their wife's lands (that is, its full use for an indefinite period) unless they had issue by them. This requirement encouraged legal interest in the events of the birthing chamber, since births did not 'count' if the child had been born dead, was never heard to cry, or was a 'monster'. In *Placitorum abbreviatio* (Summary of pleas), written in England in the time of King Edward I, it is explained that the hearing of a cry was essential because women could not testify in court and men were not allowed into the birthing chamber. Thus, in the thirteenth century exclusively male witnesses were interrogated regarding births and whether cries were heard.[23]

Corroborating the visual evidence, the *Placitorum abbreviatio* confirms that men were not usually present when their wives gave birth. It also underscores the disenfranchisement of women, who were not permitted to testify to the births of their own children.

Since infertility was commonly regarded as a punishment for sin, married women who were barren were subject to criticism and they, rather than their husbands, were often blamed for their failure to conceive.[24] While some couples struggled to have even a single child, others had a surplus of children. Birth control was not unknown, but attempts to regulate fertility contravened Church teaching and some methods were more reliable than others.[25] Partners who practiced *coitus interruptus*, a method estimated by modern doctors to have a failure rate as high as 25 per cent, often became parents. And women who placed between their breasts a pouch containing the testicles of a weasel were even more likely to get pregnant, despite its reputation as a fail-safe prophylactic.[26]

One option, which was available to poor people who could not support all of their offspring and also to relatively wealthy parents who did not want to fragment their inheritance by dividing their estates, was to leave a child, usually a newborn

Initial 'E' for *Expositus* (Abandoned child), showing an infant left outside a city gate. Two other babies, drawn in pen by the scribe and author, James le Palmer, are incorporated in the text.
James le Palmer, *Omne Bonum*, England, London, *c.* 1360–75. Royal 6 E. vii, f. 104v

baby, in a public place where it could be found and raised by others. Some parents, having arranged to give their child to an acquaintance or to a local monastery, continued to maintain contact with him or her afterwards. Boxes or hatches in which unwanted babies could be placed became a feature of some religious institutions, presumably to protect the infants from the elements and to prevent monks or nuns from tripping over the little bundles, previously deposited on their doorsteps.

The practice of giving children to a monastery or convent simply to alleviate financial pressures rather than out of religious conviction was criticised by various ecclesiastics. Some children, remarked William of Auvergne, Bishop of Paris (1228–49), are 'cast into the cloister by their parents or relatives just as if they were kittens or piglets whose mothers could not nourish them'.[27] In certain circumstances, parents genuinely could not feed their children. A famine in the region of Vendôme in France in 1161, for example, is said to have prompted desperate women 'to throw their children at the doors of the monastery'.[28]

Ideally, from the moment of birth onwards, mothers concerned themselves with the spiritual and physical welfare of their children. For Christians the rite of baptism, which ensured the salvation of the child's soul, was of paramount importance. Despite the control exercised by male authorities over ritual aspects of spiritual life, surviving laws indicate that at certain periods and in particular regions, if a baby was sickly and seemed likely to die, midwives or other female attendants at the birth were permitted to baptise the infant immediately.[29] Mothers who had given birth alone could also baptise their dying babies, if there was no alternative.[30] Scenes of infant baptism in medieval manuscripts, however, generally show the baby being baptised by a priest in an ecclesiastical setting, with the parents and godparents in attendance. By the twelfth century, babies were usually baptised at birth or within a few days.[31] The brief interval between birth and baptism is conveyed in an illustration showing the birth of Louis the Pious of France (778–840), which incorporates both events (p. 74).

Nurturing children was one of the primary responsibilities of medieval women. Medieval mothers either breastfed their children or hired wet nurses to do it for them. Tips for hiring suitable wet nurses suggest that the matter was taken seriously. The model wet nurse was characterised as a young woman, on the plump side, with ample but not pendulous breasts. She was advised to avoid pepper, salt, spicy foods, rocket, onions and, above all, garlic to avoid upsetting her charge's digestion.[32] Women who suffered discomfort from breastfeeding were

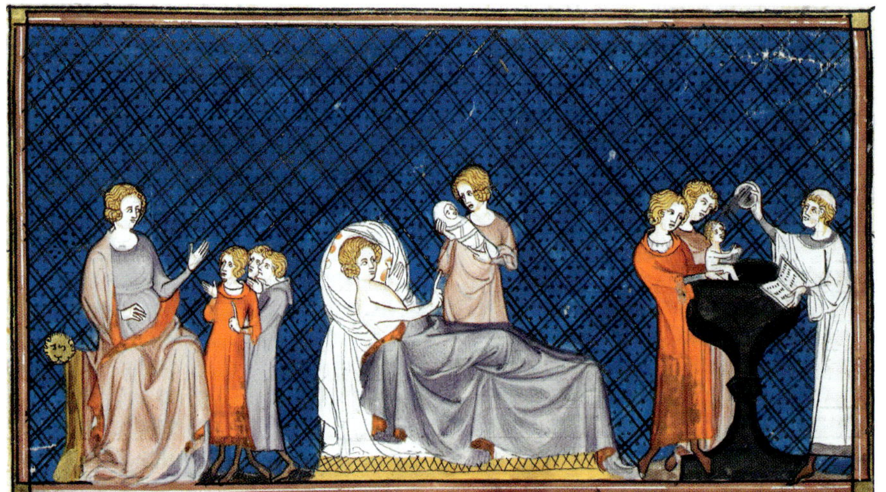

The birth and baptism of Louis the Pious,
Les Grandes chroniques de France,
France, Paris, *c.* 1332–40.
Royal 16 G. vi, f. 187v

advised to apply to their breasts a healing plaster of clay mixed with vinegar to diminish the pain. Breast milk, a vital source of nourishment, could also serve as a panacea. In one unusual image, for example, the Virgin Mary is shown offering her breast to the infant Christ to distract his attention while he is being circumcised (opposite).

Images of mothers suckling their children range from idealised depictions of the Virgin and Child to pictures of ordinary women in domestic settings. Arguably one of the most pragmatic images of breastfeeding is to be found in the fourteenth-century encyclopaedia of the London clerk, James le Palmer, which survives in a single copy written in James' own hand. Under the heading '*Lac*' ('Milk') he discusses the properties of human breast milk and that of goats, and the illuminated initial that introduces the topic shows a woman milking a nanny goat while another sits nearby nursing a baby. Comparisons between animals and humans were also sometimes employed to shed light on child development. 'The young child', claims Albertus Magnus, 'smiles on or about the fortieth day and this is the first activity which the rational soul produces in its body. For this is not a trait shared by the other animals. It dreams after two months but forgets them.'[33]

Infants required special care since they were particularly vulnerable, as attested by high mortality rates. Some scholars estimate that as many as 30 per cent of children died before reaching the age of seven.[34] Wealthy parents, wanting to ensure that their sons and daughters survived and thrived, could avail themselves of advice on childcare. One of the most widely read ensembles of medical texts, compiled in the mid-thirteenth century but based on earlier treatises, advocates the following methods to stimulate an infant's intellectual development:

This initial introduces a discussion of the care of the breast.
Aldobrandino of Siena, *Le Régime du corps*.
Cambrai or Thérouanne/St-Omer, *c.* 1265–70.
Sloane 2435, f. 28v

The Virgin Mary offers her breast to Christ as the circumcision is performed (above). *Poem on the Life of Christ*, England, *c.* 1350–60. This manuscript, which had been hidden in a wall at Pentlow, Essex, was discovered in the eighteenth century. One of the artists who illustrated it also worked on James le Palmer's *Omne bonum*. Cambridge, Fitzwilliam Museum, MS 259, f. 3r

Initial 'L' for *Lac* (Milk) showing a woman milking a goat and a mother nursing her baby (above right). James le Palmer, *Omne Bonum*, England, London, *c.*1360–75. Royal 6 E. vii, f. 404r

> There should be different kinds of pictures, cloths of diverse colors, and pearls placed in front of the child, and one should use nursery songs and simple words; neither rough nor harsh words … should be used in singing in front of the child. After the hour of speech has approached, let the child's nurse anoint its tongue frequently with honey and butter, and this ought to be done especially when speech is delayed. One ought to talk in the child's presence frequently and easy words ought to be said.[35]

In his detailed description of the duties of a wet nurse, the Franciscan friar Bartholomew the Englishman, writing *c.* 1240, describes how the nurse takes care of both the psychological and the physical needs of the child. He employs the masculine pronoun, but we have no reason to think that his description does not reflect the type of care also given, ideally, to female infants of high social standing. He writes:

> Like a mother, the nurse is happy when the child is happy, and suffers when the child suffers. She lifts him up if he falls, gives him suck when he cries, kisses him if he is sick, binds and ties him if he flails about, cleans him if he has soiled himself, and feeds him although he struggles with his fingers. She instructs the child who cannot speak, babbling, practically breaking her tongue, in order to teach him speech more readily. She uses medicines in order to cure the sick

> child. She lifts him up on her hands, shoulders and knees, and relieves the crying child. She first chews the food, preparing it for the toothless child so he can swallow it more easily, and thus feeds the hungry child. Whistling and singing she strokes him as he sleeps and ties the childish limbs with bandages and linens, lest he suffer some curvature.[36]

A similarly affectionate description of a mother playing with a toddler occurs in a thirteenth-century English guide for female religious recluses, the *Ancrene Wisse*, in which the relationship between a woman and her child is used to illustrate the relationship between Christ and his devotees. 'She runs away from him and hides herself, and lets him sit alone and look anxiously around, and call, "Dame! Dame!" and weep a while. Then she jumps out laughing, with outstretched arms, and embraces and kisses him and wipes his eyes.' The young child struggles to walk, bumps into something or stumbles against it, and knocks itself. When that happens, says the author, 'we smack the thing that it has run against, as if that had been naughty, and the child is amused and stops crying.'[37] Both Bartholomew the Englishman and the anonymous author of the *Ancrene Wisse* suggest that a woman's commitment to her child's welfare could go well beyond attending to its bodily needs and that play was as crucial to child development in the Middle Ages as it is today (opposite).

A mother holds her baby as she tends a pot at the fireside. This medallion is one of ten illustrating key stages in life, from birth through maturity to death. These stages were known as the 'Ages of Man'. The Latin caption reads, '*Mitis sum et humilis; lacte vivo puro*' ('I am gentle and humble; I live on pure milk'). De Lisle Psalter, England, probably London, *c.* 1310–20. Arundel 83, fol. 126v

Life-like paintings of the Virgin and Child, showing her as a loving young woman and Christ as an appealing little boy, underscore the tender relationship between mother and child. Paintings in manuscripts also evoke the intimacy between ordinary mothers and their young children. It is often difficult to determine the sex of the babies depicted, but in the case of older children, far more boys are portrayed than girls, an issue that calls for further research. Toddlers taking their first steps with the aid of walkers are depicted in some illustrations, like the Christ child in a marvellous book of hours made for Catherine of Cleves (1417–76).[38] Infants are also shown tucked into a cradle beside their mother's bed or seated on her lap, and some are depicted outdoors, gaining their first impressions of the wider world. Among the throngs of people gathered to watch the consecration of the biblical King David, for example, we find a mother cradling a young child in her arms (p. 78). The image occurs in an outstanding breviary made in Bruges for Queen Isabella of Castile (1451–1504), patron of Christopher Columbus. Both the young mother and her baby smile at a groom who attends one of the steeds ridden by a royal functionary. They have no bearing on the main event depicted, but they lend the biblical scene an immediacy and freshness.

Not all children were angelic. Various authors describe youngsters who had misbehaved and were duly punished. A biography of Queen Margaret of Scotland

Children playing with spinning tops (above). The Huth Hours, France, Valenciennes, S. Netherlands, Bruges, and probably Ghent, early 1480s. Additional 38126, f. 46r

Virgin and Child with Angels (above right). Book of Hours, S. Netherlands, probably Ghent, *c.* 1500. Additional 35313, f. 46r

(1046–93), consort of Malcolm III, attributed to her chaplain Turgot of Durham, contains details relating to her strict views on bringing up her royal offspring. According to Turgot, 'she charged the governor who had the care of the nursery to curb the children, to scold them, and to whip them whenever they were naughty, as frolicksome children will often be. Thanks to their mother's religious care, her children surpassed in good behaviour many who were their elders; they were always affectionate and peaceable among themselves.'[39]

The moral and spiritual instruction of older children also concerned medieval mothers. Touching evidence survives in the form of a long letter, now known as the *Liber manualis* (manual or handbook), written *c.* 841–3 by Dhuoda, a Frankish noblewoman, for her eldest son William, who was just turning sixteen. Dhuoda's manual is important for a number of reasons, not least because it is 'the only extant book-length work' written by a European woman between the late fourth and tenth

Consecration of King David by the prophet Samuel with a mother and baby among the spectators. Another child is shown, clinging to the back of the rider in the foreground. Breviary of Queen Isabella of Castile, S. Netherlands, Bruges and probably Ghent, late 1480s and before 1497. Additional 18851, f. 124r centuries.[40] Modern historians would be poorer without Dhuoda's book, but she makes it clear that she would have preferred to impart her advice to William in person. The circumstances in which she found herself were unhappy. William had gone off to war with his father, the power-hungry renegade Bernard of Septimania, and was being held as a political pawn at the court of Charles the Bald. Dhuoda feared that Bernard might abandon her, since he had also taken with him their eight-month-old baby, another boy, before she had had a chance to christen him.

Dhuoda lived in Uzès, near Nîmes, and in the absence of her husband and sons was obliged to defend the border, maintain the region under her husband's control and raise funds for his military campaigns. These concerns did not, however, eclipse her anxieties about her eldest son's welfare. The subjects covered in her book for William are broad, as if Dhuoda wished to prepare him thoroughly for the future and feared that she might not have another chance. 'In anticipation of the day when I shall no longer be with you', she wrote, 'you have here as a memento of me this little book of moral counsels.'[41]

Drawing apt quotes from classical authors, early Christian theologians and especially the Bible, she urges him to buy books, to study, to be charitable to the poor, respect his father, conduct himself well at court and, above all, to trust in God and pray. Glossing over the subject of sex, Dhuoda recommends that he read relevant books if he needs to know more and tells him to avoid prostitutes. Although her young son was destined to be a warrior, she concentrates her remarks on his civilian life, as if unable to conceive of the worst outcome, his violent death.[42] Her allusion to grandchildren suggests that she yearns for happier days.

The *Liber manualis* reveals Dhuoda's own intellectual and educational attainments as much as her hopes for her son. It is a passionate lecture, delivered by a loving mother to inculcate in her son the values that she herself esteemed. Although they were separated, writing helped bridge the gap. As Dhuoda reminded William, 'Even though I am absent in body, this little book will be present. As you read, it will lead your spirit back to those things you ought to do for my sake.'[43]

Whether or not William read his mother's words, her worst fears were realised. Although Dhuoda had admonished William to remain loyal to his feudal lord, in 850, at the age of twenty-two, he rebelled against Charles the Bald and was killed in Barcelona. Dhuoda had advised William to share her advice with his peers and also with his little brother when he had reached an appropriate age, and it is possible that a copy of her handbook was passed on to him and, consequently, preserved.

Approximately 560 years after Dhuoda had completed her book for William, Christine de Pizan, also living in a time of political unrest and violence as competing factions struggled for the French crown, wrote a handbook of conduct, entitled *Enseignemens moraux* (*Moral teachings*), for her eldest son Jean du Castel, who was

Detail. Breviary of Queen Isabella of Castile, S. Netherlands, Bruges and probably Ghent, late 1480s and before 1497. Additional 18851, f. 124r

Christine de Pizan instructing her son Jean. Christine de Pizan, Collected Works, France, Paris, *c.* 1410–14. Harley 4431, f. 261v about twelve or thirteen. He too was about to be separated from her, to take up residence at another court, that of John of Montagu, 3rd Earl of Salisbury, but he was going to England of his own volition, to establish himself among the elite and further his career.

At the time Christine was writing her handbook for Jean, *c.* 1398, the tradition of composing works of moral advice for princes and noblemen was well established. Most conduct books were addressed to men, but some offered counsel to women.[44] Three-quarters of the moral and practical advice that Christine offered to her son is conventional, but it was probably no less useful for that.[45] However, her instructions to Jean to hold his temper in order to succeed at court, and to avoid wasting his money on lawsuits, seem to be original contributions.[46]

Given Christine's passion for reading, it is not surprising that she recommended specific books to her son. She endorsed the sermons of Bernard of Clairvaux and the encyclopedic works of Vincent of Beauvais, as well as chronicles, such as the *History of Troy* and *Deeds of the Romans*, containing salutary biographies of historical figures. Books she warned Jean to avoid were Ovid's sexually explicit *Art of Love* and, of course, the *Roman de la Rose*, a book she found offensive, as discussed in the previous chapter.[47]

An image showing Christine seated at a desk with a large book lying open before her appears at the beginning of one of the surviving copies of her handbook to Jean. Her authoritative pose and the high-backed chair on which she is seated call to mind images of medieval masters, lecturing their pupils in university classrooms. If we did not know that she was the young man's mother, we would not necessarily suspect the relationship. Like Christine, the young Jean, resplendent in his dusty pink robe and red cowl, radiates confidence. With his feet spread apart and his arms crossed, he gazes directly at her as she leans forward, gesturing emphatically to make her point.

Unlike so many images of authors which are retrospective 'portraits', this one was painted in Christine's own lifetime. More importantly, we can be sure that she viewed it, since the image appears in the most highly finished manuscript of her collected works, a remarkable volume made under her supervision, which she presented to Isabeau of Bavaria, Queen of France, in 1414. In the prologue addressed to the queen, she states that her ideas are behind both the '*histoires*' (images) and '*escriptures*' (text) of the manuscript. While valuable, the words of advice issued to Jean in the *Enseignemens moraux* could not have been as influential as the model of conduct provided in the person of his indomitable mother, who established herself as a professional writer whose works were sought after by the most prestigious patrons.

[Inc]ipit almagesti ptolomei phe[ludiensis]

pnceps nomine albuguafe. in libro suo
quem scienciarum electionem et librorum no
minauit pulcritudinem: dixit quod hic p
tholomeus fuit uir in disciplinarum scien
cia preotens. preminens aliis. in duabus ar
tibus subtilibus. id est. geometria. et astrolo
gia. et fecit libros multos. de quorum numero
iste est qui megasti dicitur. cuius signifi
cacio est maior perfectus. quem ad lingu
am uolentes conuertere arabicam. no
minauerunt almagesti. Hic autem ortus
et educatus fuit in alexandria. cuius si
deri consideravit instrumentis. tempore
regis adriani. et aliorum. et super consideracio
nes abrachis quas in rhodo expertus est.

CHAPTER FOUR

LEARNING

ONE OF THE IRONIES of medieval intellectual culture is that although men controlled access to higher learning and women were barred from attending universities (the first of which were founded *c.* 1150), the subjects studied at these institutions, including grammar, rhetoric, dialectic, arithmetic, geometry, music and astronomy, were represented in medieval art as female figures. We find, for example, an array of women personifying these subjects in a manuscript commissioned by the Neapolitan native Francesco Caraccioli, Master of Theology, who rose to the rank of Chancellor of the University of Paris in 1309, the first Italian to hold the post.[1] It is not surprising that the female personifications in this book are so appealing: Francesco, intending to present it to the learned Robert of Anjou (1275–1343), King of Sicily, enlisted the services of a leading Parisian artist, an anonymous illuminator known today as the 'Meliacin Master'. Despite the fact that the manuscript contains numerous diagrams and twenty-one separate texts studied by students in the Faculty of Arts at the University of Paris, it is not a prosaic textbook, but a magnificent compendium worthy of its royal recipient.

Women, representing the different subjects discussed, are portrayed in the decorated initials at the beginning of each book. Introducing the text of Boethius' *Arithmetica*, Arithmetic completes a sum, while Music, illustrating Boethius' *De musica*, plays the bells. Geometry, pictured at Euclid's *Elementa*, draws figures with a compass, while Astronomy, who appears at the beginning of Ptolemy's *Almagest*, expounds on the constellations. A more complex image marks Priscian's *De constructione* (p. 84). It features Grammar, an elegant woman seated on a bench, who holds a flourishing branch. Each leaf is inscribed with a part of speech, and the label at the fork of the branch reads, '*Ora*' for '*Oratio*' (*Sentence*), on which all the parts of speech (i.e. the leaves) depend. Across from Grammar sits the master, armed with a ferule, a wooden paddle specifically designed to thrash dim-witted students. He clasps the hand of a student who is about to be punished, having failed to master the essentials of the lesson so coherently presented by Grammar. In many depictions, Grammar herself wields a switch or ferule in order to rain punishment on students

Female personification of Astronomy, pointing at the constellations. Miscellany of University Texts on the Liberal Arts, France, Paris, *c.* 1309. Burney 275, f. 390v

Female personification of Grammar, holding a branch representing speech (*oratio*). The Master, wielding a ferule, disciplines a student (far left). Miscellany of University Texts on the Liberal Arts, France, Paris, *c.* 1309. Burney 275, f. 94r

Female personification of Geometry, with square and compass, drawing shapes on a table (left). Miscellany of University Texts on the Liberal Arts, France, Paris, *c.* 1309. Burney 275, f. 293r

too obtuse to comprehend her. Although Grammar is not shown as a disciplinarian in this image, she towers over the male figures, including the master, suggesting that she is the ultimate authority on the subject. The treatment of the other female personifications represented in the manuscript also reveals their high status. Many are shown pointing didactically, with books open on their laps, instructing both masters and students.

In each case, a woman dispenses knowledge and the masters and students benefit from her wisdom. Writers and artists of classical antiquity first employed women as symbols of the seven liberal arts and of other intellectual disciplines, including philosophy. The rationale for depicting these subjects as women was based, in part, on the fact that the Latin words for *arithmetica*, *musica*, *geometria* and all other abstract nouns are feminine in gender. Later authors perpetuated the tradition. In Martianus Capella's fifth-century *On the Marriage of Philology and Mercury*, the seven liberal arts are portrayed as women, and in Boethius' sixth-century *Consolation of Philosophy*, which was one of the most widely read books of secular literature in the Middle Ages, the allegorical figure Lady Philosophy comforts the imprisoned author.

The positive portrayal of Grammar and her associates in medieval art and literature, which was based ultimately on classical precedents, seems to have had relatively little bearing on men's perception of the intellectual abilities of actual women. Despite the link between women and academic subjects advertised in texts and images, women were not only excluded from universities, but also from the grammar, cathedral and collegiate church schools where boys received instruction.[2]

It was one thing for women to enter the academic arena in theory, but another in practice.

In the Middle Ages education was the prerogative of a relatively small elite. Neither women nor men from the lower ranks of society would have had access to learning, and literacy was not widespread. While class largely determined whether or not a person learned to read, gender also played a part. For centuries, laymen from the ruling classes were steeped in a culture that placed greater emphasis on hunting and warfare than on scholarship. While their wives may have learned to read, they often remained illiterate.[3]

This was apparently the case for King Malcolm III of Scotland, whose wife, Queen Margaret (*c.* 1046–93), was a learned and devout woman. A posthumous biography of Margaret written by her chaplain, Turgot of Durham, sheds light on the monarchs' respective levels of literacy and gives us a glimpse of their affectionate relationship. According to Turgot, although Malcolm could not read, he 'would often leaf through and gaze upon the books that she was accustomed to use for prayer and reading; and whenever he gathered from the queen that one of them was particularly dear to her, he too considered it as particularly precious, kissing it

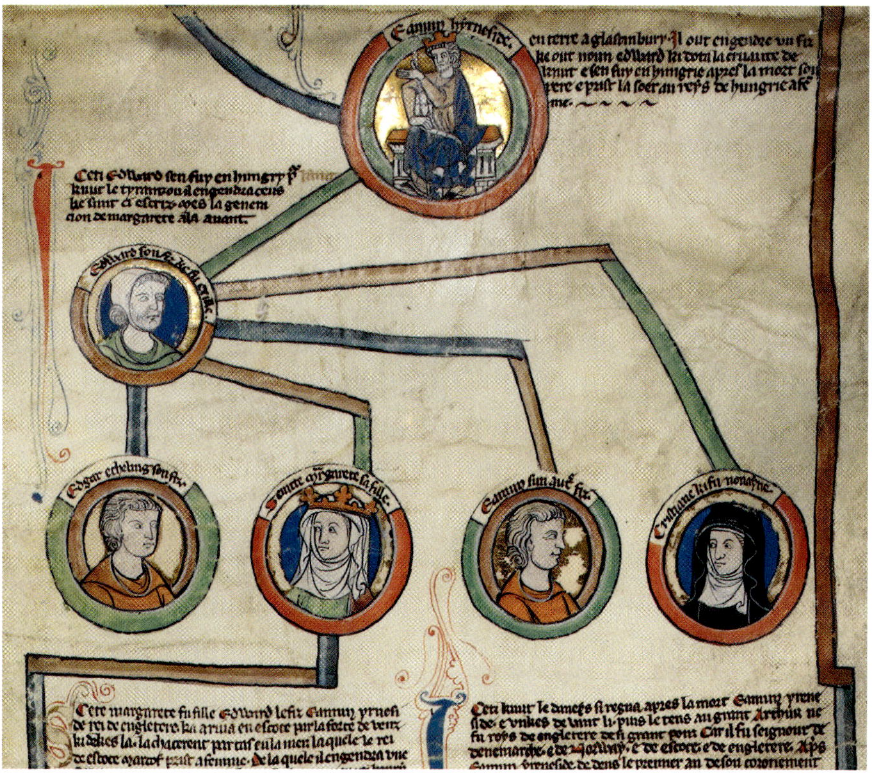

Queen Margaret of Scotland (bottom row, second from left). Genealogical Chronicle of the English Kings in roll form, S. England, *c.* 1300–1307, with addition, *c.* 1340–42. Royal 14 B. vi, membrane 4 (detail)

DIEUX QUI FAIT LA PATER NOSTRE

Christ teaching his disciples the *Pater Noster* (Our Father) (opposite). Frère Laurent, *La Somme le roi*, France, *c.* 1290–1300. Yates Thompson 11, f. 52v. In the nineteenth century, this miniature was separated from the rest of the *Somme le roi* manuscript, which is preserved in London, British Library, Additional 28162

and often touching it. Sometimes he even summoned a goldsmith and ordered him to adorn that volume with gold and gems; and when it had been ornamented, the King himself used to carry the book to the Queen as a token of his devotion.'[4] While this passage forms part of a panegyric to the saintly Queen that presents her in the most favourable terms, it reminds us that it is useful to consider the question of medieval literacy from a variety of perspectives and not reduce the issue to a question of gender. It is significant that Turgot wrote his biography of Queen Margaret at the request of her daughter Matilda (1080–1118), wife of King Henry I of England, who like her mother acquired a reputation 'as a cultured patron of learning'.[5] As an adolescent, Matilda was sent to the prestigious convents of Romsey and Wilton to be educated, but it is probable that her mother served as a positive role model in her formative years.

Mothers who had sufficient wealth and education often encouraged their daughters' intellectual development by teaching them to read. From the outset, reading was connected with a highborn girl's moral edification and spiritual development, and the first steps towards literacy were usually taken at home. Typically, a girl's first exposure to the written word, whether under the guidance of her mother, cleric or other teacher, consisted of learning her ABCs. When she had mastered the alphabet she would be taught how to recite the prayers *Pater Noster* (Our Father), *Ave Maria* (Hail Mary), and the Apostles' Creed. The primacy assigned to the *Pater Noster* reflected the belief that it was the prayer that Christ himself had taught his disciples, as stated in the Bible. Once a girl had gained sufficient knowledge, she could engage with more complex devotional texts in a psalter.

Saint Jerome in his study. Book of Hours, S. Netherlands, Bruges, *c.* 1500. King's 9, f. 240v

The psalter, a collection of poetical texts attributed to the biblical King David, played a major part in public worship because psalms were recited alongside chants and prayers during the 'Divine Office', a literal translation of the Latin *Officium divinum*, meaning a divine duty or obligation. As the term suggests, observing the eight services of prayer (also known as the canonical hours) was obligatory for members of monastic orders and the clergy. It was the responsibility of each monk, nun or cleric to participate in the *opus Dei*, the essential work of giving praise and thanks to God. The psalter was not only central to public worship, but also the principal book for private devotions before the emergence of the book of hours in the thirteenth century, and both types of prayer books were used to teach children how to read.[6]

Few medieval women who instructed their daughters to read from psalters would have been aware that the pedagogical method had ancient roots. As early as AD 403, Saint Jerome articulated his thoughts on the education of girls in a letter to Laeta, the daughter-in-law of Paula, a pious woman who had travelled with him from Rome to Bethlehem where she helped him translate the Bible into Latin and founded a monastery adjacent to his. Laeta had just given birth to a girl and Jerome advised the new mother to educate her baby in the following way:

> Have a set of letters made for her, of boxwood or of ivory and tell her their names. Let her play with them, making play a road to learning…. When she begins with uncertain hand to use the pen, either let another hand be put over hers to guide her baby fingers, or else have the letters marked on the tablet so that her writing may follow their outlines and keep to their limits without straying away…. Let her learn the Psalter first, with these songs let her distract herself, and then let her learn lessons of life in the Proverbs of Solomon…. Let her then pass on to the Gospels and never again lay them down.[7]

Saint Anne teaching the Virgin Mary to read.
Breviary of John the Fearless and Margaret of Bavaria,
France, Paris, *c.* 1410–19.
Harley 2897, f. 340v

Jerome also recommended that 'boys with their wanton frolics' be kept far from the infant and that she gain 'no comprehension of foul words'. Laeta appears to have heeded Jerome's advice, and when her baby daughter grew up she went on to run the monastery that her grandmother Paula had established in Bethlehem. More importantly, the psalter, mentioned by Jerome in his letter to Laeta, continued to be used to teach reading throughout the Middle Ages.

Not many girls learned to write, a specialised skill generally left to scribes, but a book of expenses of the English royal household shows, for example, that in 1286, writing tablets were purchased for the use of Eleanor, the eldest surviving daughter of King Edward I and Eleanor of Castile.[8] As late as the fifteenth century, however, lay women who wanted to write generally dictated their thoughts to an intermediary, usually a male secretary, rather than taking up a pen themselves. Even personal correspondence was usually dictated to a scribe. Margaret Paston (b. 1423), who composed 104 surviving letters, rarely signed them herself, and twenty-nine different scribes copied them on her behalf.[9]

The idea that a mother could play a decisive role in her daughter's education was expressed in paintings and sculptures showing Saint Anne teaching her daughter, the Virgin Mary, to read. The motif, which emerged in England in the early fourteenth century, gradually spread throughout Europe. An illustration from

King Solomon instructing his son Rehoboam. Medieval teachers employed corporal punishment and Solomon is shown brandishing a switch.
Bible, France, Paris, last quarter of the thirteenth century.
Royal 1 C. ii, f. 205r

a liturgical book, made in Paris in the first decades of the fifteenth century, shows Anne, seated on a bench with an open book on her lap, gazing benignly at the Virgin, who stands before her, focusing on the pages. The Virgin is a model of concentration, and the fact that she clutches a stylus with which to trace the words suggests that she has just begun to grasp their meaning. Her gesture calls to mind Jerome's advice to Laeta that her little daughter should follow the outlines marked on a tablet to learn to write, but in this case the Virgin Mary is following the letters on parchment to learn to read. No mention is made of Anne in the Bible, and texts describing her life, which date back to about AD 150, do not claim that she played any part in the Virgin's education. When the theme emerged in the visual arts in the early fourteenth century it was unprecedented.

Images of a father instructing his son, however, are to be found much earlier, and comparing the father/son and mother/daughter motifs sheds light on the way medieval gender roles were constructed. In most thirteenth-century French Bibles, for instance, pictures of King Solomon instructing his firstborn son and heir, Rehoboam, occur at the beginning of the Book of Proverbs, in which Solomon admonishes his child, 'My son, hear the instruction of thy father, and forsake not the law of thy mother.' Although the images of Solomon with Rehoboam and of Saint Anne with the Virgin Mary are both pedagogical, they are different in emphasis. Firstly, Solomon is presented as the author of the Book of Proverbs, imparting his own knowledge to his son, while Anne, having authored no books, teaches the Virgin to read from a sacred text, probably a psalter. The manuscripts held by Anne, Mary or both are often depicted in a generic way, so it is difficult to be specific, but they are certainly intended to represent religious texts. Secondly, the authoritative Solomon, like the female personification of Grammar discussed above, wields a rod or switch to punish his offspring, thereby following the practice of medieval masters, who routinely beat their male students to instruct and chastise them. It would, of course, have been absurd to show Anne thrashing the saintly Virgin Mary, and she is never represented as a disciplinarian. Instead, Anne generally touches or embraces her daughter, offering encouragement rather than reproof. Thirdly, Solomon dispenses general moral guidance. Anne likewise introduces her daughter to spiritual truths, but she also imparts a specific

The Annunciation, showing the Virgin Mary reading. She kneels in front of a prie-dieu, a desk designed for praying. Hours of Catherine de Valois (1401–37), daughter of King Charles VI of France and wife of King Henry V of England, S. England, *c.* 1420.
The manuscript was probably made for Catherine around the time of her marriage. Her heraldic arms are shown in the lower border.
Additional 65100, f. 27v

Mary reads while Joseph holds the Christ Child. This manuscript was made for a woman who is depicted in the volume. Book of Hours. France, Besançon, *c.* 1460–70. Cambridge, Fitzwilliam Museum, MS 69, f. 48r

practical skill – literacy. Finally, Solomon's instruction has a public dimension. He is preparing Rehoboam to rule the kingdom, while Anne's focus is more personal; she is teaching her daughter to read so that she can say her prayers.

Anne must have succeeded in doing so, because in countless Annunciation scenes Mary is shown reading at the moment that the angel Gabriel appears to her to announce that she will give birth to Jesus Christ. The literary motif of Mary reading at the Annunciation is a venerable one. We find it, for example, in the ninth-century *Evangelienbuch*, a German version of the Gospels in verse composed by the Benedictine monk Otfrid von Weissenburg, the earliest German poet known by name. In this work, which Otfrid claimed he wrote for a secular audience, including women, he states that Mary was reading a psalter when Gabriel approached her.[10]

Books appear in some Annunciation scenes predating the twelfth century, but one of the earliest images of the Annunciation to show 'the Virgin Mary unequivocally as a reader meditating on a text' occurs in a psalter made at the Abbey of St Albans *c.* 1130–40.[11] The theme grew in popularity and was widespread by the time the motif of Anne teaching the Virgin first emerged, approximately two hundred years later. Judging from some medieval images, Mary's devotional reading sometimes took precedence over her maternal duties. A Nativity scene from Besançon, for example, shows her engrossed in her book while Joseph holds the swaddled Christ Child (p. 91). Since the theme of the Virgin reading at the Annunciation predates the motif of her being taught to read, the latter can be viewed as a retrospective explanation of how Mary acquired her learning.

Saint Anne and the Virgin Mary who concentrates on her book; added prefatory miniature (*c.* 1302–16). The Alphonso Psalter, England, London, *c.* 1284. Additional 24686, fol. 2v

Some surviving images show the Virgin being educated in a classroom,[12] but these are nowhere near as common as images of her being taught to read by her mother, and her instruction of the Virgin Mary came to define Anne. While Margaret, for example, has her dragon, and Saint Catherine, her wheel, the young Virgin Mary, holding a book, often serves as Anne's attribute.[13]

Many images of Anne with both the Virgin and the Christ Child likewise allude to reading. An outstanding example occurs in a book of hours given as a Christmas gift in 1430 by Anne of Burgundy, wife of John, Duke of Bedford, to her nine-year-old nephew, Henry VI of England. The manuscript was not originally made for the duke and duchess, but significant changes were made to it after they had acquired it, including the addition of their portraits. Anne of Burgundy is shown reading from a prayer book, imitating the activity of her name saint, Anne, who reads from an open volume.[14] The words '*Domine labia mea aperies. Et os meum annunciabit laudem tuam*' ('Lord open my lips. And my mouth shall declare thy praise'),[15] inscribed on the pages of Anne of Burgundy's book, are addressed to Christ, and the infant, leaning towards her, meeting her gaze and raising his hand in blessing, responds to her entreaty. Poised precariously on her mother's lap alongside the Christ Child (who is miraculously close in age to his young mother), Mary playfully riffles the

Anne of Burgundy before Saint Anne who is shown reading to the young Virgin Mary and the Christ Child. The Bedford Hours, France, Paris, *c.* 1410–30. Additional 18850, f. 257v

pages of Saint Anne's open book, seemingly attracted to the object, but blissfully unconcerned by the serious business of reading. Images of Saint Anne teaching the Virgin to read probably reflect pedagogical practice. Presumably mothers, in particular, could identify with the motif because they wanted their daughters to achieve basic literacy as well as an understanding of the main Christian precepts.[16]

Fathers and other male mentors could also play a crucial role in the instruction of their daughters and young female relations. For example, Charlemagne (*c.* 742–814), who united most of Western Europe in his vast empire, championed educational reform and attracted to his court the finest scholars of his day, stipulated that all his children be educated, boys and girls alike. Louis IX of France (d. 1270), whose mother, Blanche of Castile, supervised his instruction,[17] also took an interest in the education of both his daughters and sons, telling them cautionary tales of good and bad kings and making 'them learn the Hours of Our Lady, and repeat to him the Hours of each day, so as to accustom them to hear these regularly when they came to rule over their own lands.'[18]

In the apparent absence of her father, whose identity is obscure, Heloise (d. *c.* 1163), after receiving her early education at the Benedictine convent of Saint Marie d'Argenteuil, went to live with her maternal uncle Fulbert, a canon of Notre-Dame, Paris, who encouraged her studies, doing 'everything in his power to advance her education in letters'.[19] He did not, of course, anticipate that Abelard, whom he welcomed into his household in order to teach his young niece philosophy, would prove to be as interested in Heloise's body as her mind.

As Abelard admitted, 'with our lessons as a pretext we abandoned ourselves entirely to love. Her studies allowed us to withdraw in private, as love desired, and then with our books open before us, more words of love than of our reading passed between us, and more kissing than teaching. My hands strayed oftener to her bosom than to the pages; love drew our eyes to look on each other more than reading kept them on our texts.'[20] Despite Abelard's wandering hands, Heloise augmented the knowledge she had already gained at the convent of Argenteuil and from her uncle Fulbert. Even before she met Abelard she had established an intellectual reputation, having gained some understanding of Greek and Hebrew as well as Latin grammar, rhetoric and philosophy. Peter the Venerable, the great theologian and Abbot of Cluny, had such a high regard for Heloise's intellect and love of learning that he said she 'surpassed all women ... [and had] gone further than almost every man'.[21]

A male mentor also played a significant role in the education of the writer Christine de Pizan. Her father, an astronomer at the court of King Charles V of France, not only recognised his daughter's intellectual precocity, but also shared with her his passion for learning and supported her early interest in books. Had she followed the advice of her mother and devoted herself to spinning 'and silly girlishness', we would lack the work of one of the most prolific female authors of the Middle Ages.[22]

Historical records and surviving manuscripts provide irrefutable proof of the interest that mothers and fathers showed in their children's education. Royal and aristocratic parents 'frequently commissioned or acquired religious and devotional manuscripts for their very young children and used them for the purpose of their children's education'.[23] For example, Isabeau of Bavaria (1371–1435), Queen of France and patron of Christine de Pizan, 'ordered the preparation of a small

Initial 'B' for *Beatus* (Blessed), the opening word of Psalm 1. David admires Bathsheba (above); David kneels in penitence (below). This Psalter, made for Louis IX, was handed down within the French royal family for generations. Eventually Charles VI gave it to his daughter, Marie (1393–1438) who became a nun at Poissy.
Psalter of St. Louis, France, Paris, *c.* 1260–70.
Paris, Bnf MS lat. 10525, f. 85v

illuminated book of hours for her seven-year-old daughter, Jeanne, in 1398, and an alphabet Psalter for another daughter, Michelle, in 1403, just before her eighth birthday'.[24] Neither book has survived, and it is tempting to think that this is because the princesses wore them out through frequent consultation.

Two of Isabeau's other daughters, Marie and Catherine, were both educated at the Dominican convent of Poissy, a royal foundation on the outskirts of Paris, where Christine de Pizan sent her only daughter. Catherine went on to marry Henry V of England, famous as the victor of the Battle of Agincourt, but Marie (1393–1438), who entered Poissy at age four in 1397, became a nun. As a young child Marie, too, was given a psalter, but in this case the gift came from her father, Charles VI of France, possibly to commemorate her entry into the convent.[25] Happily, Marie's indescribably beautiful psalter has been preserved. The volume, which contains seventy-eight full-page paintings of Old Testament scenes on backgrounds of burnished gold, was a family heirloom, originally made for her illustrious ancestor Saint Louis IX (d. 1270), the only French king to be elevated to sainthood.

Another lavish psalter, likely commissioned by Queen Isabeau for her son Louis de Guyenne (b. 1397), the heir to the French throne, is preserved in the British Library. Artists based in Paris illuminated the volume *c.* 1405–10, but Louis did not have long to appreciate it before he died in 1415, at the age of eighteen. It is possible that his sister Catherine brought the psalter to England around the time of her marriage to King Henry V in 1420. The volume was altered *c.* 1430 in order to be presented to her young son, Henry VI, on the occasion of his coronation as king of both France and England, a result of the terms of the Treaty of Troyes, signed on 21 May 1420, which ceded France to the English. Images of Louis de Guyenne praying were reconfigured to suit the new royal owner: the arms of France emblazoned on his robes were replaced by the quartered arms of England and France *ancient*, and several images of monks and nuns were added to the manuscript.[26] The elegant, full-page painting of Dominican nuns inserted in the psalter, an unusual subject for a private devotional book, may perhaps allude to the Dominican convent of Poissy where both Catherine and her sister Marie had been educated. The psalter, almost certainly ordered by Isabeau of Bavaria for her son and adapted about twenty years later for her grandson, underscores the importance of books not only as literary

Dominican nuns in choir.
Psalter of Henry VI,
France, Paris, 1405–10;
added miniatures,
France, Paris or Rouen, *c.* 1430.
Cotton Domitian A. xvii, f. 177v

Saint Catherine presenting Henry VI to the Virgin Mary (right). Psalter of Henry VI, Paris, 1405–10; added miniatures, France, Paris or Rouen, *c.* 1430. Cotton Domitian A. xvii, f. 75r

A prioress instructs two novices (far right). *La Sainte Abbaïe*, France, *c.* 1290–1300. Yates Thompson 11, fol. 1v

tools, cultural artefacts and channels of religious devotion, but also as vehicles of political and dynastic aspirations.

Convents functioned as centres of learning where books were preserved, studied, often copied and sometimes illuminated. Many were presided over by stern prioresses, like the one shown wielding a switch as she instructs two novices in a copiously illustrated copy of a treatise known as *La Sainte Abbaïe*, made in northern France *c.* 1290. Women committed to the religious life, including nuns who had taken vows of perpetual chastity in childhood and had no offspring of their own, played a significant role in caring for and educating children. For example, it was from the anchoress Jutta of Sponheim, a religious recluse, that the eight-year-old Hildegard of Bingen (1098–1179) learned to read her psalter, before going on to become an abbess and celebrated author.

Many girls, particularly from royal and aristocratic families, were educated in convents, and surviving manuscripts attest to this. A thirteenth-century psalter illuminated by a German nun incorporates several features designed for the instruction of a young reader. It contains alphabets and illustrations intended to aid a girl encountering essential prayers and liturgical texts for the first time. One page is inscribed with the Apostles' Creed, one of three prayers (along with the Lord's Prayer and Hail Mary) that every Christian was required to learn, by decree of the Fourth Lateran Council of 1215. Tradition held that the twelve apostles (Christ's disciples) had composed the Creed collaboratively, each supplying a single phrase.

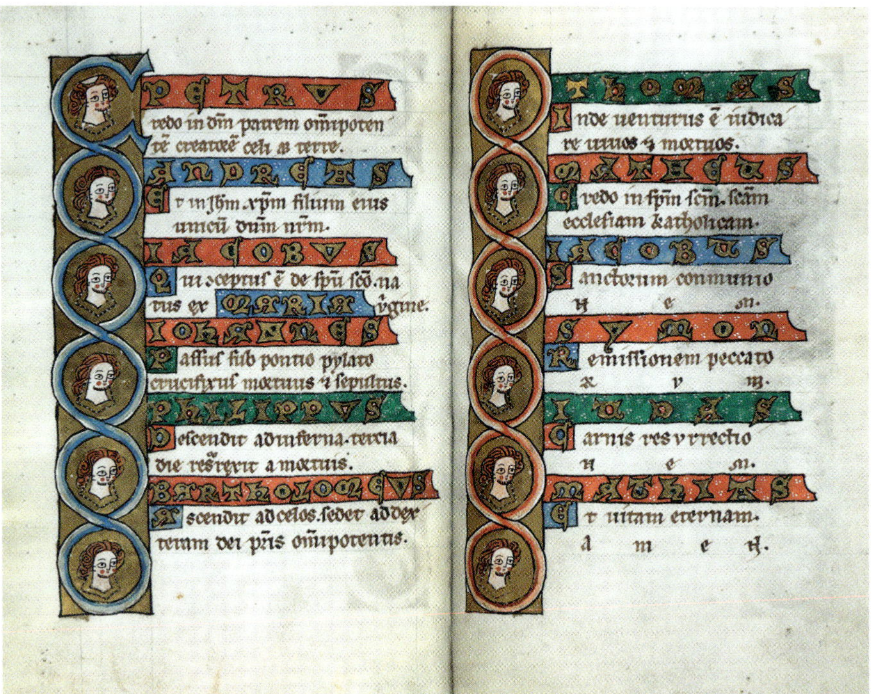

Creed with busts of apostles. Psalter for the use of a Benedictine nunnery, Germany, Diocese of Bamberg, late thirteenth century. Additional 60629, ff. 161v-162r

Alluding to this tradition, the nun who illuminated the psalter painted the bust of a different apostle before each phrase of the Creed. These 'portraits' also serve a didactic purpose; like 'bullet points', they mark off each statement of the prayer, making it easier for a beginning reader to memorise the Creed, one apostle at a time.[27] Nuns, like monks, were expected to recite the entire psalter every week over the course of the Divine Office (see p. 87 above), so having mastered the Creed, the young girl would still have had a significant task ahead.

Girls who learned to read from this German psalter could not have failed to be entranced by its illustrations, painted in vibrant colours and adorned with burnished gold leaf, including one showing the patriarch Jacob dreaming of a ladder ascending into heaven. Medallions in the border feature secular subjects, among them a stag blowing a horn, a squirrel with a piece of fruit, and a cat with a spindle and distaff. These pictures are stylistically distinct from those made by professional artists, and the nun who created them is thought to have drawn inspiration from needlework.[28]

In addition to their religious obligations, spinning and embroidering were among the central occupations of medieval nuns. If the visual evidence is to be believed, spinning also provided a diversion for their cats (p. 101). According to

Jacob's Ladder, with vignettes of men and animals, hunting or playing musical instruments. A tabby cat with a distaff for spinning, one of the main occupations of medieval nuns, is shown in the medallion on the right near the bottom of the frame. Psalter for the use of a Benedictine nunnery, Germany, Diocese of Bamberg, late thirteenth century. Additional 60629, f. 87v

rules governing the ownership of personal property, nuns were not permitted to own pets of any kind. Clerical supervisors frequently criticised nuns for this offence, which suggests that many women valued the company provided by their lap dogs and cats so much that they kept the animals regardless.

Medieval Christians believed that the Virgin Mary, as a young girl, had been educated in the Temple in Jerusalem, where she had received religious instruction and learned to weave. Praying and working were considered to be complementary activities, and nuns who devoted themselves to embroidery or spinning viewed the

Virgin Mary as a role model.[29] Some nuns were reputed to pray and spin with phenomenal zeal. 'According to the chronicle of Kirchberg, the prioress Leugard recited a thousand Ave Marias as well as the Psalter each day as she worked, laboring like the Virgin with her spindle and thread.'[30] Girls just beginning to learn to say their prayers and to grapple with their spindles may well have looked on such figures with a mixture of awe and despair.

Needlework and prayer could prove tedious for little girls and some chafed under the strict regime. The misbehaviour of one high-spirited child is the theme of a miracle recorded in the largest surviving medieval collection of miracles of the Virgin Mary, the thirteenth-century *Cantigas de Santa Maria* (*Songs of Holy Mary*), commissioned by Alfonso X, King of Castile-León.[31] Set at the Cistercian convent of Santa María la Real de Las Huelgas in Burgos, the miracle tale concerns a little girl who was being educated there by the nuns, one of whom was her aunt.[32] The girl and her companions frequently played pranks, and the nuns punished them severely. One day when the girl had been particularly naughty, her aunt sought her out in order to beat her. However, the child, in desperation, approached a statue of the Virgin Mary and beseeched it to erase the deed from her aunt's mind. Miraculously, the statue then spoke to the girl, reassuring her that all would be well, and the next day, when the girl told her aunt about her encounter with the statue, the two were reconciled.

Religious communities offered female writers the time and space to devote to their craft, as well as the requisite tools, books and secretarial staff. Female religious authors, like the prolific German nun Hrotsvitha of Gandersheim (fl. 965), who composed eight legends, six plays and two historical chronicles, often wrote with a specific audience in mind: the sisters of their own communities.[33] For the nuns in her charge, including young novices, Herrad of Landsberg (d. 1195), abbess of Hohenburg in Alsace, designed the *Hortus deliciarum* (*Garden of Delights*), an encyclopaedia with 336 illustrations, as well as polyphonic songs.[34] That convents could nurture creativity is also attested by a poem composed in the late twelfth century by an English nun. Written in Anglo-Norman French, in rhyming couplets, the poem, which is based on earlier Latin accounts, tells the story of Saint Catherine of Alexandria, the patron saint of learning, who was allegedly martyred for her faith in the fourth century.[35] Our knowledge of the female author of the poem rests solely on the epilogue, in which she states that her name is Clemence and that she is a nun at Barking. Clemence's reference to Barking Abbey, which lay just east of London, provides a crucial clue to her milieu.

The young Virgin Mary, assisted by an angel, weaves in the temple in Jerusalem. According to an apocryphal story, dating back to the late second century, the Virgin Mary helped to make a new curtain for the temple.
The Bedford Hours, France, Paris, *c.* 1410–30. Additional 18850, f. 32r

A cat plays as a nun spins. Cats were favourite pets, but nuns also kept small dogs, birds, and even squirrels. Book of Hours, Use of Liège, S. Netherlands, Liège or Tournai, *c.* 1310–20. Stowe 17, f. 34r

In 666, when no religious communities for women existed in England, Saint Erkenwald founded Barking Abbey for his sister Ethelburga, who was its first abbess. The abbey flourished, and a century later it was re-founded as a royal institution. From that time forth, the abbess of Barking was appointed by the king. For centuries Barking was a centre of learning, and its royal history, reputation, wealth and close proximity to the court made it an attractive choice for parents who wanted their daughters to receive a superior education, and for aristocratic and royal women dedicated to the religious life.

Clemence of Barking's poem is not a pedestrian biography of Saint Catherine of Alexandria, whose life had been described by scores of previous writers, but a poetic tour-de-force, showing her mastery of her Latin source (the *Vulgata*), which she must have read in Barking's well-provisioned library, and, most intriguingly, her knowledge of the latest popular stories of courtly romance and adventure, notably Thomas of Britain's *Tristan*, written only a few years earlier, possibly for Eleanor of Aquitaine.[36] Weaving together these different strands, Clemence makes herself and her subject spring to life.

According to tradition Catherine, the daughter of King Costus, was a beautiful young virgin. Most early Christian female saints are described in similar terms. What set Catherine apart was not her high social status, youth, good looks

or intact hymen, but her prodigious knowledge. On hearing that the pagan Emperor Maxentius had commanded all his subjects to make sacrifices to pagan idols, the eighteen-year-old Catherine, a devout Christian, confronted him, arguing that his gods were worthless compared to the true God she espoused.

Catherine's arguments were so sophisticated that Maxentius, realising that he was about to be outsmarted, summoned fifty philosophers to challenge her to debate. Despite their best efforts, Catherine prevailed and converted them all to Christianity. More galling still, she also converted Maxentius' wife, the empress, and spurned his amorous advances. Enraged by the philosophers' incompetence and Catherine's rhetoric and rejection, Maxentius had them executed and her tortured. A machine with four wheels, studded with blades, was erected to dismember her, but God, hearing her prayers, destroyed this contraption along with four thousand pagans for good measure. The body count continued to escalate: every person Catherine converted to Christianity, including the empress, was condemned to death, and Catherine was beheaded. After her martyrdom, angels were said to have conveyed her body to Mount Sinai and her soul to heaven.

An angel breaks the wheels designed to kill Saint Catherine and takes revenge on her torturers.
Huth Psalter, N. England, possibly Lincoln or York, *c.* 1280.
Additional 38116, f. 13r

Empowered by the story of Catherine, the most intellectual and eloquent of all female saints, Clemence of Barking transformed the narrative, incorporating phrases and ideas from contemporary romances. For example, she compares Catherine, preparing to debate with the philosophers, with a knight entering the field to sally forth in battle, and she has Maxentius express his anger over his wife's conversion in terms of a courtly lover spurned by his beloved.[37] No other version of Saint Catherine's life contains similar allusions, a feature that must have enhanced the story's appeal for Clemence's original audience – the nuns of Barking and members of the aristocracy and nearby royal court in London. Clemence's Catherine of Alexandria is fluent in Anglo-Norman French, Clemence's mother tongue, and she articulates her arguments in especially clever ways. Speaking through Catherine, Clemence reveals her own linguistic adroitness and mastery of poetic form.[38]

Catherine passionately professes her faith; having rejected all earthly lovers, she is the bride of Christ, an idea she articulates in a striking speech that echoes the biblical Song of Songs (*Cantica canticorum*). It begins:

Car Jhesu Crist le mien espus
Est de m'amur si cuveitus,
Que ja avum fait cuvenant
Que amie sui e il amant

Jesus Christ, my bridegroom,
So desires my love
That the two of us have already made a covenant
That I am his beloved and he is my lover

'He is my pleasure', Catherine continues, 'and my comfort, my sweetness and my delight. I love him so much that I cannot be parted from him; for I love him alone, and him alone do I desire [and] … he loves me in return.'[39] Catherine voices these thoughts, but the sentiments expressed are those of Clemence who, like her fellow nuns of Barking, had chosen to abstain from marriage and devote herself to God.

Clemence could not have chosen a more suitable subject for her poem than Saint Catherine, who served as a powerful model of intellectual achievement and female autonomy. Clemence's portrait of the saint was fashioned at a time when little credence was given to the idea that women could take an active role in academic discourse and public debate. Although several versions of Catherine's life were written in the twelfth century, and male authors also emphasised Catherine's learning and verbal dexterity, they, however, viewed her as an anomaly – a saint miraculously endowed with wisdom and rhetorical skill.[40] By contrast, Clemence the earliest known female author to write in French, presents Catherine's knowledge and eloquence as integral aspects of her character, worthy of emulation by women in general.

Through their written works, religious women such as Clemence shared their knowledge with their contemporaries and, on their deaths, left a literary legacy on which the next generation could build.[41] Nuns also learned from each other by example, consciously imitating the pious acts of their sisters. Nine books known as the Sister-Books, written by Dominican nuns in Germany in the first half of the fourteenth century, record the early history of their convents and describe, by name, nuns of their communities worthy of emulation. A nun from Töss wrote of Anna von Klingnau, 'She rarely spoke a superfluous word, but God had given her the grace that she was overflowing with the sweetest words. And they were so good to listen to that hearts were rightly moved by them.' The stamina of another nun, Elsbetlein, is noted in the Sister-Book from Gotteszell, which records that 'in the very cold wintertime, she studied during the night in front of her bed so much and so eagerly that she did not feel the bitter cold and paid no attention until the fingers of her hand got stiff where she held the book'. Written by women, for women, these books present a unique picture of nuns' lives.[42]

Nuns and religious recluses also disseminated knowledge by working as scribes. The richest evidence of female scribal practice is from Germany. The twelfth-century Bavarian recluse Diemut, who copied forty-five volumes single-handedly, added entire shelves of books to the monastic library of the Benedictines at Wessobrunn where she lived in isolation in a cell, supported by the community of monks and nuns.[43] Her remarkable industry shows that she was a skilled professional and points to a high demand for books among her peers.

We know that many religious communities doubled as primary schools, but relatively little about the kind of education medieval girls received from tutors and in classrooms. One item that sheds light on the subject, however, is a fourteenth-century manuscript from Bohemia. It contains an image of a little girl, seated on a bench with her tutor, holding a hornbook from which she learns the alphabet and the *Pater Noster* ('Our Father') prayer. A hornbook was a wooden panel to which a piece of parchment had been attached, usually inscribed with the alphabet. Covered with a thin, transparent sheet of horn to protect them from wear, such panels were commonly used to instruct young children. In an adjacent 'portrait' the girl is shown at a slightly more advanced age, reading a book, and the caption explains that once she had mastered the alphabet, she learned to read the psalter.[44]

Additional evidence of pedagogical practices survives in the form of a prayer book made in Bruges *c.* 1445 for a young girl. The manuscript contains an alphabet page, with the letters inscribed in large characters in alternating red and blue ink, and various elementary texts in both Latin and Middle Dutch. The cross that appears at the start of the alphabet is not a decorative motif, but a meaningful

With the help of her tutor, a young girl learns to read. On the left she studies the alphabet, and on the right, she reads from a psalter. Filled with pen drawings, this picture book contains saints' lives and legends, and other edifying texts. Krumauer Bildercodex, Krumlov, Czech Republic, *c.* 1360. Vienna, Österreiches Nationalbibliothek, cod. 370, f. 131r

Girls in a classroom with a female teacher, with the text of the alphabet on the facing page. Compilation of texts, including a Primer (*Abecedarium*), S. Netherlands, probably Bruges, *c.* 1445.
Harley 3828, ff. 27v–28r

symbol. Children were instructed to make the sign of the cross before reciting the alphabet, a practice that reveals how closely medieval learning was linked to religion in every educational setting. The fact that the book contains religious texts, rather than secular ones, demonstrates that as late as the fifteenth century, 'Christianity did not just dominate the canon of literature passively: it actively pervaded the very concept of reading a book – in secular society no less than in the Church.'[45]

On the facing page, across from the alphabet, is an image showing three girls in a classroom receiving instruction from a female schoolteacher. Dressed in blue, the schoolmistress sits before them with her ferule poised to strike the palm of the girl standing in front of her. Another woman distinguished by her blue gown, possibly an assistant, appears at the back of the classroom. If she is also an instructor, the pupil to teacher ratio is extremely favourable, as is the provision of books for the students.[46] A hornbook, like the one shown in the Bohemian manuscript, hangs on the wall. The visual evidence suggests that this prayer book was designed for use in a classroom.

In Flanders, where the prayer book was made, the educational gap separating boys and girls was less pronounced than in most other parts of Europe.[47] The poet and chronicler Jean Froissart (d. *c.* 1405), from Valenciennes, Hainault, one of whose patrons was his compatriot, Queen Philippa of Hainault, consort of Edward III of England, states that he was educated at a school attended by both boys and girls.[48] In his *Chroniques*, Jean reveals that he became infatuated with one of his female classmates, with whom he often read, and that he lent her a book with a love note concealed within its pages. Sadly, when he later declared his love in person, she rejected him so emphatically that she tore out a hank of his hair.[49]

Attending university was not an option for women, but some found ways to support higher learning. Aristocratic and royal women who had the leisure to read and the wealth to commission books were not only more likely to inspire literary interests in their children, but also to serve as benefactors of educational institutions. Eleanor of Castile, for example, was a generous patron of both the friars and the scholars at Oxford and exhibited a desire to extend her own knowledge of theology, one of the main subjects studied there. She commissioned from John Pecham, Archbishop of Canterbury (1279–92), a French translation of a Latin work that explained the heavenly hierarchy, and in the final year of her life she sent a letter to a certain Master Richard at the University of Oxford concerning a book that she owned.[50]

Eleanor of Castile's granddaughter Elizabeth de Burgh (1294–1360), Lady Clare, daughter of Joan of Acre, likewise supported higher education, exceeding by far the model of patronage offered by her grandmother. It is not surprising that Elizabeth chose to devote money to this cause, because learning played an important part in her life. She commissioned manuscripts and borrowed volumes from the royal collection, including on one occasion three books on surgery and four romances. She also purchased manuscripts in bulk, sending seven horses to transport those she had acquired on a single day in London. Some of the manuscripts she commissioned were sumptuous, including a liturgical book that she ordered for Edward III's chapel at Windsor. Like her grandmother, she had an illuminator on her payroll.[51]

Elizabeth, who administered her own estates for almost forty years after the death of her third and last husband in 1322, was ideally placed to put University Hall, Cambridge, on a firm financial footing.[52] Her initial donations to the institution, which was founded in 1326, were only the beginning of her commitment. She became patron of the college in 1336, and as early as 1339 it bore her name. On the seal she had made for Clare College she is shown presenting the statutes to the master and scholars, which she did in 1359. Her pride in her royal ancestry is manifest on the seal, which, in addition to religious imagery and her own arms, bears those of her grandparents, Edward I and Eleanor of Castile.

Marie de St Pol (*c.* 1304–77), Countess of Pembroke, kneeling before Saint Mary Magdalene. Marie founded the Hall of Valence Mary, Cambridge in 1347 (now Pembroke College). In 1342, she also founded a house for Franciscan nuns (Poor Clares) at nearby Denny. Breviary of Marie de St Pol, France, Paris, *c.* 1330–40. Cambridge University Library, MS Dd.5.5, f. 236r

When Elizabeth lent her support to University Hall, benefactions of this kind by the nobility were highly unusual. Only two noble donors endowed colleges: Elizabeth de Burgh and her friend Marie de St Pol, Countess of Pembroke, who, in 1347, founded the Cambridge college named after her.[53]

It seems astonishing that the same basic texts and educational methods advocated by Jerome in the early fifth century were still being employed eight hundred years later, and that the psalter continued to serve as the preferred book of instruction for both boys and girls. By the mid-thirteenth century, however, the psalter began to be replaced in popularity by a new type of devotional book: the book of hours, which became the chief means of instruction and edification.

De pprio angelo. Or.
Dominus custodiat te ab omni malo
Sub umbra alarum tuarum protege me
ustos p
superna
Me tib
missum
fende qui
Ergo
mentem
t labe ve
Assidu
comes michi sis vite qꝫ lucerna
Angele fide comes sapiens
rande benigne.

CHAPTER FIVE

PRAYER

MORE PRAYER BOOKS have survived than any other single type of book owned by medieval women. Having been instructed to read from psalters and books of hours as small children, countless women continued to do so throughout their lives. Priests and clerical advisors encouraged women to say the psalms, but it was not compulsory. Nevertheless, frequent mention of the practice by medieval writers down through the centuries shows that for many people it was engrained in their daily routines. For the saintly queen Margaret of Scotland (*c.* 1046–93), reciting the psalms was a catalyst for performing pious actions; when she got up in the morning and had said her prayers and read her psalter, she would habitually feed orphans. As her biographer, Turgot of Durham, reports, 'when the little ones were carried to her she did not think it beneath her to take them upon her knee, and to get their pap ready for them, and this she put into their mouths with the spoon which she herself used'.[1] It was also the custom for women to recite their prayers before going to sleep. Matthew Paris, the thirteenth-century historian and monk of St Albans, reported that a plot to assassinate King Henry III of England in 1238 was foiled by Margaret Biset, one of the queen's ladies-in-waiting, who heard the intruder break into the palace at night because she had stayed up to recite her psalter by candlelight.[2] The Latin verb *psallebat*, employed by Matthew, probably refers to reading aloud rather than silently. In his sermons, the Dominican Antoninus of Florence, elected archbishop of the city in 1446, also referred to women who stayed up late to pray, condemning those who did so to avoid having sex with their husbands.[3] Women committed to the religious life were able to devote the greatest time to saying the psalms. According to the biographer of the English visionary Christina of Markyate (*c.* 1095–1155), her constant recitation of the sacred texts irritated the devil so much that he caused toads 'with big and terrible eyes' to invade her cell and squat on the psalter that lay open on her lap.[4] Some women memorised the entire Book of Psalms. The prioress Juliana of Mont Cornillon (b. *c.* 1192) is said to have memorised the psalms, the Song of Songs and twenty sermons by the time she had reached adolescence.[5]

Margaret Beauchamp and her guardian angel. Prayers to guardian angels were included in books of hours from the late fourteenth century onwards. The Beaufort/ Beauchamp Hours, England, London, *c.* 1430–40. Royal 2 A. xviii, f. 26r

As supplementary texts were added to the psalter *c.* 1230–40, a new type of prayer book developed: the book of hours. The core texts of books of hours were derived from the breviary, the service book used by priests, monks and nuns for public worship. As its name suggests, the book of hours comprised a series of prayers to be said at specific times by lay people in imitation of members of monastic orders and the clergy, who observed eight services of prayer known as the Divine Office. The Divine Office followed a rigorous timetable: *Matins* (prayer before sunrise), *Lauds* (dawn prayer), *Prime* (prayer at the first hour: 6 am), *Terce* (prayer at the third hour: 9 am), *Sext* (prayer at the sixth hour: 12 noon), *None* (prayer at the ninth hour: 3 pm), *Vespers* (evening prayer: around 6 pm), and, finally, *Compline* (prayer at nightfall). Books of hours were organised according to this system, but in practice people did not strictly observe this schedule.

Tens of thousands of books of hours have survived, and these vary enormously. Some are profusely illustrated, but others are unadorned. Books of hours made in England and France are usually in Latin, but many produced in Germany and the Netherlands are in the vernacular. Readings and prayers included in such volumes also diverge, but typically a book of hours contains a calendar (listing the main liturgical feasts), four lessons from the Gospels, prayers to the Virgin Mary, the Hours of the Virgin, Hours of the Cross and Hours of the Holy Spirit, the Penitential Psalms and the Litany of Saints, the Office of the Dead and Suffrages (prayers to saints). Because books of hours were often tailored to the tastes and needs of particular patrons, they provide unique insights into the devotional lives of individual women.

Women who commissioned books of hours could choose which prayers to include, which to omit, and what form the decoration would take. To further personalise these volumes, they could have their arms and devices emblazoned on the pages and could write their names inside them. Many women recorded the birth and death dates of family members in the calendars that prefaced their book of hours. These manuscripts were generally handed down from one generation to the next.

The earliest known English book of hours, illuminated in Oxford *c.* 1240 by the artist William de Brailes, contains depictions of a woman at prayer, almost certainly the female patron. She appears five times, petitioning God, in the large decorated initials which mark the beginning of specific texts.[6] From the late fourteenth century onwards, medieval artists began to experiment with portraiture in the modern sense, but 'portraits' of women in devotional books, painted before that time, are not true likenesses, but idealised images of women engaged in spiritual contemplation. The primary audience for the 'portrait' was the female book owner, who would have seen herself reflected in the pages when she opened her book.

Three separate self-portraits of the artist, William de Brailes, are also incorporated in the initials of this early book of hours, including one with an inscription

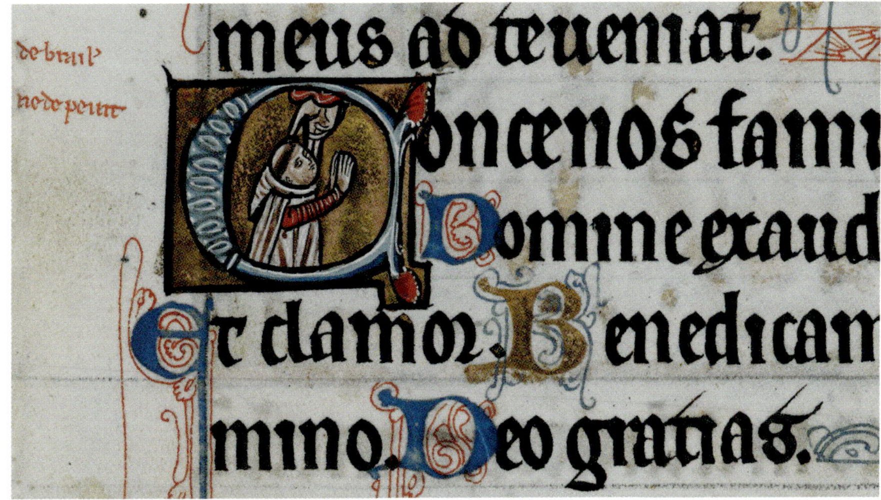

Self-portrait of the illuminator William de Brailes with an inscription in the margin, identifying him as the artist. De Brailes Hours, England, Oxford, *c.* 1240. Additional 49999, f. 43r

An image of the woman for whom this book of hours was made. De Brailes Hours, England, Oxford, *c.* 1240. Additional 49999, f. 90r

in Anglo-Norman French identifying the artist by name, 'w. de brial' q. me depeint' ('w. de brailes who painted me', f. 43r), and another signed, w. de brail' (f. 47r). It was highly unusual for an artist of the period to sign his work in this way and equally exceptional for him to include his own portraits, in addition to images of the patron. Presumably, the anonymous woman for whom he made the manuscript was not averse to having the artist depicted in her prayer book. Did she remember him in her prayers when she recited the texts? We will never know, and we will never be able to identify her with absolute certainty.

One of the images of the female patron features an Anglo-Norman French inscription in the margin that has been interpreted as a possible clue. The inscription reads, '*ele clama deu en sa tribulaciun*', which can be translated as 'she called to god in her tribulation', but an alternative reading, 'Ela called to god in her tribulation', has been advanced by Loveday Lewes Gee, who has argued that the woman is possibly to be identified with Ela Longespee (d. 1297), Countess of Warwick (in Anglo-Norman French, 'Ele Comitisse Warevykie'), who had family ties to Oxford, was buried there, and was a benefactress of both Merton and Balliol colleges.[7] Since William de Brailes inserted his own name beside one of his 'portraits' in the manuscript, the suggestion that the word '*ele*' could be translated as a proper name is congruent with the personal character of this exceptional yet enigmatic book.

A woman with prayer book kneeling beneath the enthroned Virgin and Child. Egerton Hours, England, *c.* 1250–75. Egerton 1151, f. 7r

Because she had given birth to Christ, the Virgin Mary was honoured above any other saint. One of the principal texts of the book of hours was the Office of the Virgin, a series of prayers directed to her. In books of hours made in England and France from the thirteenth century onwards, book owners are most frequently depicted petitioning the Virgin at the prayer to be said at the end of the day or on rising (Matins), which opens: '*Domine labia mea aperies / Et os meum annunciabit laudem tuam*' ('Lord, open my lips, and my mouth will declare your praise'). A portrait of this type is found in what may be the very earliest surviving book of hours commissioned by a woman. Made in Paris in the 1230s, the manuscript includes an image of the owner prostrating herself before the enthroned Virgin and Child at the start of Matins, as well as three other portraits of her marking other points in the book.[8] Similarly, in the illustration for Matins in an English book of hours made *c.* 1250–75, a woman clutching her prayer book is shown kneeling beneath the enthroned Virgin and Child in the decorated initial 'D' for '*Domine*', at the start of Matins.

The custom of using a portrait of the book owner to mark the start of Matins was maintained for hundreds of years. Images of this kind probably prompted female book owners to adopt similar postures and to focus their thoughts on the divine just before they went to sleep or when they first got up. In a book of hours made in London, *c.* 1440–43, for Margaret Beauchamp, grandmother of King Henry VII, she appears at Matins within the large initial 'D' for '*Domine*', kneeling with her open book beneath an Annunciation scene. The Virgin, whose devotions are interrupted by the angel Gabriel, is also shown with an open book, which mirrors the volume from which Margaret Beauchamp reads. Margaret's prayer, directed to Mary, is written on the narrow scroll (banderole) which she clutches between her clasped hands. It bears the inscription: '*Mat[er] ora filium ut post h[oc] exiliu[m] nob[is] donet gaudiu[m] sine fine*' (Mother, pray to your son that after this exile he will give us joy without end'). In this image, both Margaret's plea and the speech of the angel Gabriel are represented by banderoles, the medieval equivalent of the speech bubble. Margaret's banderole drifts upwards as if to signify that she is raising her voice in prayer to the Virgin. As Margaret's petition reminds us, Mary was not only venerated as the mother of Christ, but also served as the archetypal mother, the *mater misericordiae* (Mother of Mercy) to whom every individual could turn for understanding and assistance.[9]

Margaret Beauchamp praying to the Virgin Mary, who is depicted above with Gabriel. The Beaufort/Beauchamp Hours, England, London, *c.* 1430–40. Royal 2 A. xviii, f. 34r

Medieval prayers were often directed to the Virgin Mary, saints and angels, asking them to intercede with God the Father and Christ on the petitioner's behalf, a practice that reflects the hierarchical nature of medieval society. As noted by Virginia Reinburg, 'to pray was to participate in a grand network of spiritual patronage and kinship, where all exchanges and relationships were reciprocal. This was a world in which nearly everyone assumed that eternal salvation as well as most earthly business was best conducted through intercession.'[10] People who prayed expected an answer, an idea ably conveyed by another image in Margaret Beauchamp's manuscript, marking a prayer addressed to her guardian angel, which begins, '*Angele, qui meus es custos pietate superna, me tibi commissum serva, defende, guberna*' ('Angel who are my guardian by divine mercy, keep me who has been entrusted to you, defend me, and rule me').[11] An additional plea to the angel is inscribed on Margaret's banderole, which reads, '*Sub umbra alarum tuarum protege me*' ('Protect me under the shadow of your wings'). The angel does, in fact, shelter her beneath one of his brilliant pink and red wings, and his banderole bears the benediction, '*dominus custodiat te ab omni malo*' ('May the Lord protect you from all evil').[12]

Margaret Beauchamp and her guardian angel.
For detail, see p.108.
The Beaufort/ Beauchamp Hours, England, London, *c.* 1430–40.
Royal 2 A. xviii, f. 26r

Pictures like this one, showing a woman in dialogue with the divine, convey the message that it is possible to forge a direct connection to God without a male, clerical intermediary. This must have been especially emancipating for women since they were barred from the priesthood. Some images of women at prayer show the hand of God reaching down to bless them (opposite), a gesture implying that their voices have, indeed, been heard. Far more images of women actually using books survive in devotional manuscripts than in copies of secular texts, which suggests that these images 'indicate something more personal and profound than an ability to read.'[13]

Produced in the workshop of Jean Pucelle, the leading Parisian illuminator of the first decades of the fourteenth century, the Savoy Hours, which survives only in part, contains twenty-five images of its female patron, Blanche of Burgundy, Countess of Savoy and granddaughter of King Louis IX of France.[14] The contents of the book offer further evidence of its personal nature. In addition to the standard texts is a prayer, entitled, '*memoire pour moy especial*' ('prayer for myself'), which is accompanied by an image of Blanche kneeling in front of an altar on which a

A praying woman receives God's blessing. Grandison Psalter, England, 1270–80. Additional 21926, f. 135r

qui facit superbiam: qui loquitur
iniqua non direxit in conspectu o
culorum meorum.
In matutino interficiebam omnes
peccatores terre: ut disperderem de ci
uitate dñi oms operantes iniquitatem. Glia.
oracionem meam: et clamor meus
ad te ueniat.
Non auertas faciem tuam a me:
in quacumque die tribulor inclina
Iubilate deo omnis terra. Clamor meus. Amen.

crucifix rests. A stand at her feet supports her open prayer book, but she does not consult the text. Rather, she fixes her gaze on the image of the crucified Christ, as if, having recited her prayers, she is in a state of spiritual contemplation. Many royal and aristocratic women would have read their prayers in private chapels decorated with paintings and sculptures of Christ, the Virgin Mary and the saints – artworks that would have reinforced the messages of the texts and images contained in their devotional books. Less privileged women could also have performed comparable devotions in parish churches, using far plainer books of hours to guide their meditations.

One of the earliest surviving German books of hours, which was made for a woman, possibly a nun, in the mid-thirteenth century, contains explicit instructions for its owner to contemplate an image of the crucified Christ, pausing to look at each part of his body in turn. Interspersed with the Latin prayers, the instructions, written in German, direct her to 'Stand in front of the cross and gaze at it, and say this prayer with all your heart … Now look at the visage of our Lord … Now speak with all your heart to his breast … Now to his right hand … Now to his left hand … Now look at him sweetly.'[15] Not all women would have followed such a strict choreography of prayer, but these directives remind us that books could be used in concert with other forms of art to enhance the devotional practices of their owners.

Pictures in prayer books, could, of course, serve in their own right as catalysts for meditation, and they, too, could evoke profound feelings of connection with Christ. Margareta Ebner, a Dominican nun, is said to have 'pressed to her heart every image of the crucifix she encountered, large and small, including a picture painted into a small prayer book, which she also laid under her head while she slept'.[16] In a book of hours made in southern France in the last quarter of the thirteenth century, a nun, probably a Franciscan, is pictured kneeling next to Christ as he shows her the wound in his side. The proximity of the two figures expresses the intimate bond between Christ and the female suppliant. Almost certainly the nun is intended to represent the owner of the book. Presumably, each time she gazed at the image she could have turned her thoughts to his suffering.

Devotional texts focusing on Christ's birth and death were composed throughout the Middle Ages. Among the most popular were those attributed to Bridget of Sweden (1303–73), a noblewoman who experienced mystical visions. She was married at age fourteen to the nobleman Ulf Gudmarsson, and she gave birth to eight children. She also served as lady-in-waiting to Blanche of Namur, consort

Christ shows a nun the wound in his side. Miscellaneous Liturgical Offices and Prayers, S. France, last quarter of the thirteenth century.
Egerton 945, f. 237v

Saint Bridget of Sweden with the Virgin Mary and Christ Child. In 1372, a year before her death, Bridget made a pilgrimage to Bethlehem where she had a vision of the infant Christ surrounded by rays of light. Saint Bridget, *Revelations* (*Liber Celestis*), England, *c.* 1410–20. Cotton, Claudius B. i, f. 269r

of King Magnus II of Sweden. Although Bridget led a secular life, both she and her husband were extraordinarily pious, and they made a joint pilgrimage to the shrine of Saint James in Compostela. After Ulf's death in 1344, Bridget intensified her commitment to the religious life and started a new order for monks and nuns (the Bridgettines). In 1372, the year before she died, Bridget journeyed to the Holy Land and made a pilgrimage to the site of Christ's birth in Bethlehem. As she prayed at the holy place, she experienced a vision of the Christ Child, lying on the ground, with rays of light emanating from his body, and the Virgin Mary kneeling beside him, adoring her newborn child. Bridget's vision of the Nativity, which was recorded along with her other 'revelations', had a significant impact on the visual arts. From the late fourteenth century onwards, artists began to paint images of the Nativity replete with details recorded by Bridget. A fifteenth-century copy of her collected writings is embellished with an image of Saint Bridget kneeling in prayer across from the Virgin Mary, as the radiant infant lies on the ground between them, his body encircled by rays of burnished gold.[17] As this image reminds us, Saint

Bridget's prayers were the catalyst for her vision, which, in turn, changed the way artists pictured Christ's birth.

One day while Bridget was meditating on Christ's afflictions, she is said to have had a vision of Christ, who appeared to her and promised to teach her new prayers relating to his suffering and death. The fifteen prayers she allegedly learned rapidly gained popularity and were included in numerous books of hours and other compilations of sacred texts.[18] In one fifteenth-century Dutch book of hours, the prayers are preceded by a image of Bridget seated at a desk, pen in hand, as an angel, Christ's envoy, whispers the words in her ear.

Because each short prayer begins with the words 'O Jesus' or variations of the phrase, they became known as the 'Fifteen Os'. The following example is typical in its unflinching references to Christ's injuries and in its emotional appeal for clemency: 'O blessed Jesus, depth of endless mercy, I beseech you on account of the depth of your wounds, which went through your tender flesh, through your bowels, and through the marrow of your bones, that it will please you to draw me out of sin and hide me in the holes of your wounds from the face of your wrath, until the time, Lord, in which your dreadful judgement has passed.'[19] Meditating on Christ's wounds enabled medieval Christians to gain a deeper understanding of his death, which was seen as atonement for sin and the means for all believers to be reconciled to God. Gruesome descriptions of Christ's physical torments were not intended to repulse people, but rather to encourage them to reflect on Christ's sacrifice, to give thanks, to search their consciences and to repent of their sins.

Saint Bridget of Sweden writing as an angel whispers in her ear, offering divine inspiration. Bridget was an inveterate pilgrim and her staff and pilgrim's pouch are depicted at her feet.
Prayer book, S. Netherlands,
third quarter of the fifteenth century.
Harley 2850, f. 47v

The Office of the Dead, included near the end of nearly every book of hours, consists of a series of psalms and readings suitable for funerary vigils. By reciting these texts, medieval Christians believed that they could shorten the time spent by the deceased in Purgatory.[20] It was also customary for medieval Christians to recite the Office of the Dead as a reminder of their own mortality. Being mindful of death encouraged people to use their time wisely and to live moral lives.

Demons and angels were not abstract concepts, but warring entities. Hell was conceived as an actual place – as real as Provence or the Kingdom of Sicily – but no one was eager to go there. Meditations on death were intended to focus the reader's attention on the things of lasting importance – the preparation of the body and soul for their eventual reception in heaven. The point of a book of hours was to guide its owner through a set of devotions designed to bring them closer to this goal. By meditating on the words of the psalms, reciting the appropriate readings for each hour and praying to the Virgin to intercede on their behalf with her Son, the stern judge, medieval Christians sought admission to a place of eternal happiness.

Various types of illustrations were used to mark the Office of the Dead. Some catered specifically to female viewers. In a late fifteenth-century Parisian book of

A woman recoils as Death prepares to strike her (above). Book of Hours, France, Paris, *c.* 1480–90. Harley 2865, f. 86r

A female skeleton admires her reflection (above right). The Hours of Dionora of Urbino, Italy, Florence or Mantua, begun *c.* 1480; completed for Dionora *c.* 1510–20. Yates Thompson 7, f. 174r

hours, for example, a fashionable young noblewoman, standing in a churchyard, recoils in horror as Death, in the guise of a jaunty skeleton, prepares to strike her with his lethal arrow. The gaping coffin in the foreground, waiting to be occupied, and the skulls grinning from the pediment of the charnel house in the background leave no doubt as to her fate. The message that all women, regardless of their social status and wealth, are subject to death and putrefaction, a message directed at female patrons rich enough to commission prayer books, is similarly conveyed by a grisly figure depicted in a book of hours owned by Eleanor (Dionora) Gonzaga della Rovere (1490–1538), wife of Francesco Maria I della Rovere, Duke of Urbino. In the centre of a decorated initial 'D', marking the first prayer of the Office of the Dead, is a female skeleton whose hideous visage contrasts with her ornate attire and coiffure. Clutching in her bony fingers the gilt handle of a mirror, she peers at her reflection as if mesmerised by her own features.

In medieval art, significantly more women than men are depicted with mirrors. Not every image of a woman regarding herself in a mirror is misogynistic, but the idea that women are vain seductresses is often implied. In a treatise on feminine conduct and deportment written for his daughters in 1371–2, Geoffroy de la Tour Landry warned them that 'a woman should never comb her hair before a man; and even when alone she should not do so for too long, or the devil's bottom might appear in her mirror'.[21] Given the negative associations of women with mirrors, the female skeleton gazing at her reflection not only functions as a reminder of death (*memento mori*) and a comment on the ephemeral nature of physical beauty, but also as a critique of female narcissism.[22]

Temptation of Adam and Eve; Expulsion from Paradise; *Speculum consciencie* (Mirror of Conscience). The serpent is shown with the body of a reptile and the face of a woman. In his biblical commentary, the *Historia scholastica* (*c.* 1164), Peter Comestor stated that the serpent had 'the face of a virgin', and this idea had a lasting impact on the visual arts.
The Hours of Joanna I of Castile, S. Netherlands, Bruges or Ghent, between 1496 and 1506.
Additional 18852, ff. 14v-15r

Especially arresting, because it forces the viewer to contemplate his or her own mortality, is a skull reflected in a large convex mirror in a book of hours illuminated, between 1496 and 1506 for Joanna of Castile by an anonymous artist known as the Master of the David Scenes. Labelled *Speculum consciencie* (Mirror of Conscience), the object was clearly intended to prompt Joanna to evaluate her behaviour. However, because it faces the viewer, anyone who gazes at it is likewise encouraged to examine his or her conscience.[23]

The sombre image does not mark the Office of the Dead, but illustrates the first section of the devotional book, a series of texts articulating the key tenets of Christian belief, beginning with the Ten Commandments. These texts were not customarily included in books of hours, but were probably added to this one for the instruction of Joanna of Castile, who was still an adolescent when the manuscript was made for her.[24] At age sixteen, Joanna married Philip the Handsome, son of Mary of Burgundy and the Holy Roman Emperor Maximilian of Austria, and the book, which bears both Joanna's arms and those of her husband, must have been made between their marriage in 1496 and his premature death on 25 September 1506, when she was pregnant with their sixth child.

Significantly, the mirror in which the skull is reflected is positioned across from a painting of the Temptation and Adam and Eve's expulsion from Paradise – events recounted in the Book of Genesis. Because they had broken God's commandment and eaten the forbidden fruit, Adam and Eve brought sin and death into the world and were banished from Eden. By seeking redemption from God, keeping the Ten Commandments, and meditating on the prayers in her book, Joanna could hope to attain salvation.

The painting of the Temptation captures the moment after the devil, in the guise of a serpent, has persuaded Eve to eat the forbidden fruit from the Tree of Knowledge, an act forbidden by God. Her tempter is shown with the tail of a serpent and the torso of a woman, whose shapely breasts and appealing face rise above the reptilian carapace of her lower body. The serpent is not described as female in the Book of Genesis, but in his highly influential biblical commentary, the *Historia scholastica* (*c.* 1164), Peter Comestor, chancellor of the cathedral school of Notre Dame, Paris, stated that the serpent had 'the face of a virgin', and that Eve was inclined to listen to it because 'like favours like' ('*similia similibus applaudant*').[25] In other words, drawn towards the serpent because it resembled her, Eve became a victim of seduction. By endowing the serpent with female characteristics, a male theologian thus transformed it into a creature that mirrors Eve and, by extension, all women. The misogynistic motif had a lasting influence on the visual arts and can be found in images of the Temptation dating from the twelfth to the seventeenth century.[26] Although these pages of Joanna's prayer book, adorned with scenes of the Temptation and a skull in a mirror, offer a sober discourse on human frailty and failure, they also hold the key to redemption. As long as there is life to live and prayers to recite, vices can be overcome, wrongs amended, sins forgiven.

A similar message is conveyed by the cautionary tale of the 'Three Living and the Three Dead', which emerged in the mid-thirteenth century and was especially popular in England, France and Italy.[27] The story, which circulated in several different versions, centres on a conversation between three young noblemen or kings and three desiccating corpses or skeletons. On a hunting expedition, the carefree youths encounter the three macabre beings that remind them of life's transience and warn them to reform their lives. One of the most popular versions of the tale was a French poem written by the minstrel Baudouin de Condé, who served Margaret II, Countess of Flanders (r. 1244–80). Although it may have been composed to please the countess, women play no part in Baudouin's poem, *Li dis des trois mors et des trois vis*, or in any other version of the story. Consequently, it was rare (but not unknown, as we shall see) for medieval artists to portray any member of the hunting party as a woman.

One of the earliest illustrations of the tale occurs in a Parisian miscellany, made *c.* 1285, which includes Baudouin de Condé's poem (Paris, Bibliothèque de l'Arsenal 3142, fol. 311v). A strikingly similar composition is a painting made in London, *c.* 1310–20, by an exceptionally talented artist known as the Madonna Master (opposite). The two pictures are so close in detail that the only conclusion to be drawn is that the Madonna Master made use of a French model.[28] Captions in Middle English run across the top of the Madonna Master's painting. Catching sight of the worm-infested skeletons, the three kings exclaim: 'I am afraid!', 'Lo, what I see!', and 'Methinks these be devils three!' The Dead in turn reply: 'I was well fair', 'Such shall you be', and 'For God's love beware by me'.[29] Beneath is inscribed an Anglo-Norman version of Baudouin de Condé's poem, in which women play no part. Consequently, they are also absent from the accompanying illustration.

Women seldom appear in illustrations of the story, but some late medieval artists broke with convention. For example, in an illustration marking the Office of the Dead in a book of hours made in Ghent, *c.* 1480–82, for Mary, Duchess of Burgundy, a woman is depicted as one of three hunters, mounted on horseback (p. 124). Dressed in a conical headdress and luxurious gown, with a bird of prey attached to her wrist, she is aggressively pursued by the agitated skeleton in the foreground. Armed with a long arrow, the skeleton, one of three depicted, reaches for her saddle, grimly determined to dismount her. Having just released their falcons, the two male riders, facing away from her, seem oblivious to the danger and show no signs of coming to her rescue. Because the initials 'MM' are emblazoned on the harness of the horse of the female rider, scholars have convincingly argued that the woman is intended to represent the patron of the manuscript, Mary of Burgundy.[30]

The Three Living and the Three Dead. Miniature by the Madonna Master. De Lisle Psalter, England, probably London, *c.* 1310–20. Arundel 83, f. 127r

Mary died prematurely in 1482, when she was twenty-five, of injuries incurred in a riding accident, and whether the image was painted in her lifetime or was added to the book shortly after her death by her husband, Maximilian of Austria, has been long debated. It was not unusual for a patron to be represented in images for the Office of the Dead, and Mary, an enthusiastic rider and hunter, who is shown engaging in these pursuits in other manuscripts, may well have commissioned this stark *memento mori*.[31] If the image was created at Mary's behest, and there is no compelling reason to think otherwise, when she read her prayer book she would have seen herself confronting death without flinching or soliciting help from her male companions. The insertion of her portrait in the scene of the 'Three Living and the Three Dead', which audaciously rewrites the script of the venerable narrative, transforms the tale into a highly personal statement.

Evidently, the image was considered worthy of imitation, because a copy of it, illuminated by a different artist, was included in a later Flemish prayer book made, *c.* 1500, probably for Mary of Burgundy's daughter, Margaret of Austria, or her daughter-in-law, Joanna of Castile (p. 125).[32] Like Mary of Burgundy, the woman in the

Mary of Burgundy depicted on horseback in a miniature of the Three Living and the Three Dead. The Hours of Mary of Burgundy and Maximilian, S. Netherlands, Ghent, *c.* 1480–82. Berlin, Staatliche Museen, Kupferstichkabinett, MS 78 B 12, f. 220v

later version is shown elegantly attired, on horseback, in the centre of the composition, with a falcon on her wrist. A skeleton wielding an arrow likewise stalks her, and her male companions seem unaware of her plight. These late medieval images, in which the women take centre stage, are robust expressions of female autonomy; pursued by death, the women maintain their composure and urge their horses onwards.

Books of hours offer the single largest body of evidence for medieval women's devotional practices, but it is important to remember that books were not essential

A woman depicted on horseback in a miniature of the Three Living and the Three Dead. Book of Hours, S. Netherlands, probably Ghent, *c.* 1500. Additional 35313, f. 158v

A woman makes her confession to a Dominican friar and, in subsequent scenes, kneels in prayer at an altar. *Li livres de l'estat de l'ame*, France, *c.* 1290–1300. Yates Thompson 11, f. 29r

A woman praying at Vespers. Egerton Hours, England, *c.* 1250–75. Egerton 1151, f. 50r

Family members are often depicted together in books of hours. Here, a couple kneels beneath an image of Christ in the Garden of Gethsemane. The Taymouth Hours, England, probably London, *c.* 1325–35. Yates Thompson 13, f. 118v

to the act of prayer. Most women would have been able to recite by heart the three basic prayers, the Our Father, the Hail Mary and the Creed, which all Christians were enjoined to know. Communicating with God took many different forms. When she was a little girl, for example, the visionary Christina of Markyate, having heard 'that Christ was good, beautiful, and everywhere present', is said to have spoken to him at night in her bed, 'as if he were a man whom she could see.'[33]

Prayers could be uttered in private, but praying was often a collective act performed by a community of believers. Nuns' lives were structured around communal prayer and most secular women would have had opportunities to participate in public worship in local churches and monasteries. It was common, for example, for people to attend Vespers at the end of the day. In one prayer book, the image for Vespers shows two clerics in front of an altar, reciting prayers from open books while a woman with her hands clasped kneels directly behind them. Many women took their prayer books to church and used them during services, particularly the Mass.[34] Two fashionably dressed women, seated on the floor near the high altar, are depicted reading from their prayer books at the Christmas service in one of the most sumptuous books of hours ever produced, the *Très Riches Heures*.[35] In addition, numerous wealthy women employed chaplains and advisors who offered spiritual counsel, prayed with them, and heard their confessions. A woman making her confession to a Dominican friar is shown in the first panel of an exquisite, full-page miniature in a lavishly illuminated compilation of spiritual treatises (opposite).[36] As she kneels on the ground before her confessor, an angel appears, bearing a scroll inscribed, '*Si vis delere tua crimina dic Miserere*' (If you wish to efface your sins say the *Miserere*'). His advice is straightforward: recite Psalm 50, one of the seven psalms associated with penance, which opens with the words, *Miserere mei Deus …* ('Have mercy on me, O God, according to thy great mercy. And according to the multitude of thy tender mercies blot out my iniquity.')[37] The hand of Christ emerges from a cloud to bless her, a gesture echoed by her confessor. Surely her prayers have been heard and her sins forgiven. The original owner of the manuscript is unknown, but he or she may well have heeded the angel's counsel and prayed the *Miserere*, since the image offers a paradigm for anyone seeking absolution. It was widely believed that reciting the *Miserere* would protect people from the devil and from untimely death.[38]

Women are sometimes pictured in their prayer books with their husbands and/or children, which suggests that these volumes served as the focus for family devotions. For medieval women, reciting prayers, whether in private or public, alone or with others, was not an academic exercise, but a means of seeking forgiveness for their sins and ensuring that they and their loved ones would be protected in this life and welcomed in Paradise in the next.

il esteit maimes as estrnges e prira suens entre mau
ues al memes. Tote la chose ki pleyseit a deu e a ceus
ki deu amoient si desplesoit au rey e a ceus ki li rey a
moient. Il morut e fu entere a Wyncestre. A ki entere
ment tant il auoit de ioie. Le a peine il auoit vne ler
me ploree. Car en tens au celi rey seint anceaume fu
despoille de tuz ses biens e si fu exille dekes en la fin de la
vie de cetu rey Wyllam le rous. E seint Wlstan ki fu eue
ske de Willescestre e homme de seinte vie trespassa glorio
sement de ceste seccle a deu en la ioie pardurable.
Maud fille la reine de escoce e femme au prim rey henri.
Henri le clerc.
Willam son fiz. peri en la mer.
Henri le secund.

CHAPTER SIX

LITERARY PATRONAGE

PRAYER BOOKS made for medieval women survive in their thousands, but these volumes tell only part of the story of their engagement with the written word. Women encouraged and rewarded writers, commissioned works, and had manuscripts made for them, including volumes illuminated by leading artists, and these reveal the profound depth and range of their interests. In addition, female authors made significant contributions to the literary canon, and women working in the book trade helped meet the growing demand for manuscripts.[1]

The most important single factor in women's participation in literary culture was the rise of the vernacular, a development that occurred around the middle of the twelfth century. At that time, there was an increasing demand for books in everyday languages, fuelled, in part, by a growing number of women who wanted to read. To cater to this market, authors composed new works and translated Latin texts into the major languages spoken in Europe today. Women who sponsored the creation of texts in the vernacular not only provided themselves with reading material, but also helped to spark a literary revolution. By offering an alternative to Latin texts, they made reading possible for vast numbers of people who had, until then, only restricted access to written knowledge.

Women, for example, were among the most avid readers of 'romances' (tales of heroism, passion and adventure) that were first recited at royal and noble courts for the entertainment of the elite.[2] Noblewomen such as Eleanor of Aquitaine (*c.* 1124–1204) and her eldest daughter Marie, Countess of Champagne (1145–98), for whom Chrétien de Troyes wrote the first known Arthurian romance, helped to cultivate a new literary landscape.[3] As the centuries progressed, these stories reached larger and more diverse audiences. Romances were written in couplets of rhyming verse, which made them easier to recall and recite, and more entertaining to hear. Although many romances have a love interest, the term does not derive from their subject matter, but refers instead to the French language (*romanz*), in which the earliest examples were written. The exploits of Arthur and his knights, and of heroes of classical antiquity, fired the imaginations of countless readers, but

Queen Matilda (Maud) and King Henry I of England. Matilda (d. 1118), who liberally rewarded the poets and singers who entertained her, is the first identifiable female patron of French literature.
Genealogical Chronicle of the English Kings, England, c. 1340–42.
Royal 14 B. vi, membrane 5

the genre was not limited to tales of chivalry and valour. Instead, it comprised 'a rich spectrum of narratives whose themes and issues intersect[ed] with virtually every aspect of medieval social and cultural life'.[4]

Royal and aristocratic women, in particular, played a key role in the transmission of texts.[5] As John Higgitt states, 'When marriages took them far from home, they often took their books with them, thereby disseminating knowledge of book-types, texts and imagery.'[6] In most cases, when a woman married a foreign monarch or nobleman, she maintained close connections with her relatives, court and country of origin, facilitating cultural exchanges over significant periods of time. Women who moved to foreign lands not only brought their books with them, but also the practices, values and literary interests that had been instilled in them in childhood.

It could be argued that child brides, some as young as seven, did not have a chance to absorb their own culture before they were immersed in another. However, these diminutive royal brides did not migrate alone, but settled in their new homelands with large staffs of retainers from their native lands, including relatives, learned advisors, guardians and clerics, with whom they shared a common language and heritage. A frequent criticism levelled against foreign queens was that they brought far too many compatriots in their wake and showered favours on them, which angered natives competing for royal patronage.

This chapter, which charts the rise of the vernacular, focuses on the literary interests of four foreign-born women who reigned as queens of England: Matilda of Scotland (d. 1118), Adeliza of Louvain (*c.* 1103–51), Eleanor of Provence (*c.* 1223–91) and Eleanor of Castile (1241–90). In England, in particular, where three languages – English, French and Latin – jostled for space, it was a time of invention and linguistic experimentation. Writers based in England not only dedicated important works to female patrons, but were also in the vanguard of the shift from Latin to the vernacular. After the Norman Conquest of 1066, English remained the spoken language of the majority and was gradually adopted by the French invaders who intermarried with the native population. However, Anglo-Norman (the French spoken in England) 'asserted itself as the language of the ruling elites in society and the vernacular of a prolific written culture'.[7] Works in Anglo-Norman commissioned by or dedicated to female patrons include the earliest known historical chronicle in any Western European language, the earliest known bestiary, and the earliest known military treatise. Given these 'firsts' and the range of other texts written for women, it is clear that they were instrumental in changing the function of reading in Western Europe, influencing who read, what they read and how they read.

Born into a household where books were esteemed, and educated at the convents of Romsey and Wilton, both founded by royal patrons, it is not surprising that Matilda, queen of King Henry I of England, was esteemed for her learning.

The sinking of the White Ship, with King Henry I enthroned above. *Liber legum antiquorum regum* (Book of the Laws of Ancient Kings), London, *c.* 1321. Cotton Claudius D. ii, f. 45v

Matilda could trace her illustrious family back to King Alfred the Great (r. 871–99), King of Wessex, who was revered as a just ruler and great warrior who defended his kingdom from the Vikings. Alfred also promoted literacy by establishing a court school, sponsoring translations of key texts from Latin into English, and authoring at least four translations himself. Matilda's esteem for her mother, Queen Margaret of Scotland, inspired her to commission Turgot of Durham to write Margaret's posthumous biography, in which he presented her as an articulate woman with an enquiring mind, 'keen to comprehend any matter, whatever it might be', and enviably equipped with 'a great tenacity of memory, enabling her to store it up'.[8] Matilda seems to have shared her mother's intellectual curiosity, for she enlisted William of Malmesbury, the Benedictine monk and chronicler, to write in Latin an account of her ancestors of the royal house of Wessex.[9] This served as the foundation of his most important work, the *Gesta regum Anglorum* (*Deeds of the English Kings*), completed after her death.[10]

William of Malmesbury claimed that 'clerks famed in song and poetry flocked' to Matilda's court, and he implied that her patronage of foreigners was so extensive that she aggrieved the local talent.[11] That Matilda liked to entertain in style is also suggested by Anselm, Archbishop of Canterbury, one of the leading churchmen with whom she corresponded, who advised her 'to take care lest fondness for the glories of this world hinder her journey to the next one'.[12]

Tragically, on the night of 25 November 1120, Matilda's firstborn son William, the heir to the throne, was drowned when *La Blanche-Nef* (White Ship), the vessel in which he was returning to England from France, sank near the Norman port of Barfleur. It was reported that the seventeen-year-old prince, who seems to have inherited his mother's talent for entertaining, had supplied the captain and oarsmen with copious quantities of wine, rendering them unfit for purpose.[13] The sinking of the White Ship, with its cargo of royal and noble youths, heralded dark days for England. Matilda had died two years before, so she did not live long enough to grieve for her son or to witness the political instability and crisis of succession that prompted her husband Henry I, a year after the tragedy, to take as his new queen Adeliza of Louvain (*c.* 1103–51), another cultured bibliophile.

How many books did Adeliza own? We cannot say precisely, but the poet and chronicler Geffrei Gaimar, alluding to her sizable collection, boasted that he knew as many songs as she had books. A copy of the *Voyage de saint Brendan* (*The Voyage of Saint Brendan*), composed by a certain Benedeit, probably had pride of place in her library. Scholars are divided over the question of whether Benedeit dedicated the work to Henry I's first wife, Matilda, or second wife, Adeliza, since three of the four extant manuscripts with a prologue identify Adeliza as the dedicatee, and the earliest extant copy names Matilda.[14]

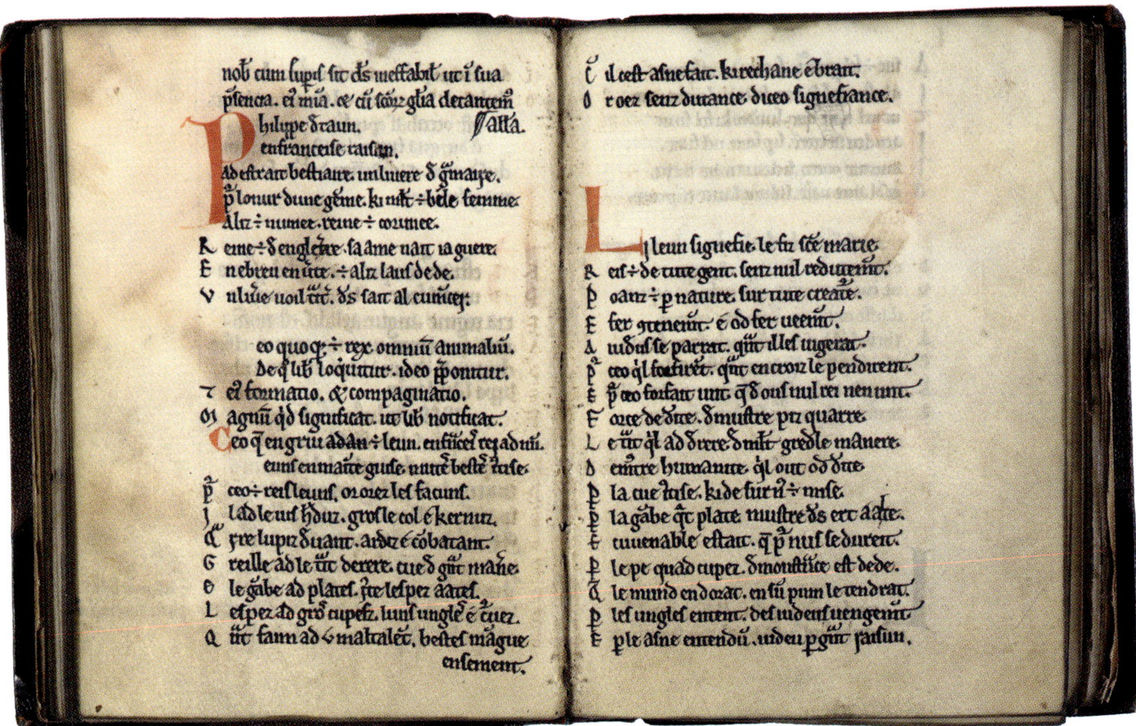

Philippe de Thaon, *Bestiaire.* Text pages with dedication to Queen Adeliza of Louvain (*c.* 1103–51), second wife of Henry I of England. The dedication begins with the large red 'P' for 'Philippe'. England, second half of the twelfth century.
Cotton Nero A. v, ff. 41v–42r

Benedeit probably composed the work for Matilda and then, after her death, rededicated it to Adeliza, hoping to enjoy her patronage as he had the former queen's.[15] Indisputably, the *Voyage de saint Brendan* was intended for one or the other of these women and, consequently, it occupies an important place in the history of female literary patronage. Written in Anglo-Norman, it is the earliest work in any French dialect to incorporate a Celtic theme, and it is also the earliest known poem written in rhyming pairs of eight-syllable verses (octosyllabic rhyming couplets), a form that became the standard for romances.[16]

Although Brendan, the Irish protagonist, is a saint and an abbot, the text is a rollicking story of adventure. Tantalised by the reports of a hermit who claimed to have once visited an island near Paradise, Brendan sets out to sea on a quest to discover heaven and hell. During the course of his voyage, he and his companions marvel at a bubbling volcano, a frozen sea and a magic spring, and encounter a dragon, a griffin and sea monsters. Most spectacularly, they dine on the back of a giant fish. Reflecting Benedeit's active imagination, it is an original story written specifically to please the queen and members of her court.

Because we usually read silently, we tend to forget that 'medieval reading (*lectio*) was primarily something to be heard rather than seen'.[17] But anyone who has had the good fortune to be read to by a parent, teacher, friend or lover knows that reading together can double the pleasure. Written in rhyme in order to be read aloud, the *Voyage de saint Brendan* is a story to be shared.[18] The fact that it was recounted in Anglo-Norman French, the language of common parlance of the English elite, meant that even members of the court who did not have the queen's command of Latin could have understood the tale.

In the twelfth century, writers met a growing demand for literature by composing new works in the vernacular and translating Latin texts. Many texts were commissioned by or dedicated to women, including a bestiary written in Anglo-Norman French verse by Philippe de Thaon for Queen Adeliza, perhaps not long after the eighteen-year-old had arrived in England to marry Henry I, in 1121.[19] That he wrote the book for her is stated in the dedication (lines 1–6):

Philippe de taun
en franceise raisun
ad estraite bestiaire. un livere de gramaire
pur l'onur d'une gemme. ki mult est bele femme.
Aliz est numee. reine est corunee.
Reine est de engleterre. sa ame n'ait ja guere.

Philippe de Thaon has distilled into a French treatise
The *Bestiary*, a book in Latin,
For the honour of a jewel, who is an outstandingly beautiful woman
She is called 'Aliz', Queen she is crowned
She is the queen of England, may her soul never know trouble!

We do not have to linger long on Philippe's praise of Adeliza's beauty – authors never claim to have written their books for unattractive women – but other aspects of the dedication are noteworthy. Philippe stresses Adeliza's coronation (*Reine est corunee*), an event that might have taken place not long before he started his translation, and one that firmly set Adeliza, a native of Louvain (in present-day Belgium), in an English royal context. In addition, in the first lines, Philippe not only identifies himself as the translator of the work, but also states that it is in French. This would have been obvious to the most inattentive reader, let alone the learned Adeliza, so we have to ask why Philippe considered this significant enough to mention.

Medieval bestiaries are collections of animal anecdotes to which morals are appended. Ultimately based on a work called the *Physiologus*, written in late antiquity, medieval bestiaries began to be compiled as early as the tenth century and gained popularity in the twelfth. The earliest bestiaries, addressed primarily to clerical and monastic audiences, were written in Latin. Philippe was justifiably proud to have broken with this long tradition and written his in Anglo-Norman French. His *Bestiaire* is, in fact, the earliest known bestiary in any vernacular language.

Bestiaries were more popular in England than in any other part of Western Europe, and a book of this type would, almost certainly, have been a novelty for Adeliza, who is unlikely to have encountered one in her native Louvain. Philippe includes several references to pictures in his text, which shows that the original manuscript made for the queen would have had a cycle of illustrations unlike any she had ever seen before. Although her original *Bestiaire* is no longer extant, the text has survived in three later copies, two with illustrations and an unfinished volume with spaces reserved for them (p. 132).[20]

After Henry I's death in 1135, Adeliza commissioned a poet named David to write a verse chronicle of the king's deeds, but no copy of the work has been preserved. We only know of David's chronicle because his rival poet, Geffrei Gaimar, mentions it, stating that his own patron, Constance Fitz Gilbert, whose husband Ralph was a Lincolnshire landowner, paid a silver mark – a considerable sum – for a copy of it, and that she often retired to her chamber to read it.[21] Though Constance is said to have read the work in private, she might also have had it performed, since the first stanza of the verse chronicle was set to music, which suggests that David intended it to be recited to courtly audiences.

A patron in her own right, Constance asked Gaimar to compose for her a chronicle of English history, which he completed *c.* 1136–7. Written in Anglo-Norman, this long poem does not survive in its entirety, but scholars have determined that the extant portion, comprising the second half, an impressive 6,532 lines of octosyllabic verse, is based on several different sources, notably the *Anglo-Saxon Chronicle*. In his epilogue, Gaimar explains that he also made use of a text that fits the description of Geoffrey of Monmouth's *Historia regum Britanniae* (*History of the Kings of Britain*), begun only a few years earlier. Because Gaimar did not have a copy of this new Latin source to hand, Constance supplied him with one. Gaimar does not present her as a remote or passive patron; on the contrary, speaking of himself in the third person, he states that '*Si sa dame ne li aidast,/ ja a nul jor ne l'achevast*' (If his lady [Constance] had not helped him, he would never have completed it').[22]

Gaimar's *Estoire des Engleis*, the oldest surviving historical chronicle in French, is an ambitious book, encompassing English history from its legendary origins to the death of William the Conqueror's son, William Rufus, in 1100. Its treatment of women is also noteworthy. According to Ian Short, 'Gaimar's depiction of women in general is noticeable for its absence of misogyny, and female members of his audience, not forgetting his patroness, must have particularly relished the prominent

Enthroned Virgin and Child with female suppliant possibly intended to represent Queen Adeliza. The Shaftesbury Psalter, England, second quarter of the twelfth century. Lansdowne 383, f. 165v roles attributed to women in the *Estoire*. While female characters are, understandably for the time, most frequently mentioned in relation to men as queens, wives and heiresses, they can be seen, in certain of the roles that they play, as foreshadowing some of the heroines of courtly romance.'[23] As the earliest surviving chronicle in French, Gaimar's *Estoire des Engleis*, commissioned by Constance Fitz Gilbert, established a precedent for popular history, and made its influence felt for the next three hundred years.[24]

Although the verse chronicle of the deeds of Henry I written for his widow, Queen Adeliza, has been lost, a psalter thought by some scholars to have been owned by her is preserved in the British Library (p. 135). Michael Kauffmann, who observed that certain features of the text and illustrations point to Adeliza's ownership, has convincingly linked the volume with the queen.[25] The manuscript, known as the Shaftesbury Psalter, contains eight full-page paintings, including two showing a highborn woman supplicating Christ and the Virgin Mary respectively. Only the wealthiest of female patrons could have commissioned a private devotional book of this quality. If the images are not of Adeliza, for whom a strong case has been made, they are, nevertheless, among the most impressive images of a female patron painted in England in the twelfth century.

The twelfth century also saw the rise of the first female authors writing in French. Since the written language was still developing, authors composing texts in French at this time faced greater challenges than those writing in Latin. As Michael Clanchy explains, 'Latin was a uniform prescribed language, articulated by its grammar and learned through schooling, whereas "Roman" or "romance" [i.e. French] diction had as many and varying forms as living speech. To write anything down in its colloquial "Roman/romance" form was therefore novel and difficult.'[26] Besides facing linguistic challenges, women had to forge a place for themselves in a field that was dominated by men. There was little encouragement for women to write, and the few who did so had to find supportive patrons and audiences. Two of the most promising settings were royal or aristocratic courts and religious communities, which had long functioned as centres of women's education and Latin literary production.

Marie de France is one of the first female writers of French texts whom we know by name. Surviving works attributed to her, written *c.* 1160–89, include twelve *lais* (brief tales in rhymed couplets), a large collection of animal fables drawn from Aesop and elsewhere, and an account of a voyage to the underworld entitled *L'Espurgatoire seint Patriz* (*The Purgatory of Saint Patrick*).[27] Marie's stories, including one about a man who turns into a werewolf and bites off his unfaithful wife's nose, are quite compelling. Her importance, however, lies not only in her strength as a storyteller with a fertile imagination and a plentiful stock of tales, derived, in large

Marie de France's *Fables*, with a portrait of the author writing. Marie de France is one of the first medieval female authors known by name.
France, probably Paris, *c.* 1285.
Paris, Bibliothèque de l'Arsenal, MS 3142, f. 256r

Cil qi seuent
de letreure
deuroient bien
metre lor cure
es bons livres
et es escris
et es examples
et es dis
Qe li philosophe trouverent
Et escrisent et ramenbrerent
Par moralite escrisoient
Les bons proverbes qil oient
Qe cil amender sen peussent
Qi lor entente en bien meissent
Ce firent li ancien pere
Romulus qi ert emperere
A son fill escrist et manda
Et par example li moustra
Com se deust contregaitier
Con ne le peust engignier
Ysopes escrist a son mestre
Qi bien connut lui et son estre
Unes fables qil ot trouvees
De griu en latin translatees
Merveille en orent li plusour
Qil mist sentente en tel labour
Mais ni a fable de folie
Ou il nen ait philosophie
Es examples qi sont apres
Ou des contes sont tuit li fes
A moi qi la rime en doi faire
Nannie noient a retraire
Plusieurs choses qi dedens sont
Mais nonporquant cil men semont

Qi flors est de chevalerie
Denseignement de courtoisie
Et quant tes hom men a requise
Ne vueill laissier en nule guise
Que ni mete travail et painne
Qi men tiegne por vilainne
Mais li doi faire por sa priere
Si comencerai la premiere
Ka son maistre manda et dist
Des fables kisopes escrist

Dun coc raconte
qi monta
sor .i. fumier
et si grata
selonc nature
porchacoit
sa viande
com il soloit
Une chiere gemme trouva
Clere la vit si lesgarda
Je cuidai dist il porchacier
Ma viande sor ce fumier
Or tai ci gemme trouvee
Ja par moi neres remuee
Se uns riches hom ci te trouvast
Bien sai qe dor te coronast
Si acreust ta grant clarte
Por lor ou mult a de biaute
Qant ma volente nai de toi
Ja nule honnor naras de moi
Autressi est de maintes gent
Se tout ne vait a lor talent
Come deu coc et de la gemme
Veu lavons domme et de femme
Bien ne honnor noient ne prisent
Le pis prendent le miex despisent

Ci dist dou leu
et de laignel
qi bevoient
a .i. ruissel
Li leus par
desour bevoit
Et li aigniaus aval estoit
Iriement parla li leus
Qi mult estoit contralieus
Par mal talent parla a lui
Tu me fais dist il grant anui
Et li aigniaus a respondu
Sire de quoi. dont ne vois tu
Tu mas si ceste aigue troublee
Nen puis boire ma saolee
Autressi men irai ce croi
Com je ving ci morant de soi
Et li aigniaus dont li respont
Sire ia beves vous amont
De vous me vint ce qe jai beu
Quoi dist li leus maudis me tu
Cil ha dit nen ai volonte
Li leus respont ien sai le voir
Ce meisme me fist tes pere
A ceste aigue ou o lui ere
Ora .vi. mois si com je croi
De ce riens nen atient a moi
Car nier pas nes si com je cuit
Et qe de ce li leus a dit
Ja me fais tu ore contraire
Chose qe tu ne dois faire
Dont prent li leus laignel petit
Et si lestrangle et si locit
Si font li riche robeour
Li visconte li iugeour
De ceaus qil ont en lor iustice
Fausse ochoison par couvoitise
Truevent asses por aus confondre
Sovent les font a plait semondre
La char lor tolent et la pel
Si com li leus fist a laignel

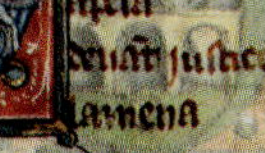

Ci conte dun chien
menteour
de male guise
tricheur
a une brebis
parla
devant iustice
la mena

part, from Breton folklore, but also in her awareness of her role as literary pioneer. She tells us, for example, that stories she had heard, rather than a written source, inspired her to write her *lais*, which she often worked on 'late into the night'.[28] They are not, she emphasises, a translation, but a new work, dedicated to a noble king (identified by most scholars as Henry II of England). Marie also discloses the source of her fables. Modern scholars are sceptical about her claim to have based them on a collection in English by a certain 'King Alfred', since they have been shown to derive from Latin sources, but they agree that her verse collection of animal fables is the earliest known in French.[29]

In *L'Espurgatoire seint Patriz*, Marie states her authorial intentions with particular clarity, writing, 'I, Marie, have put the *Book of Purgatory* into French as a record, so that it might be intelligible and suited to lay folk.'[30] This does not mean that she was writing for an unsophisticated readership; on the contrary, members of the aristocracy and royal court were her primary audience. It is little wonder that women appreciated her work; 'in contrast to much chivalric literature where women are often passive objects or marginalized temptresses, Marie's female characters are central figures who exhibit courage and ingenuity'.[31] Evidently Marie was famous in her lifetime, because a jealous rival, the author Denis Piramus, writing *c.* 1170, complained that people 'everywhere', including counts, barons and knights, were overly fond of her work, and that women, in particular, liked the *lais*.[32]

Marie expressed her desire to be remembered and was concerned that other authors might plagiarise her work. She articulates these sentiments in the epilogue to her fables, where she states, 'at the conclusion of this work, which I have written and narrated in French, I shall name myself for posterity: Marie is my name, and I am from France. It may be that many writers will claim my work as their own, but I want no one else to attribute it to himself. He who lets himself fall into oblivion does a poor job.'[33] Her statement shows that she took pride in her accomplishments and was aware that as a female author she was breaking new ground. She was, in fact, one of the first medieval women authors of vernacular literature to achieve celebrity.

Marie's reluctance to reveal anything about herself, other than 'Marie is my name, and I am from France', has frustrated scholars seeking to identify her, but she has certainly not fallen into oblivion, and her knowledge and ability to read several languages provide us with clues to her educational background. Keith Busby states, 'even though we may not be able to identify Marie with a specific historical figure, she almost certainly lived and worked in a religious community of some kind. Her learning could hardly have been acquired elsewhere.'[34] We cannot assume that Marie became a fully professed nun, but it is possible that she was educated in a convent where she could have found intellectual stimulation and books in equal measure.

Edward the Confessor carries a crippled man to the Church of Saint Peter (Westminster) where he was healed. Matthew Paris was the second author to write an account of Edward's Life in Anglo-Norman verse. The first was composed, *c.* 1163, by a nun of Barking Abbey, possibly Clemence. For Clemence, see pp. 100–3.
French Prose Translation of Edward's Life in Anglo-Norman verse written by a nun of Barking, France.
Paris, first half of the fourteenth century.
Egerton 745, fol. 91r

Among the most intriguing works written for medieval women are those that were composed to mark specific events in their lives. A prime example is the biography of Saint Edward the Confessor, dedicated to Eleanor of Provence (*c.* 1223–91), consort of King Henry III of England. Written by Matthew Paris (*c.* 1200–1259), a Benedictine monk of St Albans, the text was composed to inform Eleanor, newly arrived in England, of the glory of the English monarchy and to intensify her commitment to her new husband, Henry III of England, whom she had travelled from her home in southern France to marry, sight unseen when she was only twelve years old. The original manuscript presented to Eleanor has not survived, but, as we shall see, Matthew's text is preserved in a later copy. Entitled the *Estoire de seint aedward le rei* (*History/Story of Saint Edward the King*), the historical narrative, in Anglo-Norman French verse, recounts the deeds and posthumous miracles of the Anglo-Saxon king and saint, Edward the Confessor (d. 1066).

The first Christian saints were martyrs, men and women who died for their faith. Later, sainthood was conferred on 'confessors', individuals who lived holy lives and performed miracles, but who had not suffered martyrdom. Edward was reputedly so pious that he tended the sick, gave his wealth to the poor and abstained from having sex. Kings were naturally expected to produce heirs to the throne, but Edward's religious scruples precluded him from doing so. Edward the Confessor's death in 1066 resulted in the Battle of Hastings, fought by the rival claimants to the English throne: Harold II, who had been crowned immediately after the king died, and Edward's maternal kinsman, William the Conqueror, who challenged Harold's legitimacy to rule, events that unfurl on the famous Bayeux tapestry. William's decisive victory on 14 October 1066 changed England irrevocably. Though the conquerors carved up England, reserving the choicest portions for themselves, the Norman Conquest was not simply a tale of dominance, but one of assimilation. Edward's cult rose to prominence in the reign of Henry II (1154–89), who traced his ancestral line back to both Anglo-Saxon and French royalty and saw himself as the rightful heir to the glorious Anglo-Saxon past embodied by the Saint Edward who was enshrined at Westminster Abbey and canonised in 1161.

Although his chronicles and various other works are in Latin prose, Matthew Paris deliberately chose to write the

Estoire in Anglo-Norman French. Furthermore, he composed the work in octosyllabic rhyming couplets, by then long established as the preferred form for romances, probably to make the story even more appealing to his female dedicatee, Eleanor of Provence. It is impossible to understand the significance of Eleanor's *Estoire* without considering the mindset of her new husband, Henry III. Although Henry, who had been crowned king of England in 1216 at age nine, did not evince an early interest in Edward, by the time he married Eleanor he was becoming increasingly attached to the Anglo-Saxon king. Henry's incipient feelings of affection for the saint developed around the time of his marriage. Henry had been seeking a bride for over a decade by the time the negotiations for his marriage to Eleanor of Provence were successfully concluded in 1235. In June of that year, only days after Henry had sent his envoy Richard de Gras, monk of Westminster, overseas to negotiate the marriage, he described Saint Edward for the first time as his 'special patron' and, shortly after Richard's return in the autumn with the good news that the proposal had been accepted, Henry participated in the celebration of Saint Edward's major feast at Westminster on 13 October, 'perhaps the first time he had made a definite effort to attend it'.[35] As David Carpenter muses, 'One wonders if Henry had prayed for the Confessor's help with Richard's mission, and was now thanking him for its success. This may have been a crucial moment in consolidating Henry's attachment to his saint.'[36] This information provides a vital context for understanding why a biography of Edward the Confessor, rather than some other saint, was made for Eleanor of Provence. The choice was far from random.

Henry III marries Eleanor of Provence. Marginal sketch by Matthew Paris. A prolific and original author, Matthew wrote a series of historical chronicles that he illustrated himself. This manuscript contains the only complete copy of his *Historia Anglorum*, a history of England covering the years 1070-1253.
Matthew Paris, *Historia Anglorum*, England, St Albans, *c.* 1250.
Royal 14 C. vii, f. 124v

It is not surprising that Henry III wished to present his new bride with a new version of the story of his favourite saint, a saint he could thank for blessing his marriage. By reading the story of Edward's life, written for her by Matthew Paris, Eleanor could better understand her new husband's veneration for Edward the Confessor and gain insight into the history of one of the most significant religious institutions in the kingdom: Westminster. Before his death in 1066, Edward had built a new abbey on the site of the tenth-century monastic foundation, and he devoted considerable sums to its embellishment.

Westminster Abbey lay adjacent to the royal palace and was also the site of the most significant event in Eleanor's young life, the place where she was crowned and anointed queen of England on 29 January 1236, following her exchange of marriage vows with Henry III at Canterbury six days before. Saint Edward was not forgotten in the course of preparations for the elaborate coronation ceremony, and on the day itself, Henry presented Eleanor with a sumptuous liturgical vestment to offer at Edward's shrine.[37] Although Henry III had not yet embarked on the project when the *Estoire* was written, following Edward's example, he was soon to transform Westminster Abbey into the church we recognise today as one of London's most famous landmarks, conscripting craftsmen from all over Europe to rebuild it and to create a new jewel-encrusted shrine to house Edward's body.[38]

As stated explicitly by its author, Matthew Paris, the *Estoire* was conceived to foster Eleanor's love both for Henry III and for Edward the Confessor. Addressing the young queen directly, he writes in the preface:

> Noble, well-born lady, Eleanor, rich queen of England, flower among ladies … I who have prepared this book for you put it in your care …. I know that whatever your lord King Henry loves, you cherish and desire. A will toward shared goals renders love praiseworthy: whatever the lover wants, so should his sweetheart want …. And whatever the lady wants so should her beloved …. I tell you this for the sake of Saint Edward, whom King Henry loves, and I write in particular that it befits you to love and cherish Edward, for he was a king and proven saint who has embraced you in his love.[39]

King Henry III, holding a model of Westminster Abbey, as depicted by Matthew Paris. Matthew Paris, *Historia Anglorum*, England, St Albans, *c.* 1250. Royal 14 C. vii, f. 9r

Eleanor was indeed devoted to Henry, and she gave birth to his son and heir, Edward, on 17 June 1239, when she was just fifteen years old. She clearly responded positively to the admonition to cherish Edward the Confessor, since she agreed to name her child after the saint. Matthew's *Estoire*, which was almost certainly commissioned by Henry III, can be viewed as a polemical book, intended to shape the ideals of his young queen. It presents as potential role models virtuous Anglo-Saxon queens, including Edward the Confessor's wife Edith. But it can also be seen as the most personal of gifts, created to give Henry's new wife insight into the things he most esteemed.

Sadly, the original copy of Matthew's *Estoire*, dedicated to Eleanor, has not been preserved. It must have been an extraordinary book. As Matthew explains in the text, which survives in a later copy, he embellished it with illustrations in order to make Edward's story intelligible to people who could not read. He states, 'for laypeople who do not know how to read, I have also represented your story in illustrations in this very same book, because I want the eyes to see what the ears hear.'[40] Was Eleanor's *Estoire*, an experimental work, the first illustrated saintly biography created by this prolific author? We cannot say with certainty, but it seems significant that he articulated his intentions so plainly. If he had already produced other illustrated saints' Lives, it would hardly have seemed necessary for him to explain his rationale.

Surviving pictures in other manuscripts by Matthew Paris are quirky and expressive, and we can only regret that the images he painted in Eleanor's *Estoire*, depicting Edward's court, battles fought and the miracles performed by the saintly king, have been lost. Undoubtedly, these pictures would have made the book

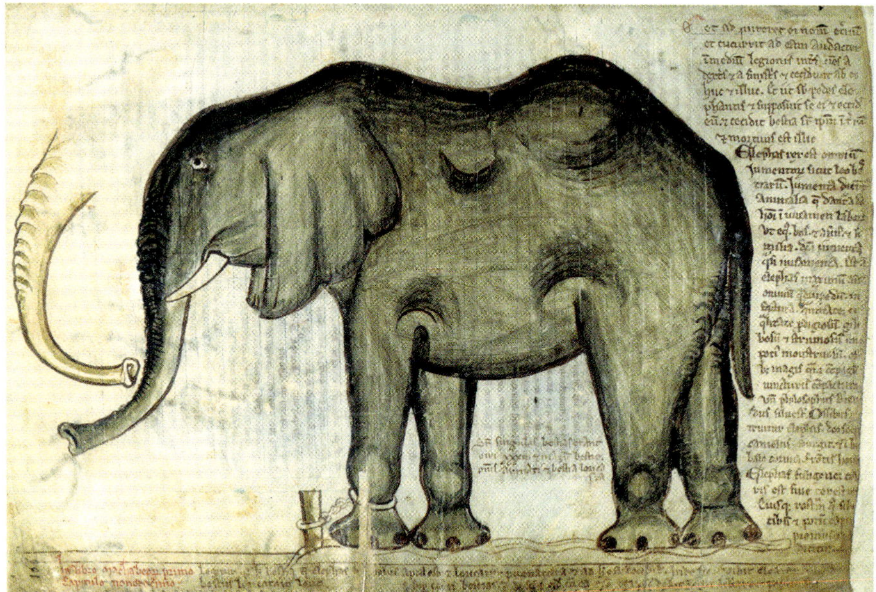

Drawing of an elephant in the royal menagerie by Matthew Paris. The elephant, which was kept at the Tower of London, was given to King Henry III by Louis IX of France in 1255. Matthew Paris is one of the very few artists of his time who can be identified by name.
Matthew Paris, *Liber additamentorum*, England, St Albans, *c.* 1250.
Cotton Nero D. i, f. 169v

especially attractive to the young Eleanor, who almost certainly received the book between the time she arrived in England at age twelve and the birth of her son Edward in 1239, when she was fifteen. The *Estoire* records the deeds of a pious king and his ancestors, but it also evokes courtly life and is not lacking in tales of adventure, potentially appealing to a young woman.

Although we cannot peruse Eleanor's original manuscript, the text of the *Estoire* has been preserved in a single copy, a handsome volume containing sixty-four illustrations painted by professional artists based in London (opposite). On the basis of the style of the paintings in the extant copy of the *Estoire*, art historians have convincingly dated the manuscript to *c.* 1255–60.[41] Given this late date, the surviving manuscript cannot be the one presented to Eleanor around the time of her marriage to Henry III in 1236. It could, however, be a later copy commissioned by her to replace the original, which may have been considerably worn after almost two decades of use, particularly if it had been passed from hand to hand by 'laypeople who do not know how to read', so that Matthew's illustrations could be viewed by all. Matthew, who alludes to the text being read aloud, evidently designed it for collective reading, a practice that must have taken its toll on even the most robust book. Even if Eleanor had kept her original manuscript in pristine condition, by the mid-thirteenth century she may have wanted another with illustrations in an up-to-date style.

It is not necessary to insist, however, that Eleanor commissioned the surviving copy of the *Estoire* for herself. Another strong possibility is that she and/or Henry

Edward persuaded by the barons to marry; Edward praying at an altar. Matthew Paris, *Estoire de seint aedward le rei (History/Story of Saint Edward the King)*, England, probably London, *c.* 1255–60. Cambridge, University Library, Ee.3.59, f. 10v

III had it made to present to Eleanor of Castile (1241–90), the new bride of their son and heir, Edward, to commemorate the couple's marriage in 1254. Many scholars have suggested that the manuscript, a deluxe copy illustrated by artists known to have worked on other royal projects, was made for the younger Eleanor, and it is possible that Eleanor of Provence, who had been given a copy of the work to introduce her to Henry's patron saint, could have presented the surviving *Estoire* to her new daughter-in-law, Eleanor of Castile, to serve a similar purpose.[42]

Would the *Estoire* have been as relevant to Eleanor of Castile as it had been to Eleanor of Provence, to whom it was dedicated? Evidently Henry III thought so, because he made plans to introduce his new daughter-in-law to his patron saint even before she had set foot in England. After Henry III and Eleanor of Castile's half-brother, Alfonso X, had conducted successful negotiations to seal the marriage between Eleanor of Castile and Prince Edward, they were married in 1254, at the Royal Monastery of Las Huelgas in Burgos, northern Spain. Henry had wanted the wedding to take place on Edward the Confessor's principal feast day, 13 October, but Edward and Eleanor, aged fifteen and thirteen respectively, were joined in matrimony about a week later.[43] After spending a year in Gascony, to which Alfonso had renounced his claims as part of the marriage agreement, Edward, who held sovereignty over the French duchy, arrived in London with his new Spanish bride.

Henry III had timed the grand entry of Eleanor of Castile to coincide with the feast of Edward the Confessor on 13 October 1255, but because Eleanor's clothes were not deemed sufficiently sumptuous and others had to be procured at short notice, plans were delayed, and the ceremony, which culminated in Eleanor of Castile making offerings at Saint Edward's shrine, was celebrated on 17 October 1255.[44] As she witnessed her fourteen-year-old daughter-in-law's ceremonial entry, Eleanor of Provence, then thirty-two, may have recalled the events of her own marriage and her arrival in a foreign country. It is perfectly plausible that on this occasion she presented the young Eleanor with the surviving copy of the *Estoire*.

Over the course of three and a half decades, Eleanor of Provence and her daughter-in-law, Eleanor of Castile, developed a close relationship. As well as the same name, they shared a common language – French – for Eleanor of Castile would have conversed in that language with her mother, Jeanne of Ponthieu. Because she did not become queen until Edward was crowned in 1272, the younger Eleanor had almost two decades to learn from the experience of her mother-in-law, and they maintained a harmonious relationship throughout their lives. We have no record of the two women exchanging book recommendations or manuscripts, but we know that they both owned saintly biographies and romances, typical reading material of women of their high status.

Knight paying homage to a king.
Drawing added to The Westminster Psalter, England, probably London, *c.* 1250.
Royal 2 A. xxii, ff. 219v-220r

Eleanor of Provence's mother, Beatrice of Savoy (*c.* 1207–66), almost certainly mediated her earliest encounters with literature. As mentioned in a previous chapter, Beatrice asked Aldobrandino of Siena to write a health treatise, the *Régime du corps*, so that she could share it with her four daughters, who are named in the preface.[45] Troubadours were welcome at the Provençal court of Beatrice of Savoy and her husband, Raymond Berengar V, and some, including Blacas, lord of Aups, and Sordello, an Italian, composed songs in Beatrice's honour.[46] As a child, Eleanor of Provence would have been immersed in the rich cultural heritage of southern France and exposed to epics and romances.[47]

No secular books owned by Eleanor of Provence have been preserved, but her household accounts show that 'within the space of six months, between 24 June and 28 October 1252, she bought two romances, one from Peter of Paris for 10s and one "done by the hand of William of Paris" at Oxford for £1 15s'.[48] Records also reveal that she ordered a binding for one of her romances.[49] Since the accounts do not supply titles, it is impossible to connect these books with specific works or gain a better understanding of the queen's literary interests. That Eleanor owned a copy of the *Roman de Guillaume le Conquerant* (*Romance of William the Conqueror*) is certain, however, because after her death it came into the possession of her son, Edward I, who gave it, in turn, to his son and heir, Edward of Caernarfon, in 1298.[50]

Eleanor of Provence's enthusiasm for tales of gallant actions and bloody conflicts seems to have exerted an influence on her home décor. In 1252, the walls of her chamber at Nottingham Castle were decorated with scenes from the Life of Alexander the Great, and previously, in May 1250, a copy of the *Geste d'Antioc*, an account of the siege of Antioch during the First Crusade, was made available for an unspecified project connected with the queen ('*ad opus regine*'/ 'for the queen's use').[51] Possibly with Eleanor's encouragement, just over a year later, in June 1251, the king had versions of the story of Antioch painted on the walls of a chamber at Westminster, and he later commissioned similar wall paintings to adorn chambers in his castle at Winchester and palace at Clarendon.[52]

Further evidence of Crusading fervour in the circle of the royal court survives in the form of a painting added *c.* 1250 to a psalter used by the monks of Westminster Abbey. Painted in a similar style to the illustrations in the extant copy of the *Estoire*, the image shows a Crusader knight paying homage to a king. Eleanor and Henry III had a vested interest in the subject, because in the spring of 1250 they had both taken vows to go to the Holy Land on Crusade. While their own plans remained unfulfilled, in March 1250, Eleanor's sister Marguerite journeyed to the Holy Land with the contingent led by her husband, King Louis IX of France.

Marguerite and Eleanor were particularly close, and in 1254, they and their other two sisters, Beatrice and Sanchia, celebrated Christmas together with their husbands at the royal palace in Paris. John Lowden has suggested that, on this occasion or a subsequent visit, Marguerite might have given Eleanor a vast three-volume *Bible moralisée*, a specialised picture bible, originally commissioned for Marguerite or for her husband, Louis IX, by his mother, Blanche of Castile. Lowden has further proposed that the *Bible moralisée*, which definitely entered the English royal library in Eleanor of Provence's lifetime, could have inspired English artists to create another type of biblical picture book, the illustrated Anglo-Norman Apocalypse, recounting, as the title suggests, events leading up to the destruction of the world.[53]

A richly painted Apocalypse made in the mid-1250s, now preserved in Trinity College, Cambridge, has been linked by some scholars to Eleanor of Provence, and by others with Eleanor of Castile, but the identity of the patron for whom it was made remains subject to speculation. Most unusually, a woman in thirteenth-century dress is featured in several illustrations. Brandishing a sword, she assails a seven-headed beast in one stunning image. Another Apocalypse, *c.* 1265–70, now in the Bodleian Library, Oxford, was indisputably owned by Edward I and Eleanor of Castile, who are portrayed in a decorated initial.[54] The idea that Marguerite's gift of the *Bible moralisée* to Eleanor may have inspired English artists to create an entirely new kind of book, the illustrated Anglo-Norman Apocalypse, which suddenly emerged in England in the mid-thirteenth century, has significant implications because it suggests that the role played by women as 'cultural ambassadors' could result in the creation of new ideas and artistic forms, in addition to the exchange of specific manuscripts.

The Lord Edward (later Edward I) and Eleanor of Castile kneeling before the Trinity (above); Saint John writing and Saint Paul preaching (below).
The Douce Apocalypse,
England, *c.* 1265-70,
Oxford, Bodleian Library,
MS Douce 180, f. 1r

Eleanor of Provence's younger sister Sanchia, Countess of Cornwall, was one of several women associated with the royal court who shared the queen's interest in the saintly biographies authored by Matthew Paris. Between *c.* 1236 and 1250, Matthew composed four saints' Lives in Anglo-Norman verse, two of which he dedicated to women. Although the chronology of these works is subject to debate, the two earliest, written in quick succession, were probably the Life of Thomas Becket and Eleanor's *Estoire*. Because Matthew's original manuscript of Becket's Life has not been preserved, we cannot identify its intended dedicatee. The *Estoire*, however, shows Matthew, perhaps for the first time, working in a language and rhyme scheme (octosyllabic rhyming couplets) appealing to a female readership. After Matthew had composed the Lives of Thomas and Edward, he wrote the *Vie de Seint Auban* (*Life of Saint Alban*), aimed primarily at the monks of his own abbey.[55] The last known saintly biography authored by Matthew in the vernacular, the Life of Saint

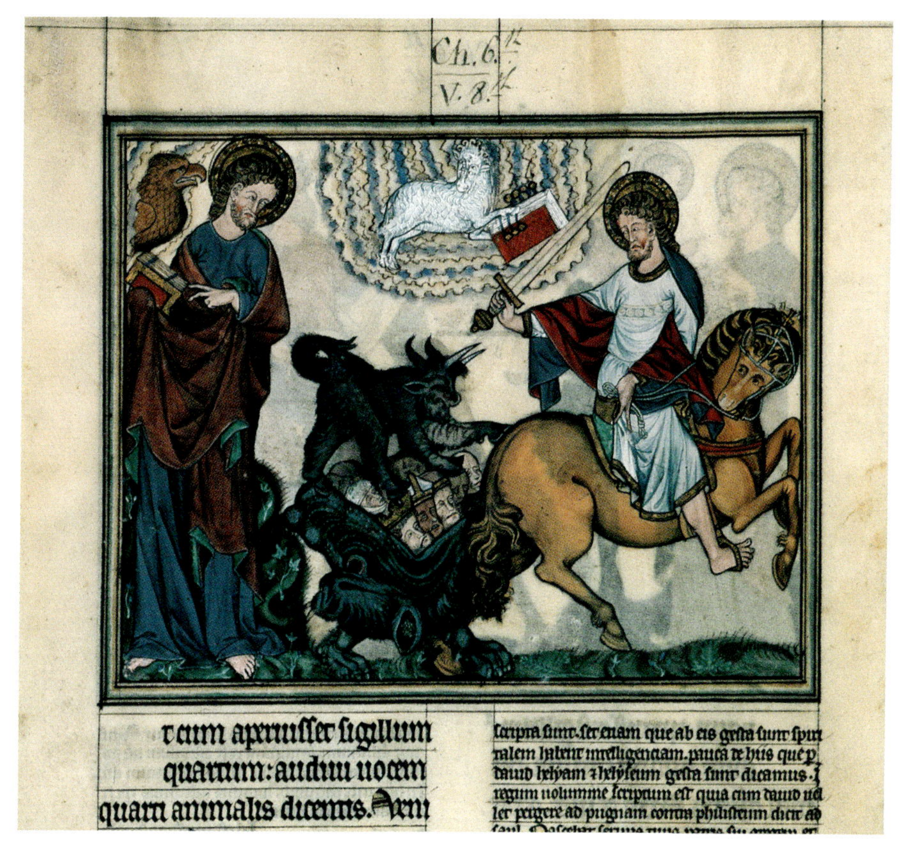

Most Anglo-Norman Apocalypses, like this magnificent example, are lavishly illustrated. This image depicts Saint John's vision of the one of the Four Horsemen of the Apocalypse; the Fourth Seal, the Pale horse (Revelation 6: 7–8). The Douce Apocalypse, England, *c.* 1265–70, Oxford, Bodleian Library, MS Douce 180, p. 16

Edmund Rich, Archbishop of Canterbury, was also written in Anglo-Norman octosyllabic rhyming couplets. In the preface, Matthew explicitly addresses the issue of language. He explains that he first wrote the Life in Latin and then translated it into French for the benefit of Isabelle de Warenne, the Countess of Arundel, to whom he dedicated it. Matthew does not seem to have composed any works in the vernacular earlier than these saints' Lives, which suggests that he did so in the first instance to accommodate the women to whom he dedicated his books.

Only one surviving manuscript, a *Life of Saint Alban*, is Matthew's original copy, written in his hand and featuring his illustrations (p. 148). A note inscribed by Matthew on a flyleaf shows that it was customary for him to loan autograph copies of his saintly biographies to aristocratic women, possibly to court their patronage, or perhaps in response to their requests. The note opens with the phrase, 'if you please, you can keep this book until Easter', referring, presumably, to the *Life of Saint Alban*, which he was about to loan to an unspecified person. The note then records Matthew's intention to lend the Countess of Cornwall (Eleanor of Provence's sister, Sanchia) 'the book about Saint Thomas the Martyr and Saint Edward' that he had translated and illustrated. Before being dispatched to Sanchia, the book was

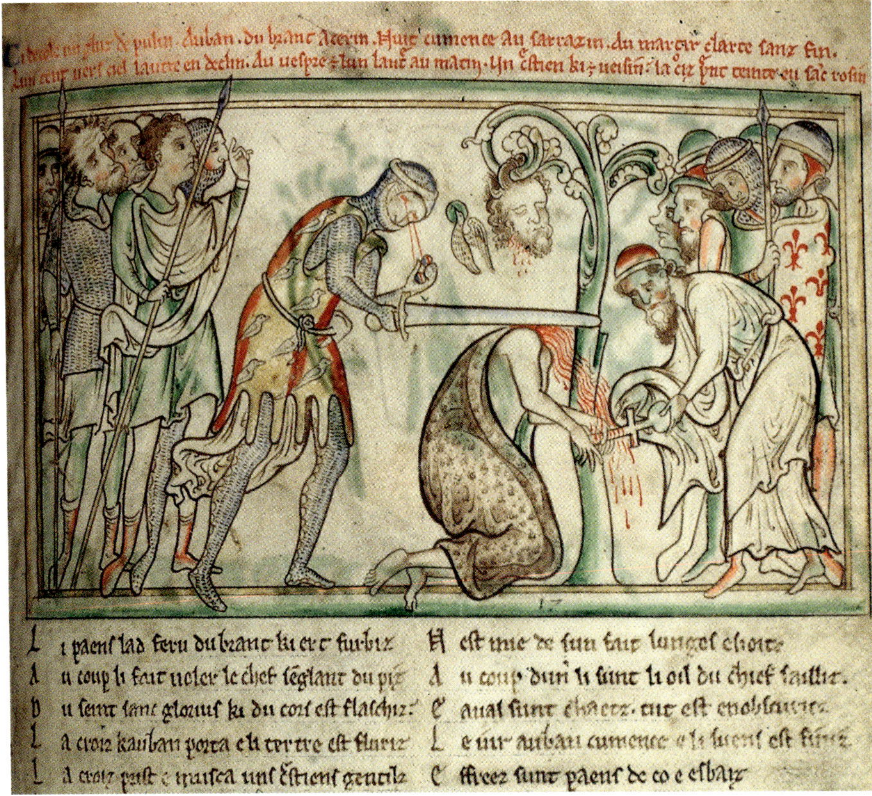

Tinted drawing by Matthew Paris showing the beheading of Saint Alban, the first English martyr. As a divine punishment, the executioner's eyeballs were torn from their sockets. Matthew Paris, *Life of Saint Alban*, St Albans, 1240–50. Dublin, Trinity College MS 177, f. 38r

to be retrieved from the Countess of Arundel, who had previously borrowed it. Matthew's note suggests that there were at least two illustrated copies of his *Estoire* in use by female patrons at the time; one bound with the *Life of Saint Thomas*, which he loaned both to Eleanor's sister Sanchia and to Isabelle de Warenne, Countess of Arundel, and another, undoubtedly a grand presentation copy, in the possession of Queen Eleanor of Provence, to whom it was dedicated.[56]

The only other surviving work with a religious theme dedicated to Eleanor of Provence is a poem composed for her by John Howden, a clerk in her service. Entitled *Rossignos* (*Nightingale*), it was probably written *c.* 1274, a few years after the death of Henry III on 16 November 1272. Based on his earlier Latin poem, *Philomena* (Latin for *Nightingale*), and reconfigured to suit his dedicatee, the widowed queen, it is an account in Anglo-Norman verse of events in the life of Jesus and the Virgin Mary, concentrating particularly on the agony experienced by the crucified Christ. Making an emotional plea to his reader, the poet asks her to identify with the suffering Christ and paints a poignant picture of his grieving mother Mary.

The precise date of composition is unknown, but if John completed the poem shortly after Henry's death, the theme would have had an additional resonance for Eleanor, who was mourning her husband of thirty-six years. Nine Latin poems by John survive, but this is the only one written for a female patron and the only one in French by a poet who is 'considered a major figure among the Anglo-Latin poets of his day'.[57] Regardless of whether Eleanor commissioned John to write it or he elected to do so himself, his deviation from his usual mode of expression – Latin – reflects his intention to craft a poem especially for the queen.[58]

By weaving motifs from courtly literature into the devotional work, John catered to Eleanor of Provence's literary tastes.[59] More remarkably, he also incorporated into the poem references to members of her family. Mentioned alongside the legendary figures of Lancelot, Gawain, Yvain, Percival and King Arthur are many of Eleanor's relatives and male acquaintances, including her deceased husband Henry III, her father Raymond Berengar V, her uncle Peter of Savoy and, of course, her son, Edward I, who is praised for his handsome appearance and heroism – comments any mother would presumably welcome. Her brothers-in-law Charles of Anjou and Louis IX are also cited, as is King Fernando III, father of Eleanor of Castile.

In the prologue, John explains that one of the reasons he called the poem *Nightingale* was because 'it was made and contrived in a fair orchard in flower where nightingales were just then singing' ('*que il estoit fez e trové en un beau verger flori ou rossignol adés chauntoient*'), and that he wrote it to inflame with love for God the heart of his reader – sentiments intended to appeal to his female patron, who would have been attuned to the echoes of romances in these lines.[60] In the poem, the nightingale appears as a symbol for Christ, so it would be unreasonable to take literally John's claim that the birds serenaded him while he was writing. It is not, however, far-fetched to think that he would have been acquainted with the song of the nightingale. The birds were probably a feature of the gardens that Eleanor of Provence maintained at Windsor, Woodstock, Kempton and elsewhere, and they are listed among the birds purchased by her daughter-in-law Eleanor of Castile, who built an aviary at Westminster in 1279.[61] In the final stanza of *Nightingale*, John addresses the poem directly, telling it to go to the queen in order to 'be read and repeated to her' ('*Va, chanson, e, se li agree, / Soiez leüe e recordee*').[62] This suggests that he expected that it would be read aloud to her. Perhaps he anticipated doing so himself.

Few extant manuscripts can be associated with Eleanor of Castile, but a wealth of evidence points to her engagement with books. Crucial information is provided by her *Liber Garderobe* (Household Account Book), preserved in the British Library, which covers 1289–90, the final year of her life.[63] Two damaged accounts in roll form, dated 1287–8 and 1288–9 respectively, provide the only other records of her personal expenses. Since most accounts relating to the queen's household have been lost, it is all the more impressive that the ones that have survived include multiple references to book production.

Among the entries, for example, are references to two scribes, Roger and Philip, who were based at the palace in Westminster and copied manuscripts for her. A painter, Godfrey, who supplied illustrations, is likewise mentioned, and expenses relating to materials, including quills, ink, parchment and gold leaf, are duly noted.[64] Eleanor's accounts also reveal that her scribes and illuminators sometimes accompanied her on her travels and bought supplies in far-flung places.[65]

That Eleanor had her own scribal workshop was unparalleled – 'she maintained the only personal scriptorium documented at a northern European court at this period'.[66] Her half-brother, King Alfonso X, one of the most active literary patrons of the thirteenth century, almost certainly inspired her to do so.[67] The itinerant king employed scribes and artists who travelled with him and also worked at his palace in Seville. Eleanor's respect and affection for Alfonso was such that she named her firstborn son after him, and they corresponded throughout their lives.

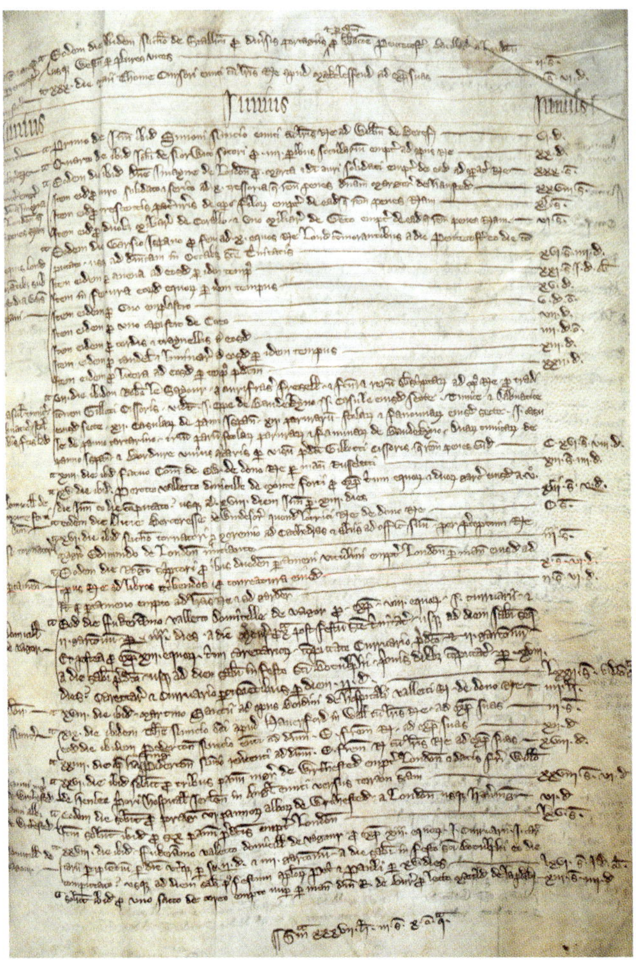

Household Account Book of Eleanor of Castile. Expenses include materials for making manuscripts and payments to her scribes and illuminator.
England, London, 1289–90.
Additional 35294, f. 10r

Because references to Eleanor's scribes and illuminator are found in her financial accounts of 1290, the year she died, it is clear that until the end of her life, despite intermittent periods of illness, she continued to have books made for her. After her death from fever, possibly caused by malaria, on 28 November 1290, the workshop was disbanded, which confirms that it was Eleanor's personal undertaking, created to meet her needs.

In addition to shedding light on her scribal workshop, Eleanor's accounts also show that a psalter and seven books of hours (*primers*) were acquired for her on a single trip to Cambridge (perhaps to give to her children or young relatives to learn to read), and that a chest was purchased *pro romanciis regine* (for the queen's romances), so that she could transport them on her travels.[68] The volumes in the chest may well have included *un romanz de Isembart* made in Ponthieu in 1280.[69] The timing of the purchase of this now lost tale of Isembart, who was celebrated by chroniclers as the Count of Ponthieu, is significant, because in 1279, on the death of her mother Jeanne, Eleanor had become the countess of the northern French county. As John Carmi Parsons remarks, 'Eleanor's interest in Isembart, shortly after she succeeded in Ponthieu, implies that she saw him as an ancestor, or at least a predecessor'.[70]

The chest in which Eleanor stored her books might have also contained a copy of *Escanor*, a tale of the Arthurian knight Gawain, composed around 1280 for Eleanor by Girart d'Amiens, who claimed that the queen supplied its subject matter. Medieval writers often made claims of this sort to ingratiate themselves with their patrons, but we should not dismiss the idea that Eleanor had developed a particular interest in *Escanor*, a story about two warring adversaries who are reconciled.[71] In 1277, shortly before Girart embarked on *Escanor*, his earliest known work, Edward I had conquered the Welsh ruler Llewelyn ap Gruffyd, causing him to capitulate and sign a peace treaty, and it is conceivable that this event was the catalyst for the commission. Richard Traschler has, in fact, suggested that the battle tactics employed by King Arthur in the narrative, as described by Girart d'Amiens, resemble those actually put into practice by Edward I on his Welsh campaign against Llewelyn.[72]

It is possible that Eleanor, who had been raised in the militaristic atmosphere of the Castilian court and had taken a Crusader vow at the age of twenty-six, was genuinely fascinated by stories of chivalry and may well have encouraged her husband's interest in Arthur.[73] Certainly they both visited Glastonbury in April 1278. There, according to one chronicler, 'the King caused the tomb of Artour to be opened, whose bones he caused to be removed out of the said tomb, to behold the length and bignes of them, and then returned to London'.[74]

King Alfonso X of Castile–León (r. 1252–84), half-brother of Eleanor of Castile. Alfonso, known as 'el Sabio' ('the Wise'), was one of the most active royal literary patrons of the thirteenth century. Alfonso X, *Cantigas de Santa Maria*, El Escorial, Real Monasterio de San Lorenzo, MS T.I.1, f. 5r

Among the most intriguing entries in Eleanor's account book is one dated 16 May 1288, which records money spent on gold leaf, ink, an inkwell, and on parchment to repair the bindings of two books: a Life of 'the Blessed Thomas' and a Life of Saint Edward.[75] As we know, Matthew Paris wrote a life of Edward the Confessor (the *Estoire*), as well as a life of Thomas Becket, the martyred Archbishop of Canterbury. Evidently, Eleanor of Castile owned copies of both texts.[76] Furthermore, she or other members of the royal household had consulted these manuscripts so frequently that they had incurred damage. An aspect of this record that seems to have been overlooked is that the expenditure was converted into shillings from a foreign currency – the chipotensis of Bigorre – the local currency of Gascony, the French duchy ruled by Eleanor's husband, Edward I. Eleanor, who was with Edward in Gascony from May 1286 to August 1289, must have taken along her copies of the Lives of Saint Thomas and Edward the Confessor and had them repaired there. Whether the extant *Estoire*, illuminated *c.* 1255 by artists working in the ambit of the English royal court, was one of the manuscripts Eleanor had repaired in France in May 1288 is an open question. It is certainly possible.

Eleanor of Castile's accounts also reveal that earlier that same year she had parchment purchased for the purpose of writing a Life of Saint Thomas.[77] Since this record is dated 3 January 1288, it seems unlikely to refer to the copy of Thomas' Life Eleanor sent for repairs just over three months later. More likely, she wanted a second copy, possibly to give to a member of her family. That the Confessor continued to be upheld as a role model for the next generation is strongly suggested by the purchase, in 1302, twelve years after Eleanor of Castile's death, of a deluxe copy of the saint's Life in French for her youngest son, Prince Edward (the future Edward II), who was then eighteen. Royal records show that a payment of 58 shillings was made to a London craftsman for the volume, which was handsomely illuminated and bound.[78]

Among the most remarkable books connected with Eleanor of Castile is a military treatise preserved in the Fitzwilliam Museum, Cambridge. The volume consists of two related parts: a copy of *De re militari* (*On Military Matters*), composed in the late fourth or early fifth century by the Roman author Publius Vegetius Renatus, and an Anglo-Norman translation of the work, the earliest known version of the Latin text in any Western European language.

Why was Eleanor drawn to a nine-hundred-year-old treatise concerning every aspect of military life, from the recruitment of soldiers to battle formations and strategy? It is possible that Eleanor of Castile's half-brother, King Alfonso X, who incorporated sections of the text in his great law code, the *Siete Partidas* (*Seven Divisions*), called Eleanor's attention to the work, and it is conceivable that she would have found the subject matter compelling. A keen equestrian and hunter, she was, moreover, the daughter of Fernando III, the great warrior of the Reconquest who had united the Christian and Muslim kingdoms of Spain under his sovereignty. She was also the niece of John of Brienne, King of the Crusader Kingdom of Jerusalem.[79] It was not, however, primarily her own interest in the subject that inspired her to commission the translation, but that of her husband Edward, to whom she presented the volume.

Having taken a Crusader vow in 1267 and journeyed with Edward to the Holy Land, Eleanor of Castile resided in Acre from May 1271 to September 1272.[80] There she witnessed an attempt on Edward's life by a knife-wielding assassin whom the king, though badly wounded, grappled with and killed. She also gave birth to two daughters in quick succession. Only one of the babies, Joan, born in April 1272, survived. Against the backdrop of these events, Eleanor ordered for Edward the

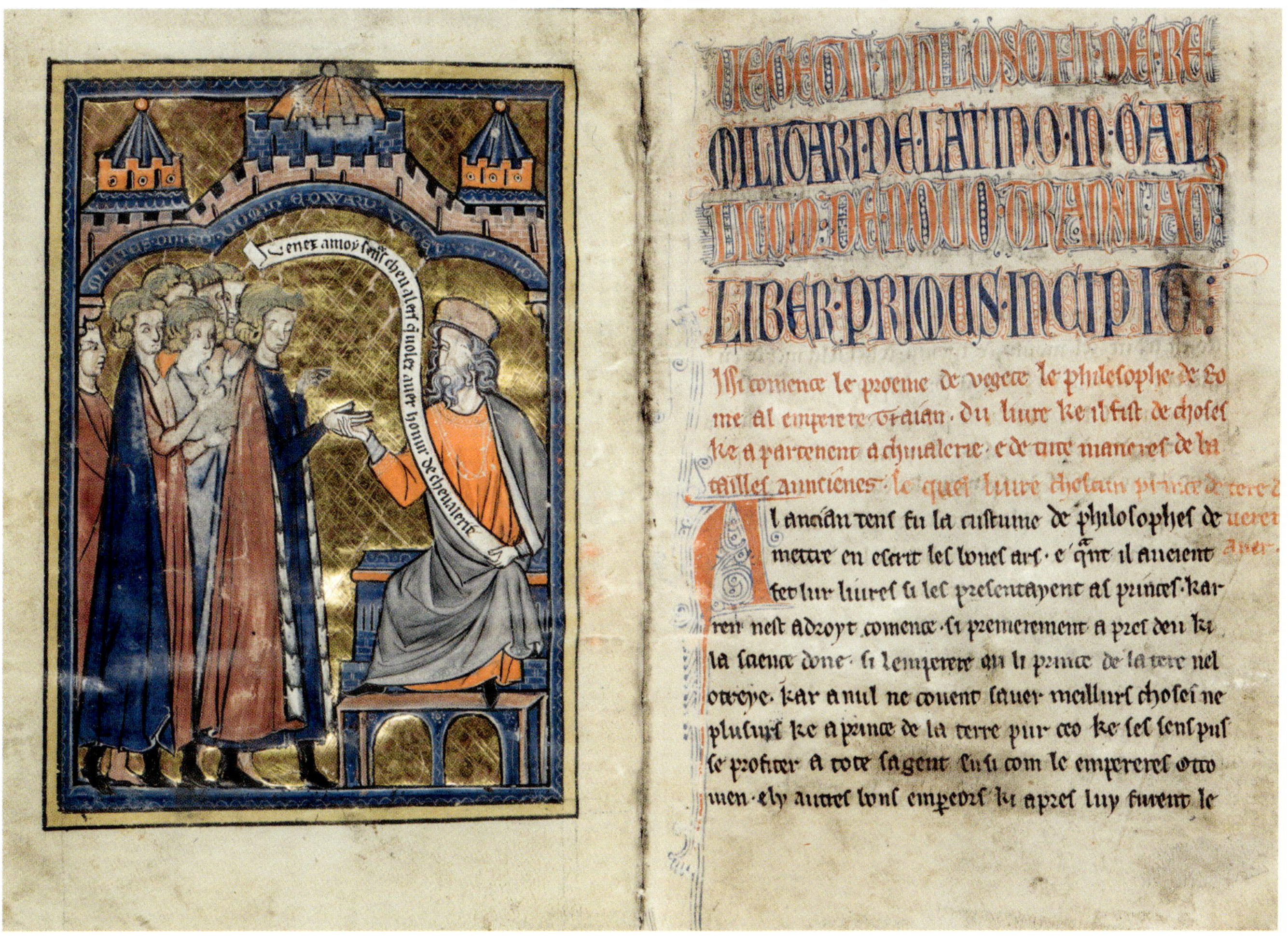

The Lord Edward (the future Edward I) and his knightly companions with the Roman author, Vegetius. Vegetius, *De re militari*, probably Acre, *c.* 1265–72. Cambridge, Fitzwilliam Museum, MS Marlay Add. 1, ff. 2v–3r

translation of *De re militari*. A more suitable book to give to a prince who was waging war would be difficult to conceive. Surviving in a single copy, the translation of *De re militari* commissioned by Eleanor of Castile for Edward is evidence of her literary patronage, her engagement with the vernacular and her affection for her husband.

The manuscript opens with the following heading inscribed in capital letters: 'VEGETII PHILOSOFI DE RE MILITARI DE LATINO IN GALLICUM DE NOVO TRANSLATUS.' This alerts us to the novelty of the text: it is '*de novo*' – a new translation made from the Latin into French. The translator states that Vegetius' treatise is '*quel livre chescun prince de tere devereit aver*' ('that book every prince of the world must have'). Evidently, Eleanor agreed. When Edward read the Anglo-Norman translation commissioned by his wife, he would not have had to struggle to understand

arcane terms, for the translator adapted the Latin text, tailoring it for the prince and using 'the terms of chivalry to replace those of the Roman armies'.[81] Evidently intending to flatter his reader, he also incorporated a fleeting reference to Edward's surprise assault on the rebel baron Simon de Montfort at Kenilworth on 1 August 1265.[82]

It is rare to find medieval manuscripts containing bilingual editions of secular texts. Most vernacular translations circulated as independent volumes. The Fitzwilliam Vegetius containing both French and Latin versions, one bound after the other, was probably designed to flatter its intended recipient, Edward I, since it implied that his command of Latin was sufficiently good that he would want to have recourse to the original. It is also significant that the translation is in prose rather than rhyming couplets, which suggests that it was designed for private study rather than communal reading. Indeed, there would have been little point in broadcasting military tactics.

Map of the Holy Land by Matthew Paris, showing Acre and Jerusalem. East is at the top. Eleanor of Castile, who traveled to the Holy Land with the Lord Edward (later Edward I), stayed in Acre from May 1271 to September 1272. On this map, the city is shown within a walled enclosure beneath the jaunty camel.
England, St Albans, *c.* 1250.
Royal 14 C. vii, ff. 4v-5r

Naval combat.
Vegetius, *De re militari*,
probably Acre, *c.* 1265–72.
Cambridge, Fitzwilliam Museum,
MS Marlay Add. 1, f. 86r

A full-page painting at the front of the volume, probably painted by an English artist, shows Edward, accompanied by six young men, standing before the Roman author, who is portrayed in thirteenth-century dress (p. 153). An inscription on the arch above identifies 'Lord Edward', his knights, and the grey-bearded sage Vegetius (*Vegetius Philosophus*), who holds a scroll inscribed with the words, '*Venez a moy, senurs chevalers qui volez aver honur de chevalerie*' ('Come to me lord knights who wish to have the honour of chivalry'), which implies that they have already been knighted and are now ready to receive his counsel. The inscription is couched in contemporary language; Vegetius, it appears, has sprung to life to impart his knowledge directly to Edward, who steps forward, as instructed, to clasp the Roman author's hand.

A second, smaller image, in a different style, shows knights in ships engaged in combat. It was painted on a separate piece of parchment, possibly by Western artists working in Acre, and then pasted into the volume. From the style of the script, we can deduce that the scribes were English, probably clerks in Eleanor's service who had travelled overseas with her.

According to a verse inscription on a flyleaf at the end of the manuscript, written in a late thirteenth-century hand, a certain Master Richard wrote the work in Acre at the request of his female patron. Although he does not identify her by name, he is undoubtedly referring to Eleanor of Castile. Significantly, the verse inscription, which is addressed to Eleanor, is written in continental French, her mother tongue, whereas the translation, made for her English husband, is in Anglo-Norman prose. More importantly, the first line of the inscription was modified by the writer, who changed his original phrase, '*ceste lettre*' ('this letter'), and wrote in its place '*vostre livere*' ('your book'). This suggests that, in the first instance, Richard might have presented his verses to Eleanor as an independent document, a brief letter. Later it must have been considered expedient to preserve in the manuscript itself his description of the circumstances of the commission.

In the verse inscription, Richard expresses his intention to be reunited with his female patron in France after his departure from Acre. The word 'France' supplies the rhyme in the final line, but Richard's allusion to France could be more than a case of artistic licence. On Edward and Eleanor's journey back from the Holy Land in 1272, Eleanor, who was four or five months pregnant, stayed in France where she gave birth to her son, Alphonso. He was named after her half-brother, Alfonso X, King of Castile-León, who travelled to Bayonne in November 1273 to attend the child's baptism and to serve as his godfather. It was not until 2 August 1274, after a four-year absence, that Eleanor and Edward returned to England.

Whether Edward I benefited from Vegetius' wisdom is unknown, but he probably treasured the manuscript given to him by his wife, and it is possible that it came to be held among several other royal manuscripts in the Privy Wardrobe of the King in the Tower of London, where other valuables, including arms and armour, textiles, plate and jewels were stored.[83] Books kept there were loaned to various members of the royal household and, according to a record made by John Fleet, who supervised these transactions in the second quarter of the fourteenth century, a handsomely bound copy of Vegetius' *De re militari* in French was among seven 'romances' issued to the Queen Mother, Isabella of France, on 5 March 1327, on the orders of her son, Edward III. He had ascended to the throne only three months earlier, after Isabella and her powerful lover and ally, Roger Mortimer, 1st Earl of March, had toppled King Edward II from power and forced him to abdicate. By 1327, when Isabella of France borrowed the copy of Vegetius' *De re militari* from the royal stores, the writer Jean de Meun had translated the work into continental French, but it seems much more likely that the sumptuously bound copy, held under lock and key alongside other treasures in the Tower of London, was a family heirloom, the manuscript of the Anglo-Norman translation presented by Eleanor of Castile to Edward I in the early 1270s, rather than a copy of Jean de Meun's translation.

Further evidence of Eleanor's provision of books for her family members survives in the form of a psalter commissioned, *c.* 1284, to mark the marriage of her son Alphonso. Like the military treatise she gave to her husband, the psalter, made for the ten-year-old prince and emblazoned with his arms, was conceived especially

Combat between a knight and a giant; a lion attacking a man.
The Alphonso Psalter, England, London, *c.* 1284.
Additional 24686, f. 17r

for him. Combat scenes abound, surely designed to excite the imagination of a young boy who had his own falcon and saddle, and whose playthings included a toy castle and siege engine. When he was five, in July 1278, his father gave him a suit of armour. This was not so that he could stage a sword fight with his playmates, but so he could attend a tournament in Windsor Park, alongside seasoned knights who had accompanied his father on Crusade.[84] The life-like lions in Alphonso's psalter could have been inspired by animals in the royal menagerie, and the naturalistic birds by specimens in his mother's aviary at Westminster, home to an array of birds including nightingales, swans and Sicilian parrots.[85] Other features of the manuscript also reflect Eleanor's interests, including an image of a woman hunting with hounds, one of her favourite pastimes. The inclusion in the litany (prayers to saints) of Dominic de Guzmán, the Spanish founder of the Dominican order, and his fellow friar Peter Martyr, reflect her devotional allegiances, for her confessor (private chaplain), Walter de Winterbourne, was a Dominican, and she was one of the main patrons of the order, having founded Dominican priories in Chichester, Rhuddlan and London.[86]

Alphonso sadly died at age ten on 19 August 1284, a week after the marriage contract was signed and only months before the planned wedding.[87] His body was buried in Westminster Abbey and his heart enshrined at the Dominican priory in London, founded by his mother. Eleanor's attachment to him was such that she made arrangements to have her own heart interred with his on her death. After the young prince died, his psalter lay unfinished. There was no impulse to continue and the manuscript languished for over a decade. It was, however, retained at the

A noblewoman hunting with hounds. The Alphonso Psalter, England, London, *c.* 1284. Additional 24686, f. 13v

court and, remarkably, in 1297, it was completed by a different group of artists to present to Alphonso's younger sister Elizabeth (1282–1316), on the occasion of her marriage to John I of Holland, the brother of Margaret, Alphonso's intended bride.

Eleanor could have played no part in the decision to give the psalter to her daughter, for she had died seven years before, on 28 November 1290. It is probable that Edward I himself arranged for it to be given to Elizabeth. He was, indeed, so attached to her that after her marriage, when she expressed her reluctance to leave home and move to Holland, he permitted her to stay with him in England. Nine months after the wedding, her fraught husband John sent a letter to the king, pleading with him to send Elizabeth to Holland so he could enjoy her company. It was not his first request. Eventually, Edward conceded and escorted her there.[88]

Elizabeth kept the psalter throughout her life, a legacy of the brother who had died when she was just two years old and of her mother, the queen, who died when she was eight. While the volume was in her possession several illustrations were added to it, including a full-page image of four female saints. Suitably for a book that may well have been used by Elizabeth to instruct her own children, an image of Saint Anne teaching the Virgin to read is paired with an image of Saint Catherine. It is an unusual but meaningful juxtaposition of the two most important patron saints of female learning. Elizabeth's psalter must have had symbolic resonance for her as well as practical value. It was a royal book, probably presented to her by her father, and it was a link to the people she loved and to whom she rapidly returned when her husband, John of Holland, died in 1299, two years after their wedding. The calendar, added to the book, includes, in a fourteenth-century hand, the obits of three women named Eleanor: Elizabeth's grandmother, her mother, and her older sister. Her own date of death was inserted after she passed away at age thirty-four, shortly after giving birth to her eleventh child by her second husband, Humphrey de Bohun, 4th Earl of Hereford, on 5 May 1316.

Apart from the Alphonso Psalter, no manuscript presents such a personal glimpse of Edward I and Eleanor of Castile's relationship with their children, but Eleanor's influence can be discerned in other ways. Her daughter Mary (*c.* 1279–1332), for example, who was a Benedictine nun, is associated with a major work, a historical chronicle written by the Dominican friar Nicholas Trevet (d. *c.* 1334), Master at the University of Oxford. Given her mother's staunch support for the friars, Dominicans would have been familiar figures in Mary's life, but not all of them would have enjoyed Trevet's international reputation. Trevet was a prolific scholar with wide-ranging interests, and his writings, encompassing theology, law, astronomy, history, literature and the exposition of Christian and classical texts, gained him prestigious patrons, including Pope John XXII (r. 1316–34) and Cardinal Nicolò da Prato.[89] How he came to write a historical chronicle for Mary is unknown, but that it

Saint Anne and the Virgin Mary with Saints Catherine, Margaret, and Barbara; added prefatory miniatures (*c.* 1302–16). The Alphonso Psalter, England, London, *c.* 1284. Additional 24686, fol. 2v was intended for her from the start is indicated by the preface, in which she is named, and confirmed by the character of the work.

While sketching the history of mankind from Adam up to the fourteenth century, Trevet's sweeping chronicle, dedicated to Mary, also includes information of personal relevance to her. He describes the reign of her father, Edward I, in more detail than that of any other ruler, and, tracing maternal lines of kinship including that of Matilda of Scotland, he stresses connections between Anglo-Saxon and Norman kings. More remarkably, he also mentions Mary by name and tells how on 15 August 1285, at the age of six, she entered the nunnery of Amesbury in Wiltshire.[90] Trevet reports that Eleanor of Castile was reluctant to part with her young daughter, but she complied at the insistence of the girl's grandmother, the elderly Eleanor of Provence, who was planning to retire to the convent and wanted the child to live with her there. According to John Carmi Parsons, the discussion over Mary's future resulted in 'the only recorded disagreement between the two queens'.[91]

Eleanor of Provence died at Amesbury in 1291, the year her granddaughter Mary, then aged twelve, formally became a nun. Although she took the veil, Mary led a luxurious life; she had private quarters at the nunnery, a generous allowance, and was given, among many other royal provisions, firewood to keep her chambers warm and bright as well as copious quantities of wine from the royal stores.[92] She also travelled widely and made extended visits to the royal court. Both her indulgent father and her brother, Edward II, grew resigned to paying the bills that she left in her wake on shopping sprees. They also covered the phenomenal debts that Mary accrued playing dice.

Trevet's chronicle, his final work, is the only known text composed by him in French, a language he obviously employed as a concession to the young woman for whom he was writing. Occasionally, for dramatic effect, he employs English expressions, but he supplies translations in French, Mary's mother tongue. As noted by Ruth Dean, it was not his preferred mode of expression and is 'couched awkwardly in a vernacular in which he is unable to write with the sweep and rhythm to which his Latin had sometimes attained'.[93] Although Trevet's text could not be more different in form and tone from Eleanor of Provence's *Rossignos* (*Nightingale*), it is notable that the authors of both works embedded in their texts references of personal significance to their patrons. It is tempting to think that Mary, who had every opportunity to read her grandmother's poem while they both lived at Amesbury, might have been motivated by it to commission Trevet's chronicle, a work commemorating her own family members. Although Eleanor's *Nightingale* restricts its references to prominent men, Mary's chronicle mentions both male and female members of her family, including her sisters. Although the specific circumstances of the commission are unknown, it has been argued that the impetus for writing it came from Mary, because Trevet 'as an internationally renowned scholar, had no need to court Mary's patronage with an unsolicited work'.[94]

As outlined in this chapter, women played a significant role in the literary developments of the twelfth and thirteenth centuries. Growing numbers of male authors, including Matthew Paris, John Howden and Nicolas Trevet, who had forged a reputation on the strength of their Latin works, catered to highborn women by composing works in the vernacular. And female authors, such as Marie de France, also employed everyday languages in order to make their work 'intelligible and suited to lay folk'. Texts, including those of a historical or 'scientific' nature, were invariably composed in rhyming couplets, which must have made them more entertaining to declaim and less difficult for audiences to digest. That writers like Geffrei Gaimar transformed arid Latin sources into romping poems with irresistible rhymes is a tribute to their ingenuity and patience.

Several of the literary works discussed above reflect key moments in their owner's lives. At least three texts associated with Eleanor of Castile – the romance of Isembart (purchased shortly after she became Countess of Ponthieu), Girart of Amiens' *Escanor* (commissioned around the time Llewelyn ap Gruffyd capitulated to Edward I), and the translation of Vegetius' *De re militari* (made when she and Edward were on Crusade) – suggest that her reading matter reflected important events in her life.[95] In addition, as we have seen, copies of Matthew Paris' Life of Edward the Confessor, the *Estoire*, were probably commissioned to commemorate two royal marriages: that of Eleanor of Provence to Henry III, and of her son Edward I to Eleanor of Castile. That the Anglo-Saxon king continued to be upheld as a role model for members of the next generation is indicated by the purchase, in 1302, of a deluxe copy of the saint's Life in French for Edward of Caernarfon (the future Edward II). Although the chaste Anglo-Saxon king had died without issue, he was, nevertheless, evoked as a 'special patron' who would bless the monarchy and help to perpetuate the royal line. For the members of the English court who read and re-read Edward the Confessor's Life in private, or gathered to hear it recited in great assemblies, he was not a shadowy figure from the historical past, but an ever-present ally who could intercede with God on their behalf.

It is striking that so many of the works commissioned by, or dedicated to, women served as a testament to family members. Turgot's biography of Queen Margaret was written at the request of her daughter Matilda, and the now lost poem by David was commissioned by Queen Adeliza to commemorate her husband, Henry I. Personal references embedded in both Eleanor of Provence's *Rossignos* and Trevet's *Chronicles*, written for Mary of Woodstock, similarly reflect an interest in dynastic history and a desire to preserve, through writing, reading and recitation, the memory of people they held dear.

CHAPTER SEVEN

WORK

WOMEN PLAYED a vital role in the medieval economy, but two main obstacles prevented them from making an even greater contribution: first, a lack of formal education and professional training comparable to that available for men of the privileged classes; and second, the idea that women's work differed from men's in fundamental ways. Though some women were surely capable of using a plough or axe, they were generally denied these opportunities. The fact that jobs were largely socially determined is suggested by the fact that a task like sowing was rarely relegated to women although it was less arduous than weeding, which they were permitted to do. Divisions of labour varied from region to region and period to period. Some women performed tasks traditionally assigned to men, but the reverse was rare.

Only a fraction of the jobs accomplished by women are represented in medieval manuscripts. Illustrations of women at work are not, of course, straightforward reflections of historical realities, but paintings governed by artistic conventions. The proliferation of shepherdesses in scenes of the Annunciation to the Shepherds in French books of hours of the late fifteenth century is, for example, a reflection of changing artistic styles and tastes, rather than proof of a burgeoning female workforce schooled in livestock management.[1] Because medieval artists tended to portray styles of dress according to fashions worn by their contemporaries, and to base agricultural implements and other tools on items in use in their own day, images of women at work are, however, grounded in the real world.

Women were responsible for domestic chores, including childcare, cooking and cleaning, dressing flax and combing and spinning wool, and, when required, nursing the sick and elderly. Women also planted and tended vegetable gardens, harvested crops, cared for poultry, guarded and milked livestock, churned butter and made cheese. Since ewes weigh an average of 60–90 kg and rams 90–130 kg, cleaning and shearing sheep is arguably more strenuous than sowing or ploughing, but it was a task considered suitable for women because they were the primary custodians of small livestock, and the washing and processing of the wool was also their responsibility.[2]

Annunciation to the Shepherds. Shepherdesses do not appear in the earliest depictions of the subject, but they are represented in many fifteenth-century French miniatures. Book of Hours. France, Tours, fifteenth century. Additional 11865, f. 32v

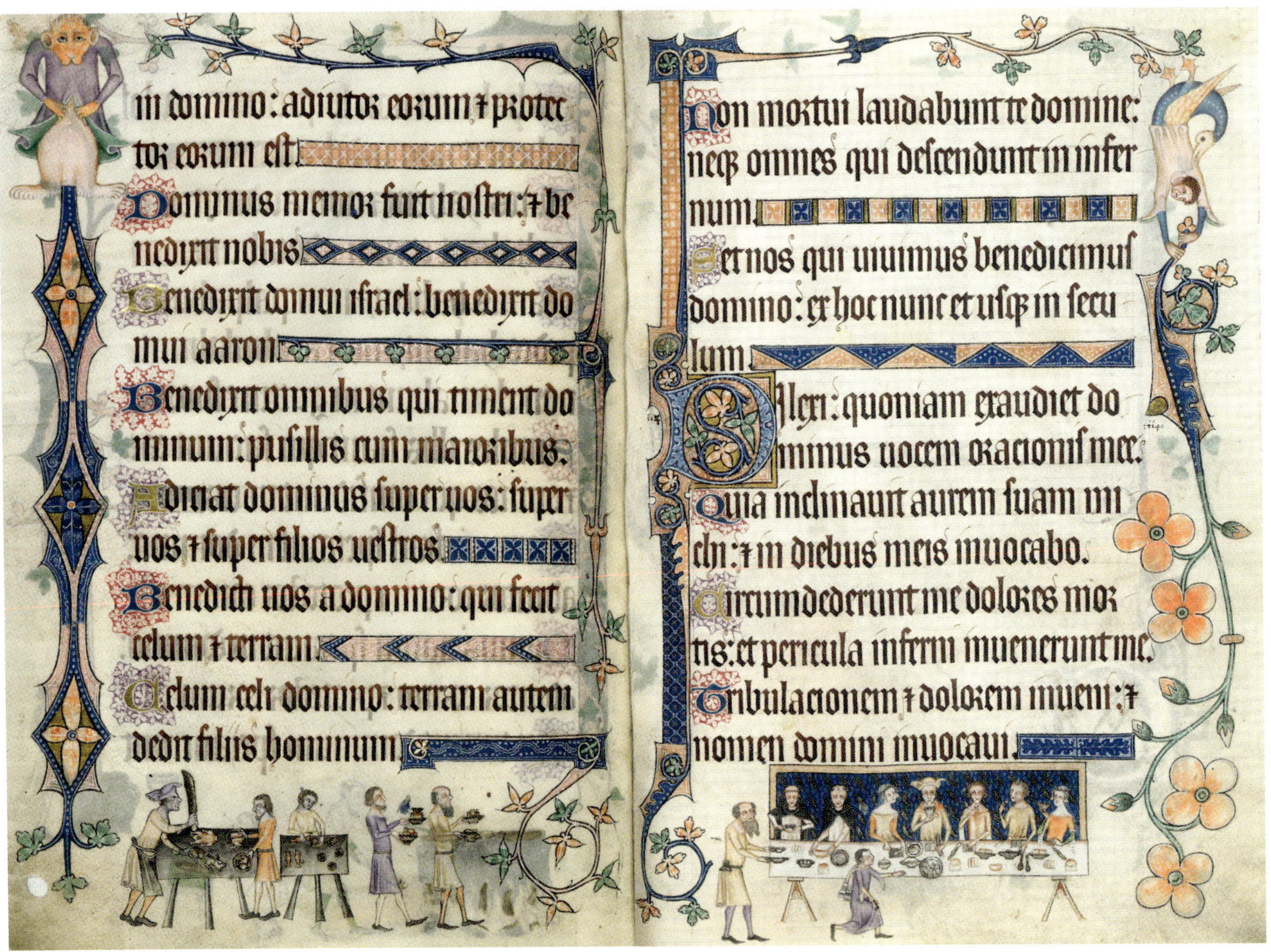

The Luttrell family feasting. Geoffrey Luttrell is pictured at the centre of the table with his wife, Agnes Sutton, on his right. The Luttrell Psalter, England, Lincolnshire, c. 1320–40. Additional 42130, ff. 207v–208r

Sheep were valuable commodities, providing manure, milk, wool and meat. Alfonso X's *Cantigas de Santa Maria* (*Songs of Holy Mary*) contains an anecdote underscoring the value of even a single sheep. According to the tale, a poor woman entrusted her only sheep to an unscrupulous shepherd, who hid it and told her that it had been eaten by a wolf. Miraculously, the sheep, which had been eavesdropping on the conversation, disclosed its location by bleating, 'Here I am!', and the grateful woman sheared it, took the wool to church and offered it to the Virgin Mary.[3]

A richly decorated English psalter commissioned by the landowner Sir Geoffrey Luttrell, lord of the manor at Irnham, Lincolnshire, *c.* 1320–40, includes idealised portraits of him, his wife and daughter-in-law, and many images of people engaged in tasks necessary for the successful running of his estates. In one border scene, for example, three women wielding sickles cut grain, followed closely by a man who bundles it into sheaves. The harvesters' countenances are grim, but the majority of the people depicted in the manuscript, including Geoffrey Luttrell himself, wear similar expressions, so this alone is not indicative of the strenuous nature of their job. More telling is the pose of the woman who takes a brief rest, arching her back to relieve the strain imposed by bending over the crop. 'Let the fields be jubilant, and everything in them' reads Psalm 95:12, inscribed above the workers' heads, but they seem unlikely to break out in songs of praise.[4] Whether Geoffrey himself appreciated the irony when he perused this page of his devotional book is impossible to say, but the deliberate juxtaposition of this psalm and image bears witness to the level of sophistication of the anonymous artists who illuminated this devotional book and responded to the ancient texts of the psalms in original ways. Not every image is as closely related to the text as the harvest scene, and some bear no relation to the text at all, but each page of the manuscript reflects the active imaginations of the artists who painted candy-coloured monsters alongside scenes evoking daily life.

Occasionally, the illuminators combined the fantastic and naturalistic, offering for their readers' delectation such sights as a monkey in a jaunty cap, driving a team of horses. In the harvest image, the male reaper is not shown in the principal role (he has a sickle tucked into his belt, but does not use it). The prominence assigned to the female harvesters is almost unparalleled in medieval art made before 1400 and has intrigued scholars who have sought to explain it.[5] Some have interpreted the image as a symbol of fertility and procreation, with sexual allusions suggested by the women bending forward in front of the male reaper, and the corn dolly, resembling a phallus, positioned near his feet.[6]

Harvesters. The Luttrell Psalter, England, Lincolnshire, *c.* 1320–40. Additional 42130, f. 172v

An elderly woman climbs up the steps of a windmill.
The Luttrell Psalter,
England, Lincolnshire, *c.* 1320–40.
Additional 42130, f. 158r

The physical demands of agricultural labour expressed in the harvest scene are also conveyed by other images, including one depicting a man and a woman breaking up clods of earth, another of a couple weeding and yet another showing an elderly woman balanced precariously on the steps of a windmill, shouldering a heavy sack of grain or flour. Her stooped figure provides a stark contrast to the man behind her, who rides to the mill on horseback with an empty sack. In the Luttrell Psalter, male labourers are shown playing various games, but women of the same class do not engage in recreational activities.[7] Apart from a few images of noblewomen at leisure, women are invariably shown working.

Among the richest sources of imagery of women at work are the calendars, recording major Church feasts and saints' days, placed at the beginning of liturgical and devotional books. Each month of the calendar was generally illustrated with the appropriate zodiac sign and an additional image showing a typical task or pastime for that month, from feasting by the fireside for January to slaughtering a pig for December. Male workers predominate in the earliest surviving illustrated calendars. These customarily contain small medallions or scenes featuring a single worker engaged in an agricultural task, painted by artists who relied on traditional pictorial models (e.g. a man pruning a tree for March). As artists began to devote more space to calendar illustrations and to explore their narrative potential, they incorporated more figures into these compositions and gradually introduced more women.[8] A pair of women, for example, rake the hay cut by their male companion in the illustration for the month of June in a book of hours made in Paris, *c.* 1440–50. At first glance, this appears to be a conventional image of agricultural

Man mowing and two women raking.
The Dunois Hours,
France, Paris, *c.* 1440–50 (after 1436).
Yates Thompson 3, f. 6r

labour, but the arrangement of the figures is peculiar. Logic dictates that the man with the scythe should stand in front of the raking women, and that they should follow behind. The fact that he is positioned behind permits him to stare at his female companions who are bending forward in front of him, and his gaze implies he has more on his mind than the task at hand. As in the image of harvesters in the Luttrell Psalter, it is possible to discern a sexual subtext in this example, painted over a hundred years later.

Calendar scenes offered artists tremendous scope for invention, and in the late Middle Ages, especially in northern Europe, painters depicted workers in increasingly naturalistic ways, often devoting two facing pages to each month and creating complex compositions replete with details inspired by daily life. In the illustration for the month of December in a sumptuous book of hours made in Bruges, *c.* 1540, now known as the 'Golf Book', of which only thirty leaves survive, a woman kneeling with a skillet catches the blood flowing from the throat of a protesting pig as it is butchered by her male companion (p. 168). While they slaughter the pig, other workers occupy themselves with baking bread, another traditional task for December. In the background a woman kneads the dough in a large trough; a man balances on his shoulder a tray of unbaked loaves, and another woman breaks branches to feed the fire raging in the oven. A sense of peace and order prevails; the men and women work together in apparent harmony. Painted by artists from the workshop of the leading Flemish illuminator Simon Bening (*c.* 1483–1561), this calendar scene offers a typically idealised picture of rural life. No sleet or rain impedes the workers and the women's aprons are implausibly white. Moreover, there are sufficient adult workers to accomplish the requisite tasks without calling on the assistance of the boys in the lower border, who are free to frolic on their sleds.

Women in rural communities were faced with a multiplicity of chores that they frequently had to complete by themselves: rising in the night to comfort a crying child, milking at dawn, feeding the fowl, baking and brewing, carding and spinning wool, and preparing meals. These tasks and numerous others are enumerated in a fifteenth-century ballad in which a wife, accused by her husband of having an easy life ('wast hast thou to do but sit here at home?'), readily agrees to exchange jobs with him. Having sabotaged the milk so that it will never turn to butter no matter how long he churns it, she goes out to plough in his stead.[9] The anonymous author of a thirteenth-century treatise, written to encourage girls to become nuns, describes a farm wife who enters her house only to find her child screaming, the pot boiling over, the cakes burning, the cat, dog and calf making mischief, and a grumpy husband.[10] The treatise is an exaggerated portrait of domestic anarchy written for a polemical purpose, but it is indisputable that women in rural communities had to be adept at multi-tasking. Sundays and feast days were no exception; women had to provide food for members of their households and look after their children regardless.

Peasants making bread and slaughtering a pig. Book of Hours (The Golf Book), S. Netherlands, Bruges, probably early 1540s. Additional 24098, f. 29v

Wealthy women who supervised large households were not compelled to perform such demanding physical jobs and had more varied routines. Even so, they had considerable responsibilities. In *Le livre des trois vertus* (*Book of Three Virtues*), *c.* 1405, dedicated to the young princess Margaret of Burgundy, Christine de Pizan recommended that a woman know the yearly income from her estate and discuss matters of finance with her husband. According to Christine, a woman should understand every aspect of property management down to the smallest detail. She should avoid unpleasant encounters with bailiffs by living within her means, watch out for napping workers, and instruct her maids 'to look after the animals, prepare food for the workers, take care of the milk, weed the gardens, or hunt for herbs, even though it may muddy them to the knees'. Her tone is sober and admonitory; 'things rarely go well in a household where the mistress lies abed late',

A woman supervises her male gardener. Book of Hours (The Golf Book), S. Netherlands, Bruges, probably early 1540s. Additional 24098, f. 20v

chides Christine. It is significant that she thought it essential for a woman to learn 'the best way to have furrows run according to the lay of the land; their proper depth, straightness, and parallel layout; and the favorable time for sowing with seed suited to the land.'[11] Armed with this knowledge, a woman could make informed decisions and give lucid instructions to men; the fact that she had never ploughed or sowed would not exclude her from the discourse. An independent knowledge of estate management was imperative for such women because their husbands were often absent for long periods on business, at court or on military campaigns. If her spouse were to die prematurely, as Christine's had done, a woman had to be capable of governing her own affairs, defending her property in legal disputes and, if need be, rebuffing armed attacks.

As Christine de Pizan emphasised, managing workers was a job in itself. Although the theme is relatively rare, some medieval manuscripts contain images of highborn women exercising authority over their subordinates.

A portrait of a woman overseeing her female gardener occurs, for example, in the calendar page for the month of March in the 'Golf Book', illuminated in Bruges, *c.* 1540, by members of Simon Bening's workshop. In this image, an aristocratic woman, wearing a fur-trimmed robe and clutching her lap dog, pays a visit to her gardener, who leans on his spade in the foreground. He doffs his cap in deference and does not meet her gaze. She is clearly the mistress of the estate, working in partnership with her husband, the lord of the manor, who is depicted nearby conversing with another worker, possibly the foreman in charge of the men felling a tree. Instead of leaving her spouse to manage their affairs, she demonstrates a comparable interest in their property. Both she and her husband are shown pointing authoritatively as they issue instructions to their subordinates.

Simon Bening and his older contemporary Gerard Horenbout, with whom he collaborated on several commissions, both used the motif of owners supervising gardeners to illustrate March calendar pages. The subject was not invented by them, however, but was ultimately derived from illustrations in a popular treatise on estate

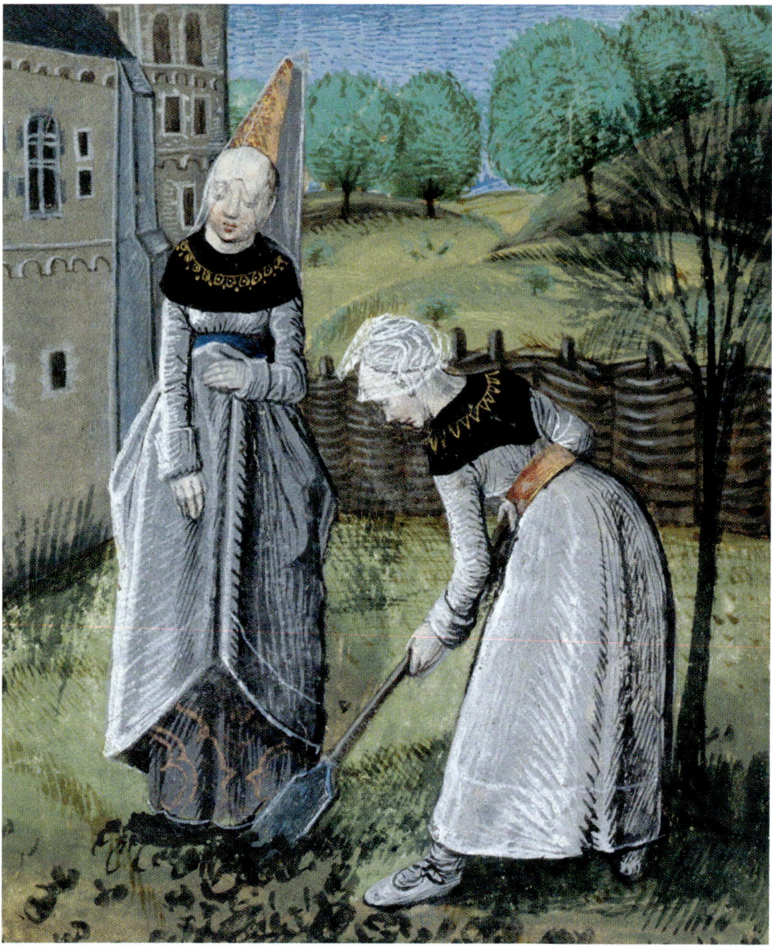

This allegorical illustration shows Christine de Pizan with the spade, and a female personification of Reason. This is the only surviving copy of the Dutch translation of Christine's most famous work.
Het Bouc van de De Stede der Vrauwen (Christine de Pizan, *Livre de la cité des dames*), S. Netherlands, Bruges, 1475.
Additional 20698, f. 17r

management, the *Liber ruralium commodorum*, written by a Bolognese lawyer, Piero de' Crescenzi, *c.* 1304–9. Translated into Italian and French, this work circulated in many copies, including richly illustrated manuscripts made in Flanders in the late fifteenth century, containing scenes of a lord, accompanied by his advisor, managing his estate.[12] Using variations on the motif to illustrate a calendar page was, however, a novelty, and including an aristocratic female landowner was also a departure from the Crescenzi illustrations, in which only a man is depicted in a supervisory role.[13]

In a fifteenth-century copy of Christine de Pizan's, *Cité des Dames* (*City of Ladies*), a noblewoman is also depicted supervising her female gardener. This image is actually an allegorical illustration, showing Christine and a female personification of Reason clearing the Field of Letters of misogynist opinion in preparation for building the utopian 'City of Ladies'. Reason, wearing a conical headdress,

Eve offered fruit by the serpent, who is shown with the body of a reptile and the face of a woman. Unusually, Adam is nowhere to be seen, which places the burden of guilt for sinning on Eve alone (above).
Book of Hours,
France, Brittany, 1451.
Additional 19962, f. 29r

Eve spins and Adam digs (above, right).
The Taymouth Hours,
England, probably London, *c.* 1325–35.
Yates Thompson 13, f. 23v

hoists up her gown to avoid getting it sullied, while Christine digs with the 'spade of her intelligence'.

Spinning was a job that women of every social class were taught to perform and one that came to define them. 'God made woman to lie, cry and spin' ('*fallere, flere, nere, statuit deus in muliere*') was a popular saying, and one poet wrote, 'with women we are blessed, / by their work we are dressed; / they spin, weave and prepare / the clothes that people wear.'[14] No single, reductive task defined men; 'while knights never ploughed and any peasant who mounted a warhorse would have been ridiculed and reviled, the wives of knights and ploughmen were both at home spinning.'[15]

For Christians, the connection between women and spinning went back to Eve. After they had eaten the forbidden fruit, Adam and Eve were struck by shame, and they used fig leaves to hide their genitals until God made them more durable clothing from the skins of animals. As punishment for their sin, they were expelled from Paradise. God told Adam to till the earth, but assigned no specific job to Eve, apart from bearing children. No mention of Eve spinning occurs in the Bible, but the idea that she must have done so to provide her family with clothing was a commonplace, and she is shown engaged in this task in numerous illustrations. In some images, both Adam and Eve are shown naked as she spins, which lends her task a particular urgency. It was a given that women would spin, having been taught the skill in childhood. Witnesses at the rehabilitation trial of Joan of Arc (*c.* 1412–31), held almost twenty-five years after she had been burned at the stake, testified to her good character, stating that as a girl in her hometown of Domrémy she had been especially pious, and willingly engaged in all 'work suitable for women' (p. 172). Almost

Joan of Arc.
This richly illustrated manuscript was illuminated by Jean Pichore for Anne of Brittany, duchess of Brittany and queen of France, for whom Antoine Dufour composed the work in 1504.
Antoine Dufour, *Vie des Femmes célèbres* (*Lives of Famous Women*) France, Paris, 1506.
Nantes, Musée Dobrée, MS 17, f. 76r

without exception, the witnesses emphasised spinning.[16] To counter the charge of heresy, it was critical for witnesses to stress Joan's religious orthodoxy, and because Joan's accusers saw her adoption of male clothing as a sign of her subversion of gender roles – a transgression that led directly to her execution – it was crucial for witnesses speaking in her defence to stress that she had been a normal girl who occupied herself with jobs habitually assigned to women.

Tools for spinning are among the many implements depicted in the Luttrell Psalter. A woman works at a large spinning wheel while another cards wool nearby, and several women hold distaffs, rods on which the raw wool fibres were wound before being spun with the whorl of the attached drop spindles. A distaff from which a drop spindle dangles, for example, is shown tucked under the arm of a woman feeding chickens, reminding us that women and girls frequently did their spinning whilst performing other chores (opposite).

Woman with a distaff pursuing a fox. The Queen Mary Psalter, England, probably London, *c.*1310–20. Royal 2 B. vii, f. 158r

Woman feeding chickens with a distaff tucked under her arm (below). The Luttrell Psalter, England, Lincolnshire, *c.* 1320–40. Additional 42130, f. 166v

Various manuscripts contain images of women brandishing distaffs with which they attempt to chase foxes away from ducks, chickens or geese. Other pictures show them, armed in the same fashion, winning duels against knights. Although some women, like Joan of Arc, actually served as combatants, generally speaking, the idea of a woman entering the fray of battle would have been met with hilarity and derision. A picture in the Luttrell Psalter, showing a disgruntled woman beating a man over the head with her distaff, was surely intended to evoke a similar response (p. 174). Medieval images of women triumphing over men are not advertisements for female emancipation, but serve instead as satirical comments on the discourse of power between the sexes.

More than any other job, apart from childcare, spinning was viewed as women's work, and the distaff with drop spindle, more than any other tool, was viewed as a symbol of femininity. A distaff serves as an unequivocal sign of gender in a tinted drawing found in a copy of the *Topographia Hibernica*, an account of a journey to Ireland, written *c.* 1186 by the ecclesiastical author Gerald of Wales, who dedicated the work to Henry II of England. Among the oddities Gerald claimed to have encountered while traveling in that country was a bearded lady with a hairy spine who belonged to the king of Limerick, and 'followed the court wherever it went, provoking laughs as well as wonder'.[17] Gerald assured his readers that she was 'not hermaphrodite, and was in other respects sufficiently feminine', but supplied no further details regarding her appearance or activities. The anonymous artist who illustrated the earliest surviving copy of the work, made *c.* 1196–1223, possibly in Lincoln, was thus faced with the challenge of depicting a bearded individual with a hairy back who would, nonetheless, be instantly recognizable as female. He or she arrived at an ingenious solution. Seated on a rock, the bearded lady holds a distaff in her left hand and a drop spindle in her right. Despite her excessive facial hair and inconspicuous breasts, original viewers of the image would have had no trouble identifying her as female because she is shown spinning.

Woman beating a man with a distaff.
The Luttrell Psalter,
England, Lincolnshire, *c.* 1320–40.
Additional 42130, f. 60r

As illustrated by the story of Sardanapalus, legendary king of Assyria, a man who took up spinning was suspect and represented a threat to the status quo. Notorious for dressing and speaking like a woman, as well as wearing make-up, Sardanapalus was said by the Greek writer Diodorus Siculus to have 'exceeded all his predecessors in sloth and luxury' and to have 'led a most effeminate life', spinning 'fine wool and purple amongst the throngs of his whores and concubines'.[18] His voracious sexual appetites extended to both men and women, and he was reputedly 'more lascivious than the most wanton courtesan'. A manuscript made in Paris in the last quarter of the fifteenth century contains a full-page miniature with an image of Sardanapalus, divided into two compartments which extend across the bottom of the page.[19] On the left side Sardanapalus, endowed with breasts and wearing a long gown, holds a distaff and spindle. He is seated among a group of women, presumably his concubines, who likewise spin. Although the woman at the king's side places her hand on the back of his neck in a gesture of intimacy, the king's sexual excesses are not alluded to; instead his depravity is signaled solely by his spinning. Eventually his rebellious subjects laid siege to the palace, disgusted by his dissipation and ineffectual government. In response, as shown in the right side of the picture, Sardanapalus ordered his soldiers to kill his female companions and immolated himself along with his possessions. In the image described above, which is based on a brief account of the king's life by the Roman historian Justin, rather than Diodorus' more sensational description, Sardanapalus is not portrayed as a sodomite, but as a spinster, which is sufficient

Bearded lady spinning.
Gerald of Wales, *Topographia Hibernica*,
N. England, possibly Lincoln, *c.* 1196–1223.
Royal 13 B. viii, f. 19r

grounds for scandal. For its medieval audience, the story of Sardanapalus would have underscored the dangers inherent in blurring the boundaries between the sexes, challenging the prescribed divisions of labour and inverting the natural order.

The patriarchal nature of medieval society presented major obstacles for career advancement for women, excluding them from attending university and pursuing careers in law, civic government, academe and the Church. Various other avenues for employment were open to women, nonetheless. Huge numbers of women, including girls as young as eight as well as married women and widows, worked as domestic servants, a job requiring a strong back and a high boredom threshold, but little or no specialised training.

Some were paid a wage and lived apart from their masters and mistresses, while others received board and lodging and a single payment when their employment ended. Freedom and privacy were among the things forfeited by female servants who lived with their employers. One Parisian householder advised his young wife:

> if you have girls or chambermaids of fifteen to twenty years, since they are foolish at that age and have seen nothing of the world, have them sleep near you, in a closet or chamber, where there is no dormer window or low window looking onto the road, and let them go to bed and arise at your own time, and you yourself (who, if God please, will be wise by this time) should be near to guard them.[20]

Sardanapalus spinning with his concubines. *Les Fais et les Dis des Romains et de autres gens* (Valerius Maximus, *Facta et Dicta Memorabilia*, translated by Simon de Hesdin and Nicholas de Gonesse), France, Paris, *c.* 1473–80. Harley 4375, f. 179r

There must have been many occasions when chambermaids considered the escape routes suggested by open doors and windows and imagined more fulfilling lives.

Construction sites also offered opportunities for unskilled casual labour for women, including digging ditches and latrines. Women, for instance, hauled sand for the construction of the cathedral of Siena in 1336, and stones and bricks for the college of Périgord in Toulouse, during a building campaign lasting from 1365 to 1371.[21] Fifty-eight women helped lay the roof tiles on the Parma Charterhouse in 1396, but they were paid at half the rate earned by their male counterparts.[22]

Many women earned a living by doing jobs that men could not do, such as serving as wet nurses, or were not inclined to do, such as washing clothes. Surnames cited in urban records sometimes denote a woman's occupation, as is the case for Peronnelle l'Espicière, a Parisian spice merchant of the 1290s, who counted the king of France among her customers.[23] The surnames of some English women listed in tax records also reflect their occupations, including Beatrice le Wimplewasher and Massiota la Lavendere, who both worked as laundresses in London in the late fifteenth century.[24] The unusual surname of another Londoner, Elizabeth Scolemaystres, who paid her taxes in 1441, points to the fact that she was a teacher.[25] Legal documents also offer evidence of many women who worked in the manuscript trade, including Agnes la Lumenore of Oxford, Dionisia le Bokebindere of London, and Isabella le Luminurs of Bermondsey.[26] In English tax records, the surnames Brewster and Webster often indicate women who worked as brewers of ale and weavers respectively, and it would be possible to cite many more surnames, with the feminine ending 'ster', that refer to occupations.[27] A famous female acrobat who entertained English royalty over the course of fourteen years during the reigns of Edward I and Edward II was called Matilda Makejoy. Though her surname was apt, it has been argued that it was her family name, not one adopted to reflect her career choice.[28] If so, the coincidence is remarkable.

Prostitution was a job requiring little or no overheads. Some women practised the trade independently, while others worked in brothels. These could be disguised as bathhouses without much effort, but attempts were not always made to do so. An inventory for one 'bathhouse' in Avignon lists beds but no facilities for bathing whatsoever.[29] Parisian guild regulations, compiled by Etienne de Boileau *c.* 1270 in his *Livre des métiers* (*Book of Crafts*), include statutes relating to bathhouses, which were operated by both men and women. One injunction, highlighting the risk of moral and physical contamination associated with public bathing, forbade keepers of bathhouses to harbour vagabonds, lepers or prostitutes.[30] James le Palmer's fourteenth-century encyclopedia *Omne Bonum* includes an entry for *Balneum* (*Bath*), in which he states that women should not serve as bath attendants. In the accompanying illustration, which hints at the temptations to be avoided, a woman

Initial 'A' for *Ancilla* (Maidservant). James le Palmer, *Omne Bonum*. England, London, *c.* 1360–75. Royal 6 E. vi, f. 107r

Salome, depicted as a fourteenth-century female acrobat, dancing before Herod. The Holkham Bible Picture Book. England, probably London, *c.* 1330. Additional 47682, f. 21v

embraces a naked man who stands in a tub. Judging from the position of his hand, he is clearly enjoying her attention.

Large numbers of women were involved in commercial enterprises. Of the forty chartered guilds in Cologne in 1397, for example, three for manufacturers of thread and silk had only female members. Women were also represented in guilds for wood, metal and leather workers, as well as those for smiths.[31] In some cities, a wealthy woman could invest her income in the merchant trade and achieve a high degree of autonomy operating as a businesswoman in her own right, legally independent of any relative by blood or marriage.[32] More modest enterprises were legion; some women managed taverns, breweries or inns while others sold goods in the street or market, including fish, candles and clothing.

Initial 'B' for *Balneum* (Bath), showing a female bath attendant washing a man. James le Palmer, *Omne Bonum*, England, London, *c.* 1360–75. Royal 6 E. vi, f. 179r

In an outstanding book of hours made in Bruges *c.* 1496–1506 for Joanna I of Castile, wife of Philip the Handsome, whose arms, mottos and initials appear with hers in the volume, the December calendar illustration features traders selling meat, with their wares arrayed on tables in front of narrow houses on a cobbled street (p. 178). The table in the foreground is presided over by a woman who offers a choice piece to a female customer. Equal in status, the sole female trader takes her place beside her male counterparts. We can be sure that their wares are fresh because two butchers, curing and trimming meat, are depicted in a hut across the street, and on the facing page men kill a pig, the traditional labour for the month of December. It is not surprising that this portrait of an autonomous tradeswoman was painted in the late fifteenth or early sixteenth century in Flanders, where artists were especially interested in documenting quotidian details and women were relatively independent. Prosperous towns on vital trade routes and a successful textile industry made Flanders one of the chief commercial centres in Western Europe. Women were among the beneficiaries of the booming economy and they found employment in a wide variety of jobs. They 'tanned hides, ran inns, sold fruit, and butchered meat … [and] were indispensable to the textile industry as carders, spinners, warpers, dyers, and even as weavers. They were also drapers, employing both men and women in the manufacture of cloth sold as far away as Novgorod.'[33] They helped men run family businesses, as did women in other regions, but 'were commonly regarded as merchants and tradespeople in their own right'.[34] As Ellen E. Kittell has noted, 'the extent of their public activity repeatedly surprised foreign visitors to the region'.[35] Two daughters of the leading Flemish illuminator Simon Bening, for example, pursued careers in the arts, as did Susanna, the daughter of his fellow artist Gerard Horenbout.[36]

One of the few industries dominated by women throughout Europe was the manufacture of textiles, particularly luxury items such as gold thread and silk. Women worked at all levels of the luxury textile industry, and some all-female guilds, headed by a mistress rather than a master, existed in a few northern European cities, including Cologne, Paris and Rouen. Mistresses were often married to men who either imported the raw silk or sold the finished articles, and men generally controlled the administration.[37] Typically, girl apprentices were eight to eleven years old and learned the craft for four to six years. In return for their work they received basic necessities, and bed and board.

One of the tales recorded in Alfonso X's *Cantigas de Santa Maria* (*Songs of Holy Mary*) provides insight into the production of silk as a cottage industry. It

December calendar page with butchers and a woman among the traders selling meat.
The Hours of Joanna I of Castile (1471–1555), S. Netherlands, Bruges or Ghent, between 1496 and 1506.
Additional 18852, ff. 12v-13r

concerns a female silk worker in Segovia whose silkworms fell ill. Taking the silkworms with her to church, she knelt in front of a statue of the Virgin Mary and promised to adorn it with a silk veil if the Virgin answered her prayers and cured her insects (p. 180). The woman's silkworms were duly cured, but she neglected to fulfil her vow. Later, praying in front of the statue, she recalled her broken promise and was filled with regret. Returning home she found that her silkworms, with a little prodding from the Virgin, had woven not one, but two veils. This miracle was celebrated by the citizens of Segovia and came to the attention of King Alfonso X, who enshrined the extra veil in his own chapel. King Alfonso X and the tradeswoman, from opposite ends of the social spectrum, were united in their acknowledgement of the miracle. The king did not dismiss it as a fanciful tale, but recorded it for posterity in his book of miracles, which is how the story has come down to us today.[38]

Women who worked in family businesses owned and operated by their fathers, or engaged in crafts and trades in partnership with their husbands, had more autonomy than servants, greater stability than casual workers, and more chance of earning a decent income than petty traders. In addition, their work was often more fulfilling, and the guild membership conferred on their spouse raised their own social status. Husbands and wives who worked together in burgeoning towns and cities often spent their entire lives in close proximity, plying their crafts in ground floor workshops before retiring to their private quarters upstairs for the night, an enviably short commute. In ideal cases, the couple worked together in a genuine partnership, and the woman had a high level of responsibility, taking care of accounts, conferring with her husband on important business decisions, and overseeing apprentices.

Many female artisans who had mastered their trades continued to run their businesses independently after their husbands had passed away, including Johanna Hill of London, whose husband Richard, a bell maker, died in 1440. Although she survived him by only one year, she kept the foundry going, managing a staff of several servants, four workmen, four apprentices, a professional bell maker and a clerk. Seven of the church bells she cast in 1441 survive; these bear a distinctive stamp: her husband's mark of a cross and circle within a shield, surmounted by Johanna's own lozenge-shaped shield containing a floret.[39]

The production of manuscripts in Paris from the thirteenth to the fifteenth centuries is especially well documented, and it was a trade in which women played significant roles as suppliers of parchment, illuminators and *libraires* (people who supervised scribes and artists, sold the finished products, and usually had a hand in making manuscripts themselves). Evidence of husbands and wives joining forces in the commercial book trade in Paris survives in various forms. In the case of Richard and Jeanne de Montbaston, we are fortunate to have both documentary proof of their existence and a large number of surviving manuscripts, fifty having been

Alfonso X, *Cantigas de Santa Maria* (Songs of Holy Mary), *Cantiga* 18. King Alfonso X of Castile–León (r. 1252–84) commissioned the largest medieval collection of the miracles of the Virgin Mary. Each tale, written in Galician-Portuguese verse, is set to music and has an accompanying illustration. These pictures tell the story of a woman in Segovia whose silkworms fell ill. She prayed to the Virgin Mary, asking her to cure them, and vowed to make her a silk veil to adorn her statue. Although the woman forgot her promise, the silkworms recovered and made two veils without any prompting. Impressed by the miracle, Alfonso X, who is depicted in the final panel, enshrined one of the veils in his palace chapel.
El Escorial, Real Monasterio de San Lorenzo, MS T.I.1, f. 30v

attributed to their workshop. Jeanne, who worked as an illuminator and *libraire*, kept their business going after Richard's death *c.* 1353.[40] Living near the cathedral in the rue Neuve Notre-Dame, a street populated by book trade workers, the couple specialised in secular books written in French and containing long cycles of illustrations, including copies of the *Roman de la Rose* (*Romance of the Rose*), one of the most popular of all medieval poems.

A man and a woman making manuscripts. Finished pages are shown drying on the racks behind them. The couple is probably intended to represent husband and wife, Richard and Jeanne de Montbaston, who worked in the trade in Paris and produced this copy of the *Roman de la Rose*, France, Paris, mid-fourteenth century. Paris, Bnf, MS fr. 25526, f. 77v

One manuscript of the *Roman de la Rose* made in the workshop of Richard and Jeanne de Montbaston *c.* 1350 contains, among numerous lively scenes in the margins, two tiny ones related to the commercial book trade. The first depicts a man writing at a desk while a woman works at a nearby table, possibly grinding pigments, and the second shows a man and woman seated at desks writing or painting on the unbound pages of a manuscript. Rods on which completed pages have been placed to dry are positioned behind each of them, an unusual detail which probably reflects actual practice.[41] We cannot be certain that these are portraits of Richard and Jeanne, as some scholars have assumed, or even that the images represent a husband and wife team. But there is no reason to dismiss these possibilities.

Unlike printed books, every manuscript is unique. Contents vary, and sometimes texts or combinations of texts are found in only a single surviving copy. This is the case with a unique compendium of eight different texts (including an account of the exploits of Alexander the Great and the travels of Marco Polo) produced in Richard and Jeanne's workshop (p. 182). The compendium bears no marks of its original owner, but Richard and Mary Rouse have suggested that it was designed as a handbook for Philip VI of France (r. 1328–50), who aspired to lead an expedition to Jerusalem, since it contains a treatise on routes to the Holy Land dedicated to him. Written by an anonymous Dominican friar in 1332, this Latin treatise was translated in 1333 by Jean de Vignay (*c.* 1282–*c.* 1350), who 'worked predominantly and perhaps exclusively for the French royal family'.[42] Although the illustrations, with their riotous patterned grounds and clumsy figures, lack refinement, the manuscript, with its unique juxtaposition of texts, was certainly created for a discriminating patron. Such high-level patronage reflects the success of the de Montbaston workshop in which Jeanne played an indispensable part.

How many other women made an equal contribution to the Parisian book trade? A relatively small percentage of women are mentioned in surviving records

of taxes paid and oaths sworn dating from the late thirteenth century onwards, but it was customary to record only the names of the male heads of workshops, leaving no trace of the women with whom they may have collaborated. 'Jeanne did not appear in the written record before the death of her husband, after which she became head of their workshop. No doubt other women worked alongside their husbands or fathers without ever figuring formally as members of the atelier.'[43] If Richard had not predeceased Jeanne and if she had not been obliged, in 1353, to take two oaths in front of the authorities of the University who regulated the commercial book trade, we would probably have no record of her.[44] The majority of

Exploits of Alexander the Great. This manuscript was made in the workshop of Richard and Jeanne de Montbaston. *Roman d'Alexandre en prose* and other texts, France, Paris, *c.* 1340 (after 1333). Royal 19 D. i, ff. 31v–32r medieval women left no trace in the historical record. Others, such as Jeanne de Montbaston, only made their mark after their husband's death, when they were no longer subsumed under their spouse's identity.

Many of the women discussed in this book experienced personal losses that disrupted their lives and caused them to chart a different course. Separated from their husbands or children by death or difficult circumstances, they channelled their energies in different directions. If the ninth-century Frankish noblewoman Dhuoda had not been separated from her eldest son William, she would not have written a handbook for him, the only lengthy work composed by a European woman between the late fourth and tenth centuries.[45] If Heloise (d. *c.* 1163) and Abelard had stayed together, we would not have her letters to him, revealing her innermost thoughts. By her own admission, Christine de Pizan (*c.* 1364–1431), the most prolific female writer of the Middle Ages, did not dedicate herself to scholarship or compose any of the poems or books for which she is famous until after her husband's sudden, premature death. And we have the formidable fourteenth-century widows, Elizabeth de Burgh and Marie de St-Pol, to thank for founding two Cambridge colleges at a time when benefactions of this kind by noble men and women were extremely rare.

Women who experienced the loss of personal freedom and possessions when they became nuns frequently gained opportunities for intellectual advancement in religious communities where they could converse with women who shared their vocation and interests, and where books were preserved, studied and often made. Hrotsvitha of Gandersheim, Hildegard of Bingen, Herrad of Landsberg and Clemence of Barking composed works ranging from scientific treatises and historical chronicles to devotional books, poems and plays. Other less famous women who took the veil also found the monastic environment conducive to creativity and developed their literary and artistic talents with the support of their superiors and sisters.

Whether single or married, religious or secular, women made key contributions to medieval culture. The manuscripts they left behind give us a deeper understanding of their lives and retain the power to move, captivate, puzzle and delight us. To turn the pages of a book made hundreds of years ago is like reading over the shoulder of a person who betrays no rising sense of irritation, and is, at any rate, in no position to object. Among the most personal of possessions, manuscripts are also among the most eloquent. Luxurious volumes made for privileged patrons and modest volumes alike offer us insights into a world that seems at once foreign and familiar.

NOTES

INTRODUCTION

1 Rouse and Rouse, *Manuscripts and their Makers*, I, 266.
2 For a comparative cross-cultural study of Jewish, Islamic and Christian manuscripts, see, for example, Jackson, *Marvellous to Behold*.
3 Wiesner-Hanks, *Women and Gender*, 174.
4 Dronke, *Women Writers of the Middle Ages*, 175.
5 Christine de Pisan, *The Treasure of the City of Ladies*, 35 and 147.
6 Paris, Bibliothèque Mazarine, MS 508 (Book of Hours, Use of Paris, 1490s, with sixteenth-century additions). Cited by Reinburg, *French Books of Hours*, 60.
7 Parsons, 'Of Queens, Courts, and Books', 177–8.
8 Mahaut's book purchases are particularly well documented. See Bell, 'Medieval Women Book Owners', 750, and Rouse and Rouse, *Manuscripts and their Makers*, I, 112, 174, 178–9, 182–3, 188–9, 193, 195–8, 201–2, 217, 264, 370 n. 36, 371 notes 39, 42 and 44, 374 notes 119 and 132, 381 n. 97, and II, 62, 92, 93, 102, 137.
9 Adams, *The Life and Afterlife of Isabeau of Bavaria*, 229.
10 Vallet de Viriville, *La bibliothèque d'Isabeau de Bavière*, 16.
11 Adams, *The Life and Afterlife of Isabeau of Bavaria*, 232.

CHAPTER ONE SEXUALITY

1 Montaiglon, *Le livre du chevalier de La Tour Landry*; trans. Larrington, *Women and Writing*, 209–10.
2 For a discussion of styles of dress see, for example, Scot, *Medieval Dress*, and van Buren, *Illuminating Fashion*.
3 II Samuel 11:2–27.
4 See, for example, Stahl, 'Bathsheba and the Kings'.
5 Costley, 'David, Bathsheba, and the Penitential Psalms'; Kren, 'Looking at Louis XII's Bathsheba'; Kren, 'Bathsheba Imagery in French Books of Hours'.
6 On the incongruity between the moralising message of the story and the seductive imagery, see Caviness, *Visualizing Women in the Middle Ages*, 99.
7 Quoted by Eco, *On Beauty*, 154.
8 *Aucassin and Nicolette*, 35.
9 *The Etymologies of Isidore of Seville*, XII, i, 14, p. 247.
10 New York, Morgan Library, MS M.1001, f. 98r.
11 *Carmen* 50, Hildebert of Lavardin, *Carmina minora*, 40–41; trans. Jaeger, *Ennobling Love*, 84.
12 The theme is discussed by Smith, *The Power of Women*.
13 Montaiglon, *Le livre du chevalier de La Tour Landry*, 154–5; trans. Kren, 'Looking at Louis XII's Bathsheba', 50.
14 Wolfthal, 'Sin or Sexual Pleasure?', 285. For ivory combs and mirrors, see the Gothic Ivories Project at the Courtauld Institute of Art, London, www.gothicivories.courtauld.ac.uk.
15 Chrétien de Troyes, *Lancelot*, 46–7. For combs as fetishes, see Wolfthal, 'The Sexuality of the Medieval Comb'.
16 Bethlehem, *Guinevere, A Medieval Puzzle*, 163.
17 Chrétien de Troyes, *Lancelot*, 48.
18 Caballero-Navas, 'The Care of Women's Health and Beauty', 154.
19 Green, *The 'Trotula'*, 143.
20 Jacquart and Thomasset, *Sexuality and Medicine*, 122. See also Green, *The 'Trotula'*, 189.
21 *Robert de Blois, son oeuvre didactique et narrative*, lines 381–4, cited by Udry, 'Robert de Blois and Geoffroy de la Tour Landry', 95.
22 Walters, *Lancelot and Guinevere*, xix.
23 Samples, 'Guinevere: A Re-Appraisal', 227.
24 Chrétien de Troyes, *Lancelot*, 147.
25 Stones, 'Illustrating Lancelot and Guinevere', 139.
26 Rouen, Bibliothèque municipale, MS 1054 cited by Kennedy, 'The Scribe as Editor', 524.
27 Guillaume de Lorris and Jean de Meun, *The Romance of the Rose*, trans. Robbins, 277–9.
28 Camille, *The Medieval Art of Love*, 148.
29 Guillaume de Lorris and Jean de Meun, *The Romance of the Rose*, trans. Robbins, 445–8.
30 *Robert de Blois: son oeuvre didactique et narrative*, lines 110–20 cited by Udry, 'Robert de Blois and Geoffroy de la Tour Landry', 93.
31 Jacquart and Thomasset, *Sexuality and Medicine*, 125.
32 Thomasset, 'The Nature of Women', 47.
33 Clark, *A Medieval Book of Beasts*, 219–20.
34 Albertus Magnus, *On Animals*, I, 777.
35 Albertus Magnus, *On Animals*, I, 776–7.
36 Albertus Magnus, *On Animals*, I, 581.
37 Sandler, *Omne Bonum*, I, 18.
38 Sandler, *Omne Bonum*, I, 97.
39 Payer, *Sex and the New Medieval Literature of Confession*, 187 n. 68.
40 Rupp, *Sapphistries*, 57.
41 Karras, *Sexuality in Medieval Europe*, 144.
42 Karras, *Sexuality in Medieval Europe*, 142. See also Clark, 'Jousting without a Lance'.
43 Quoted by Flanagan, *Hildegard of Bingen*, 69–70.
44 The manuscript is Munich, Bayerische Staatsbibliothek, Clm 19411, ff. 69r–70r. Dronke, *Rise of the European Love-Lyric*, II, 478–81. A poem from a different collection, entitled *Na Maria, pretz e fina valors*, attributed to a female troubadour from southern France, Bieiris de Romans, which expresses her feelings of love for a noblewoman named Maria, has been interpreted by some scholars as an expression of same-sex desire, but others argue that the language and tenor of the song are typical of aristocratic women of that time and place. See Rieger, 'Was Bieiris de Romans Lesbian?', and Canadé Sautman and Sheingorn, 'Introduction: Charting the Field', in *Same Sex Love and Desire*, 1–47, at 30–31.
45 Radice, *Letters of Abelard and Heloise*, 133. For a discussion of their relationship, see, for example, Mews, *Abelard and Heloise*.
46 Jacquart and Thomasset, *Sexuality and Medicine*, 147, citing *Opera Arnaldi de Villanova* (Lyon: F. Fradin, 1504), f. 176v. In the seventh century, Isidore of Seville described the ailment in the same terms: '*Satiriasis iuge desiderium Veneris cum extensione naturalium locorum. Dicta passio a Satyris*' ('Satyriasis (*Satiriasis*) is continual sexual desire accompanied by erection of the natural places. This affliction is named after satyrs.'). *The Etymologies of Isidore of Seville*, IV.vii.34, p. 112.
47 Green, *The 'Trotula'*, 121.
48 McNamara and Halborg, *The Rule of Donatus of Besançon*, 51.
49 Rupp, *Sapphistries*, 57.
50 For Icelandic Marian miracles, see, for example, Wrightson, *Icelandic Verse on the Virgin Mary*, and for Spanish, Gonzalo de Berceo, *Milagros de Nuestra Señora* and English translation, *Miracles of Our Lady*.
51 Smith, *The Taymouth Hours*, 13–14.
52 The saints and apostles on ff. 34v–46r bear scrolls with Latin texts, and three noblemen and three skeletons converse in English in the Tale of the Three Living and The Three Dead (ff. 179v–180r). See Brantley, 'Images of the Vernacular in the Taymouth Hours'.
53 Smith, *The Taymouth Hours*, 294.
54 Hamburger, 'Review of *Image on the Edge*', 320.
55 The images are found in Heidelberg, Universitätsbibl. Cod. Sal IX, 51, f. 272v, Paris, Bibliothèque nationale de France, MS. fr. 25526, f. 106v, and Manchester, John Rylands Library MS fr. 2, f. 212r, cited by Randall, *Images in the Margins*, 191. See also Camille, *Image on the Edge*, and Mattelaer, 'The Phallus Tree'.
56 London, British Library, Stowe 17, ff. 18, 130v, 140, 157v, 256. For a full description of the manuscript, see Stones, *Gothic Manuscripts (I)*, Vol 2, no. III-73.

CHAPTER TWO MARRIAGE

1 D'Avray, 'Marriage Ceremonies', 517.
2 Larrington, *Women and Writing*, 11. See also Leyser, *Medieval Women*, 106, and Gottlieb, 'Clandestine Marriages'.
3 A rare image of a 'Clandestine' marriage occurs in James le Palmer's *Omne Bonum*, Royal 6 E vi, f. 28v. The scene is described by Lucy Freeman Sandler, who states, 'the clandestine nature of the marriage is indicated by the presence of a friar rather than a priest and by the irregular joining of the hands'. Sandler, *Omne Bonum*, II, 108 (see also Sandler, *Omne Bonum*, I, 104–5). An entry for wedding banns with the image of a cleric in the 'B' for *Banna* (Banns) is found on f. 179v. See also Musson, 'Images of Marriage'.
4 D'Avray, 'Marriage Ceremonies', 517.
5 Karras, *Sexuality in Medieval Europe*, 95; Payer, *Sex and the New Medieval Literature of Confession*, 186.
6 Karras, *Sexuality in Medieval Europe*, 95.
7 See, for example, Fasoli, 'Body Language'.
8 Camille, 'Manuscript Illumination and the Art of Copulation', 70.
9 Camille, 'Manuscript Illumination and the Art of Copulation', 63.
10 Landouzy and Pepin, *Le régime du corps de maître Aldebrandin de Siénne*.

11 Stones, *Gothic Manuscripts (I)*, Vol 2, no. III-55.
12 Camille, 'Manuscript Illumination and the Art of Copulation', 60, n. 6. For the manuscripts, see Fery-Hue, 'Le *Régime du corps* d'Aldebrandin de Sienne: Tradition manuscrite et diffusion', and Fery-Hue, 'Le *Régime du corps* d'Aldebrandin de Sienne: complément à la tradition manuscrite (suite)'.
13 Camille, 'Manuscript Illumination and the Art of Copulation', 64.
14 Kline, 'Girls and Boys', 327.
15 Brereton and Ferrier, *Le Ménagier de Paris*.
16 Brereton and Ferrier, *Le Ménagier de Paris*; English version adapted from the translation by Power, *Goodman of Paris*, by Amt, *Women's Lives in Medieval Europe*, 317–30, at 321.
17 Simons, *Cities of Ladies*, 61–90.
18 McDonnell, *Beguines and Beghards*, 6.
19 Henderson, *Piety and Charity*, 169.
20 Christine de Pisan, *The Treasure of the City of Ladies*, 53.
21 Stuard, 'Dowry and Other Marriage Gifts', 229.
22 Orme, *Medieval Children*, 334.
23 Goodall, 'Heraldry', 180.
24 Deirdre Jackson, 'The Alphonso Psalter', in McKendrick, Lowden and Doyle, *Royal Manuscripts*, no. 17, with additional bibliography.
25 The manuscript measures approximately 470 × 370 mm.
26 See Taylor, 'French Self-Presentation'; Scot McKendrick, 'The Shrewsbury Book', in McKendrick, Lowden and Doyle, *Royal Manuscripts*, no. 143; and four essays devoted to the manuscript in Fresco and Hedeman, *Collections in Context*.
27 Walker-Meikle, *Medieval Dogs*, 17.
28 See Mandach, 'A Royal Wedding Present in the Making'.
29 Krinsky, 'A View of the Palazzo Medici and the Church of San Lorenzo'. Sciacca, *Building the Medieval World*, 24.
30 The wedding took place between 18 October and 1 November 1254. Medieval chroniclers supply divergent dates. Parsons, *Eleanor of Castile*, 15.
31 Although 'Charing Cross' is sometimes said to derive from the phrase '*chère reine*' ('dear queen'), 'Charing' comes from the Saxon word 'char', meaning 'turn', 'referring either to the bend in the Thames or in the westward road from the City [of London]', Willey, *London Gazetteer*, 87. For the Eleanor crosses, see Coldstream, 'Eleanor of Castile and the New Jerusalem', and Alexander and Binski, *Age of Chivalry*, 361–4, with additional bibliography.
32 Prestwich, *Edward I*, 125.
33 Alexander and Binski, *Age of Chivalry*, 363.
34 For a digitised version of the Aberdeen Bestiary, with Latin transcription and English translation by Colin McLaren, see http://www.abdn.ac.uk/bestiary/index.hti. A similar description of a viper mating with a lamprey is found in Cambridge, University Library, MS Ii. 4. 26. For additional bibliography, see Morgan, *Early Gothic Manuscripts (I)*, no. 17.
35 *Quinze Joies de marriage* (*c.* 1400) (Prologue, 1–5), trans. Burgwinkle, 'The Marital and the Sexual', 234.
36 Rigg, *Gawain on Marriage*, 81, 83, 89, 91.
37 Blamires, *Women Defamed and Defended*.
38 Blamires and Holian, *The 'Romance of the Rose' Illuminated*, xviii.
39 Guillaume de Lorris and Jean de Meun, *The Romance of the Rose*, trans. Dahlberg, 159.
40 Guillaume de Lorris and Jean de Meun, *The Romance of the Rose*, trans. Dahlberg, 165.
41 Hult, 'The *Roman de la Rose*', 186–7.
42 *Ballade 26*, in Varty, *Christine de Pisan's Ballades, Rondeaux and Virelais*, 3; trans.: http://mw.mcmaster.ca/scriptorium/cdpizan5.html. For a discussion of the poem, and others on a similar theme, see Deyermond, 'Sexual Initiation', 149–53.
43 Desmond, 'Christine de Pizan', 132. For the full text, see Christine de Pizan, *Le livre de l'advision Cristine* and *The Vision of Christine de Pizan*.
44 Christine de Pizan, *L'Epistre au dieu d'Amours*, in Blamires, *Women Defamed and Defended*, 279; for an edition and translation of both the *L'Epistre au dieu d'Amours* and *Dit de la Rose*, see Christine de Pizan, *L'Epistre au dieu d'Amours*, in Fenster and Erler, *Poems of Cupid, God of Love*, 34–75.
45 See, for example, Christine's *La Mutacion de Fortune*, in which she describes her metaphorical transformation from a woman to a man after her husband died. Christine de Pizan, *Le livre de la mutacion de Fortune*; Blumenfeld-Kosinski and Brownlee, *Selected Writings of Christine de Pizan*, 88–109.
46 Christine de Pizan, *The Vision of Christine de Pizan*, 105.
47 Heloise thought that scholarship was equally incompatible with being a father. She counselled Abelard not to marry her, stating, 'who can concentrate on thoughts of Scripture or philosophy and be able to endure babies crying …? Will he put up with the constant muddle and squalor which small children bring into the home? The wealthy can do so … but philosophers lead a very different life'. Radice, *Letters of Abelard and Heloise*, 71–2.
48 Roff, '"Appropriate to Her Sex"?', 110.

CHAPTER THREE MOTHERS

1 Green, 'Women's Medical Practice and Health Care', and Green, *Making Women's Medicine*.
2 Blumenfeld-Kosinski, *Not of Woman Born*, 57.
3 For other medieval miniatures depicting caesarean births, see Blumenfeld-Kosinski, *Not of Woman Born*.
4 See, for example, Sellevold, 'Child Burials and Children's Status', 64.
5 Albertus Magnus, *On Animals*, I, 802.
6 Green, *The 'Trotula'*, 101.
7 Countless examples include a book of hours made *c.* 1340–50 for an English noblewoman, Isabel de Byron and her husband, Robert I de Neville, which contains three different prayers concerning pregnancy and childbirth, addressed to the Virgin Mary. Smith, *Art, Identity and Devotion*, 255–6.
8 The idea that Mary bore Jesus without suffering pain can be traced back to Syriac Christian writings of the end of the first century and was universally accepted by medieval Christian commentators. *The Odes of Solomon*, ed. and trans. James Hamilton Charlesworth (Oxford: Oxford University Press, 1973), Ode 19, 81–4, at 82 cited by Rubin, *Mother of God*, 35.
9 Archambault, *A Monk's Confession*, 10.
10 Alfonso X, *Cantigas de Santa María*, II, 68, lines 41–2; trans. Kulp-Hill, *Songs of Holy Mary of Alfonso X*, 150.
11 Wilson, *The Magical Universe*, 228. See also *Cantigas* 221 and 315. The first describes how Fernando III, as a young child, was healed at an altar of the Virgin at the Benedictine monastery of Oña; the second reports the cure of a child at the altar of Holy Mary of Atocha (now part of Madrid).
12 O'Callaghan, *Alfonso X and the Cantigas de Santa Maria*, 47. Her sisters, María and Leonor, died in infancy. Martínez Díez, *Fernando III*, 242.
13 *Crónica de Veinte Reyes*, facsimile edition of Escorial MS X-I-6 (Burgos: Excmo. Ayuntamiento de Burgos, 1991), Chapter 14, 324. Queen Beatriz, who was buried in Las Huelgas, died in 1235 when Berenguela was only seven years old.
14 Charter of 1254 cited by Ballesteros Beretta, *Alfonso X, el Sabio*, 962, 1030–31. See also O'Callaghan, *Alfonso X and the Cantigas de Santa Maria*, 48.
15 Ward, *Women of the English Nobility*, 68–9. The Virgin's girdle continued to be venerated at the Abbey until 1535, when Henry VIII's reformers confiscated it. Harvey, 'The Monks of Westminster', 11–12, and Breeze, 'The Girdle of Prato and its Rivals'.
16 Jacobus de Voragine, *The Golden Legend*, I, 369.
17 Lowden, *Treasures Known and Unknown in the British Library*.
18 Lowden, *Treasures Known and Unknown in the British Library*. The image is also discussed briefly in Larson, 'Who is the Master of this Narrative?', 102.
19 Weston, 'Women's Medicine, Women's Magic', 291.
20 Elsakkers, 'In Pain You Shall Bear Children', 182.
21 Elsakkers, 'In Pain You Shall Bear Children', 195.
22 Winstead, *Chaste Passions*, 93.
23 Harris-Stoertz, 'Pregnancy and Childbirth', 276.
24 Harris-Stoertz, 'Pregnancy and Childbirth', 277. There are salient exceptions. The *Book on the Conditions of Women* (*Liber de sinthomatibus mulierum*) in the ensemble of medical texts known as the *Trotula* states, 'Conception is impeded as much by the fault of the man as by the fault of the woman'. Green, *The 'Trotula'*, 113.
25 See Noonan, *Contraception* and Biller, 'Birth-Control in the West'.
26 Green, *The 'Trotula'*, 97–9.
27 William of Auvergne, *Guilielmi Alverni opera omnia* (Paris, 1674), 1:234; cited by Boswell, '*Expositio* and *Oblatio*', 244.
28 Boswell, '*Expositio* and *Oblatio*', 244. The Latin, '*ut matres projicerent infantulos ad portas monasteriorum*', could also be understood to mean that the mothers abandoned their children near the doors of the monastery, rather than literally hurled them there. I am grateful to Barry Taylor for his advice on the translation.
29 Taglia, 'Delivering a Christian Identity', 83 and 88.
30 Sellevold, 'Child Burials and Children's Status', 62.
31 Orme, *Medieval Children*, 25.
32 Green, *The 'Trotula'*, 111.
33 Albertus Magnus, *On Animals*, I, 826.
34 Kline, 'Girls and Boys', 326.
35 Green, *The 'Trotula'*, 109.
36 Goodich, 'Bartholomaeus Anglicus', 81.
37 Orme, *Medieval Children*, 68.

38 New York, Morgan Library MS M. 917, p. 149. See Rudy, 'Children and Domestic Interiors'.
39 Hinde, *Vita S. Margaretae*; trans. Forbes-Leith, *Life of St Margaret*, 33.
40 Neel, 'Dhuoda', 209.
41 Thiebaux, *Dhuoda*, 28. See also Neel, *Handbook of Dhuoda*.
42 Thiebaux, *Dhuoda*, 2.
43 Thiebaux, *Dhuoda*, 43.
44 For example, 'the *Miroir de l'ame* (*Mirror of the Soul*) dedicated to Blanche of Castile (d. 1252) and the *Instructions* composed by St Louis for his daughter Isabel, later Queen of Navarre (*c.* 1267–70)', Joanna Frońska, 'Miroir des Dames', in McKendrick, Lowden and Doyle, *Royal Manuscripts*, no. 68.
45 Roy, *Oeuvres poétiques de Christine de Pisan*; for the Enseignemens see vol. III, 27–44. See also Schulze-Busacker, 'Christine de Pizan, *Les Enseignemens moraux*', and Reno, 'Christine de Pizan's *Enseignemens moraux*', 8.
46 Reno, 'Christine de Pizan's *Enseignemens moraux*', 8.
47 Reno, 'Christine de Pizan's *Enseignemens moraux*', 8.

CHAPTER FOUR LEARNING

1 For a full description of the manuscript, see Stones, *Gothic Manuscripts (I)*, Vol 2, no. I-42.
2 Morgan and Thomson, *Cambridge History of the Book*, 32.
3 Green, *Women Readers*, 98.
4 Hinde, *Vita S. Margaretae*, 241; trans. Gameson, 'The Gospels of Margaret of Scotland', 158.
5 Gameson, 'The Gospels of Margaret of Scotland', 157.
6 Books of hours are discussed in more detail in the following chapter.
7 Jerome, letter CVII, in Kersey, *Classics in the Education of Girls*, 14.
8 Byerly and Byerly, *Records of the Wardrobe and Household, 1285–1286*, 41, no. 403.
9 Davis, *Paston Letters*, I, xxxvii–xxxviii, cited by Orme, *Childhood to Chivalry*, 159.
10 Green, *Women Readers*, 12.
11 Clanchy, *Memory to Written Record*, 191. For the manuscript, see Collins, Kidd and Turner, *The St. Alban's Psalter*, and Bepler and Heitzmann, *The St Albans Psalter*.
12 Sheingorn, '*The Wise Mother*', 69–70. See also Scase, 'St Anne and the Education of the Virgin'.
13 Sheingorn, '*The Wise Mother*', 72–3.
14 Sheingorn, '*The Wise Mother*', 74.
15 The opening words of the Office of Matins in the Hours of the Virgin.
16 For mothers as teachers, see Clanchy, 'Learning to Read', and, more recently, Clanchy, 'Did Mothers Teach their Children to Read?'.
17 A psalter, made in England *c.* 1200 and now preserved in Leiden, contains a fourteenth-century inscription stating that Louis used it to learn to read: '*Cist psaultiers fuit mon seigneur saint looys qui fu roys de france, ou quel il aprist en senfance*' ('This was the Psalter of my lord Saint Louis, who was king of France, from which he learned in childhood') (Leiden, Bibliotheek der Rijksuniversiteit, MS Latin 76A, f. 30v). Clanchy, 'Did Mothers Teach their Children to Read?', 130 n. 4.
18 Joinville, *Vie de Saint Louis*, 344–54; Joinville and Villehardouin, *Chronicles of the Crusades*, 336–7.
19 Radice, *Letters of Abelard and Heloise*, 66.
20 Radice, *Letters of Abelard and Heloise*, 67.
21 Radice, *Letters of Abelard and Heloise*, 278.
22 Willard, *Christine de Pizan*, 33. For the roles played by Christine's father and husband in her intellectual development, see also Ross, *Birth of Feminism*, 19–30.
23 Smith, *Art, Identity and Devotion*, 264–5.
24 McCash, *Cultural Patronage*, 23.
25 Stahl, *Picturing Kingship*, 6, 242, 248.
26 Scot McKendrick, 'The Psalter of Henry VI', in McKendrick, Lowden and Doyle, *Royal Manuscripts*, no. 141. See also Backhouse, 'The Psalter of Henry VI'.
27 Oliver, 'A Primer of Thirteenth-Century German Convent Life', 269.
28 Oliver, 'A Primer of Thirteenth-Century German Convent Life', 260.
29 Hamburger, *Nuns as Artists*, 187.
30 Hamburger, *Nuns as Artists*, 186.
31 Alfonso X, *Cantigas de Santa María*, III, 102–3; trans. Kulp-Hill, *Songs of Holy Mary of Alfonso X*, 367.
32 On the education of girls in Cistercian female houses see Lekai, *The Cistercians*, 353.
33 For Hrotsvitha of Gandersheim, see Green, *Women Readers*, 17, 121, 137, 211, 219, 221–4, 232–5, 245–6, 248.
34 Monroe, 'Dangerous Passages and Spiritual Redemption in the *Hortus Deliciarum*'.
35 Wogan-Browne and Burgess, *Virgin Lives*.
36 Legge, *Anglo-Norman Literature*, 71; Robertson, 'Writing in the Textual Community', 6, 11, 18–22, 24, 27–8.
37 Legge, *Anglo-Norman Literature*, 67.
38 Foster, 'Clemence of Barking'. See also Zimbalist, 'Imitating the Imagined'.
39 Wogan-Browne and Burgess, *Virgin Lives*, 23.
40 Foster, 'Clemence of Barking', 15.
41 Herrad's manuscript, which had survived for centuries at Hohenburg Abbey, was transferred during the French Revolution to the Bibliothèque Municipale of Strasbourg. There it was destroyed in the Franco-Prussian War, during the siege of 1870. Copies made beforehand reveal how much we have lost. See Herrad of Lansberg, *Hortus deliciarum* (ed. Green), and Herrad of Lansberg, *Hortus deliciarum* (ed. and trans. Caratzas).
42 Lewis, *By Women, for Women, about Women*, 195 and 271. For Sister-Books from the Netherlands, see Scheepsma, '"For herby I hope to rouse some piety"'.
43 Beach, *Women as Scribes*, 32–64. For other nuns who worked as scribes, see Cyrus, *Scribes for Women's Convents*.
44 Stejskal, 'Die wundertätigen Bilder und Grabmäler in Böhmen zur Zeit der Luxemburger', 263–4 and fig. 141. On hornbooks, see also Clanchy, 'The ABC Primer', 20–21.
45 Gameson, 'The Gospels of Margaret of Scotland', 164.
46 Rudy, 'An Illustrated Mid-Fifteenth-Century Primer'.
47 Kittell, 'Flanders'.
48 Meale, 'Literacy and Reading'.
49 Buchon, *Les chroniques de sire Jean Froissart*, III, 482.
50 Unfortunately, only the payment to the courier has been preserved, rather than the letter itself. For Pecham's translation of Pseudo-Dionysius' *De celesti hierarchia*, see Legge, 'John Pecham's *Jerarchie*'.
51 For all of the above, see Underhill, 'Elizabeth de Burgh', 270, 273, 275.
52 For Elizabeth's enormous wealth, see Ward, *Elizabeth de Burgh, Lady of Clare (1295–1360)*.
53 Underhill, 'Elizabeth de Burgh', 277, and Field, 'Marie of Saint-Pol', 2.

CHAPTER FIVE PRAYER

1 Hinde, *Vita S. Margaretae*; trans. Forbes-Leith, *Life of St Margaret*, 61.
2 Luard, *Matthei Parisiensis*, III: 1216–1239 (1876), 497.
3 Shahar, *The Fourth Estate*, 72.
4 Talbot, *Life of Christina of Markyate*, 99.
5 Walters, 'The Feast and its Founder', 6.
6 London, British Library Additional 49999, ff. 64v, 75r, 87v, 88r, 90r. See Morgan, *Early Gothic Manuscripts (I)*, no. 73
7 Gee, 'Patterns of Patronage', 581–3.
8 New York, Morgan Library MS M.92, f. 21r. See Bennett, 'Some Perspectives on Two French Horae', 37, and Sand, *Vision, Devotion, and Self-Representation*, 163.
9 On this theme, see, for example, Oliver, 'The Many Roles of Mary', and Oakes, *Ora pro nobis*.
10 Reinburg, 'An Archive of Prayer', 236.
11 For prayers to guardian angels, see Sutton and Visser-Fuchs, 'The Cult of Angels'.
12 Both phrases are taken from the psalter: Psalm 16:8 and Psalm 120:7. Prayers to guardian angels are found in books of hours dating from the late fourteenth century onwards. Morgan, 'English Books of Hours', 86. For Margaret Beauchamp's book of hours, see Joanna Frońska, 'The Beaufort/Beauchamp Hours', in McKendrick, Lowden and Doyle, *Royal Manuscripts*, no. 25, and Scott, *Later Gothic Manuscripts*, no. 37.
13 Clanchy, 'Images of Ladies with Prayer Books', 113. The literature on this topic is extensive. See, for example, Naughton, 'A Minimally-intrusive Presence'; Morgan, 'Patrons and their Devotions'; Bennett, 'Making Literate Lay Women Visible'; Reinburg, 'An Archive of Prayer'.
14 New Haven, Yale, Beinecke 390, f. 25r. Blanche is depicted in twenty-five of the forty-three illuminated initials of the original artistic campaign. Before the manuscript was damaged by fire in 1904, it probably contained as many as eighty images of her. See Wieck, 'Bibliophilic Jealousy', and Sand, *Vision, Devotion, and Self-Representation*, 240.
15 Biblioteca Apostolica Vaticana, Vat. lat. 4763; Hamburger, 'Another Perspective', 105.
16 Hamburger, *Nuns as Artists*, 178.
17 Friedman, 'MS Cotton Claudius B.I'.
18 The prayers were universally attributed to Bridget in the Middle Ages, but modern scholars think that they were composed in England, possibly by a member of the Brigettines order. Duffy, *The Stripping of the Altars*, 249.
19 Krug, 'The Fifteen Oes', 116.
20 For a lucid explanation of the doctrine of Purgatory, see Binski, *Medieval Death*, 24–7.
21 Grössinger, *Picturing Women in Late Medieval and Renaissance Art*, 13.

22 For the association between mirrors and death, see, for example, Sand, 'The Fairest of them all', 536–9.
23 Marrow, *Pictorial Invention*, 28. A similar effect is achieved by an image of a skeleton holding a mirror that faces the viewer in a Flemish book of hours, *c.* 1480s, attributed to the workshop of Simon Marmion (Baltimore, Walters Art Museum, MS W. 431, f. 115r). See Wieck, *Time Sanctified*, 134 and 136, fig. 131.
24 Elizabeth Morrison, 'Hours of Joanna of Castile', in Kren and McKendrick, *Illuminating the Renaissance*, no. 114 (with additional bibliography).
25 Peter Comestor, *Historia Scholastica*, *PL* 198, XCVIIm col. 1072, cited by Henderson, 'Bede and the Visual Arts', 65–6. According to Peter Comestor, Bede said that the serpent had a virgin's face, but the comment is not found in any of Bede's extant works.
26 For the female-headed serpent, see, for example, Flores, 'Effigies Amicitiae ... Veritas Inimicitiae', and Gussenhoven, 'The Serpent with a Matron's Face'.
27 For a recent discussion of the tale, summarising previous scholarship, see Kinch, *Imago Mortis*.
28 For Paris, Bibliothèque de l'Arsenal 3142, see Stones, *Gothic Manuscripts (I)*, Vol 2, no. I-35.
29 Sandler, *The Psalter of Robert de Lisle*, 42.
30 A second image, showing a similarly dressed woman praying to her guardian angel, appears on f. 355r of the same manuscript. She is almost certainly the patron, Mary of Burgundy. See König et al., *Das Berliner Stundenbuch*, and Thomas Kren, 'Leaves from the Hours of Mary of Burgundy and Maximilian', in Kren and McKendrick, *Illuminating the Renaissance*, no. 38 (with additional bibliography).
31 For example, Mary of Burgundy is shown hunting with hawks in the *Chronik van Vlanderen*, *c.* 1481 (Bruges, Openbare Bibliotheek, MS 437, f. 372v, cited by Kralik, 'Death is Not the End', 68, n. 18.
32 See Thomas Kren, 'Book of Hours', in Kren and McKendrick, *Illuminating the Renaissance*, no. 109 (with additional bibliography).
33 Talbot, *Life of Christina of Markyate*, 4.
34 Morgan, 'English Books of Hours', 75. Some books of hours made for women contain specific instructions about which prayers to recite during the Mass. See Walters, 'Introduction to Mosan Psalters'.
35 Chantilly, Musée Condé, MS 65, f. 158r.
36 For a discussion of each of the four panels comprising the image, see Kumler, *Translating Truth*, 230–35. See also Stones, *Gothic Manuscripts (II)*, Vol. I, no. IV-20b.
37 Psalm 50 (Vulgate/Douai), Psalm 51 (King James Version).
38 Duffy, *Marking the Hours*, 28.

CHAPTER SIX LITERARY PATRONAGE

1 As outlined in the following chapter.
2 'Numerous dedications to historical women and to unidentified "*dames*" grace the Prologues and Epilogues of romances and other vernacular texts.' Krueger, 'Questions of Gender', 135.
3 Wheeler and Parsons, *Eleanor of Aquitaine*, with additional bibliography.
4 Krueger, 'Introduction', 2.
5 For elite women as 'cultural ambassadors', see Bell, 'Medieval Women Book Owners', and McCash, 'The Cultural Patronage of Medieval Women: An Overview', 1–49, in McCash, *Cultural Patronage*.
6 Higgitt, *The Murthly Hours*, 178.
7 Lusignan, 'French Language in Contact with English', 19.
8 For Turgot's *Life of Saint Margaret*, commissioned by her daughter Matilda, see Hinde, *Vita S. Margaretae*; Forbes-Leith, *Life of St Margaret*, 28.
9 Thomson, 'Monastic and cathedral book production', 162.
10 William of Malmesbury, *Gesta regum Anglorum*.
11 William of Malmesbury, *Gesta regum Anglorum*, I, 757.
12 Schmitt, *S. Anselmi Cantuariensis*, V, 284–5.
13 Chibnall, *Ecclesiastical History of Ordericus Vitalis*, VI, 295–302, and William of Malmesbury, *Gesta regum Anglorum*, I, 759–63.
14 The earliest copy is Oxford, Bodleian Raw. D. 913. See Benedeit, *The Anglo-Norman Voyage of Saint Brendan*, 4–5, and Barron and Burgess, *The Voyage of Saint Brendan*, 65–7. On the question of patronage, see Huneycutt, who connects the work with Matilda: Huneycutt, *Matilda of Scotland*, 139–40. See also Careri, Ruby and Short, *Livres et écritures*, no. 65/II.
15 Legge, *Anglo-Norman Literature*, 13.
16 Legge, *Anglo-Norman Literature*, 14, and Crane, 'Anglo-Norman Cultures in England', 45.
17 Clanchy, *From Memory to Written Record*, 293.
18 Huneycutt, *Matilda of Scotland*, 141.
19 Walberg, *Le Bestiare de Philippe de Thaün*, 1; trans. Wright, *Popular Treatises on Science*, 74–131. The English translation quoted here is by O'Donnell, Townend and Tyler, 'European literature and eleventh-century England', 630. See also Dean and Boulton, *Anglo-Norman Literature*, no. 347 and Careri, Ruby and Short, *Livres et écritures*, no. 33.
20 Copenhagen, Kongelige Bibliotek, Gamle kgl. samml., 8°.3466, ff. 3r–51r; Oxford, Merton College, MS 249, ff.1r–10v; and London, British Library, Cotton, Nero A V, ff. 41r–82v (with spaces left for illustrations that were never completed). The British Library manuscript also contains a copy of Philippe de Thaon's *Comput*. Dedicated to his uncle, Honfroi de Thaon, it is the earliest surviving 'scientific' text in French. Philippe de Thaon, *Comput*. For the bestiary illustrations, see Muratova, 'The Decorated Manuscripts of the Bestiary of Phillipe de Thaon'.
21 Geffrei Gaimar, *Estoire des Engleis*, 350–53.
22 Geffrei Gaimar, *Estoire des Engleis*, 348–9. See also Dean and Boulton, *Anglo-Norman Literature*, no. 1 and Careri, Ruby and Short, *Livres et écritures*, no. 21.
23 Geffrei Gaimar, *Estoire des Engleis*, xli.
24 Legge, *Anglo-Norman Literature*, 28–9.
25 Kauffmann, 'British Library, Lansdowne Ms. 383'.
26 Clanchy, *Memory to Written Record*, 216–17.
27 Marie de France, *Les Lais*; Marie de France, *Fables*; Marie de France, *L'Espurgatoire seint Patriz*; Marie de France, *Saint Patrick's Purgatory*. Dean and Boulton, *Anglo-Norman Literature*, nos. 179, 547.
28 Whalen, 'Prologues and Epilogues', 14.
29 Whalen, 'Prologues and Epilogues', 21 and 24.
30 Whalen, 'Prologues and Epilogues', 27.
31 Krueger, 'Marie de France', 176.
32 Whalen, 'Introduction', viii, in *A Companion to Marie de France*, and Busby, 'Manuscripts of Marie de France', 303, citing Kjellman, *La vie seint Edmund le rei*. See also Short, 'Denis Piramus and the Truth of Marie's *Lais*'.
33 Whalen, 'Prologues and Epilogues', 25.
34 Busby, 'Manuscripts of Marie de France', 306. Only one manuscript with all of the *lais* survives: London, British Library, Harley MS 978, made in England, possibly Oxford, *c.* 1265. Busby thinks that it is 'the earliest manuscript containing any of the *lais*'. For Harley MS 978, see also Taylor, *Textual Situations*, 76–136.
35 Carpenter, 'King Henry III and Saint Edward the Confessor', 875–6.
36 Carpenter, 'King Henry III and Saint Edward the Confessor', 876.
37 Carpenter, 'King Henry III and Saint Edward the Confessor', 885.
38 On the building programme, see Binski, *Westminster Abbey and the Plantagenets*.
39 Matthew Paris, *La Estoire de seint Aedward le rei*, 2–3. Matthew Paris, *The History of St Edward the King*, 54.
40 Matthew Paris, *The History of St Edward the King*, 105.
41 Morgan, *Early Gothic Manuscripts (II)*, no. 123.
42 Binski, 'Reflections on *La Estoire de Seint Aedward le Rei*', 340.
43 The wedding took place between 18 October and 1 November 1254. Medieval chroniclers supply divergent dates. Parsons, *Eleanor of Castile*, 15. Neither Henry III nor Eleanor of Provence attended the wedding, nor did Eleanor of Castile's mother, Jeanne of Ponthieu, who was then living in France. Curiously, Henry III came very close to spending his life with Jeanne of Ponthieu rather than Eleanor of Provence. In fact, technically, since she and he had exchanged a pledge of marriage in 1235, the year before he married Eleanor, he had committed himself to Jeanne. Very shortly afterwards, when Eleanor of Provence seemed like a better prospect, Henry III had the marriage annulled on grounds that he and Jeanne were too closely related to marry. She did not object. Howell, *Eleanor of Provence*, 10–11 and 58–9.
44 Parsons, *Eleanor of Castile*, 17.
45 See Chapter Two.
46 Howell, *Eleanor of Provence*, 6.
47 Howell, *Eleanor of Provence*, 7.
48 Howell, *Eleanor of Provence*, 82.
49 Howell, *Eleanor of Provence*, 82.
50 Parsons, 'Of Queens, Courts, and Books', 179 n. 28. Cavanaugh, 'Royal Books', 307.
51 *Calendar of the Liberate Rolls, 1251–1260*, 18; *Calendar of the Close Rolls, 1247–1251*, 283, 464; Tristram and Bardswell, *English Medieval Wall Painting*, I, 89, 575; Howell, *Eleanor of Provence*, 60.
52 Howell, *Eleanor of Provence*, 60. Tristram and Bardswell, *English Medieval Wall Painting*, I, 215, 477, 528, 575, 611. Whatley, 'Romance, Crusade, and the Orient'.
53 Lowden, 'The Holkham Bible Picture Book and the Bible Moralisée', 79. See also Lowden, 'The Apocalypse in the Early-Thirteenth-Century Bibles Moralisées', 198, 207–12, 216, pls 20, 26–8, 31, and Lowden, *The Making of the Bibles moralisées*, I, 185–6 and II, x, 202.

54 McKitterick et al., *The Trinity Apocalypse*, and Morgan, *The Douce Apocalypse*. On the commissioning of Douce, see Binski, 'The Illumination and Patronage', 127–34. For additional bibliography, see Morgan, *Early Gothic Manuscripts (II)*, nos. 110, 153.
55 The fact that Matthew wrote the *Vie de Seint Auban* in alexandrines (an archaic verse form), rather than in rhyming pairs of eight-syllable verses, lends weight to the argument that he consciously tailored his compositions to suit different audiences.
56 The note appears in a manuscript of the *Lives of Saints Alban and Amphibalus* (Dublin, Trinity College MS 177). On its significance, see Morgan, *Early Gothic Manuscripts, (I)*, no. 85 and *(II)*, no. 123, and Binski, 'Reflections on *La Estoire de Seint Aedward le Rei*', 336–7.
57 John of Howden, *Rossignos*, 6.
58 John of Howden, *Rossignos*, 7.
59 John of Howden, *Rossignos*, 9.
60 John of Howden, *Rossignos*, 33.
61 Parsons, *Eleanor of Castile*, 53.
62 John of Howden, *Rossignos*, 177.
63 See Parsons, *Court and Household*.
64 Parsons, 'Of Queens, Courts, and Books', 178.
65 Parsons, 'Of Queens, Courts, and Books', 178.
66 Parsons, 'Of Queens, Courts, and Books', 177–8.
67 Parsons, 'Of Queens, Courts, and Books', 178 n. 14.
68 Parsons, *Court and Household*, 13.
69 Parsons, 'Of Queens, Courts, and Books', 181.
70 Parsons, 'Of Queens, Courts, and Books', 181.
71 Rouse and Rouse, *Manuscripts and their Makers*, I, 103.
72 Girart d'Amiens, *Escanor*.
73 Denholm-Young, *History and Heraldry*, 47.
74 Stowe's Chronicle, AD 1278, cited by Lysons, 'Copy of a Roll of Purchases', 301.
75 'Eodem die [16 May 1288] solutum magistro J. de Stella [i.e. John de Estella, a scribe of the queen, mentioned in several records] pro foliis auri emptis anno preterito, percamenis ad remanentes libros regine cooperiendos de vita Beati Thome et Sancti Edwardi, incausto et vaso ad idem, xxxvij s. x d. chipotensium.' PRO E101/352/11 mem. 2, Byerly and Byerly, *Records of the Wardrobe and Household 1286–1289*, p. 379, no. 3217.
76 Parsons, *Court and Household*, 13 n. 39; Binski, 'Reflections on *La Estoire de Seint Aedward le Rei*', 339–40.
77 'Item eodum die Januarii ... [una] duodena paracementi caprioli empta ad scribenda vita Beati Thome, vj d. sterlingorum'. PRO E 101/352/11, Byerly and Byerly, *Records of the Wardrobe and Household 1286–1289*, no. 3208.
78 Cavanaugh, 'Royal Books', 308.
79 Hamilton, 'Eleanor of Castile', 92.
80 Hodgson, *Women, Crusading and the Holy Land*, 117.
81 Thorpe, 'Mastre Richard, a Thirteenth-century Translator', 44. See also Allmand, *The De Re Militari of Vegetius*, 152–6. and Morgan, *Early Gothic (II)*, no. 150.
82 The reference comes in a section of Vegetius' Latin text in which he recommends that attackers strike enemy troops when least expected, when they are eating or sleeping and their horses are feeding. The Anglo-Norman translation is slightly abridged, but conveys the same meaning: '*Quant il pessoient lor chivaus ou quant il dormeient e nul mal ne soschoient, donc soleient ester fait les assauz, com a Kenelingworthe*'. The last three words, 'as at Kenilworth', are the only contemporary reference inserted in the lengthy text. See Thorpe, 'Mastre Richard at the Skirmish of Kenilworth?', 120–21.
83 Cavanaugh, 'Royal Books', 309.
84 Lysons, 'Copy of a Roll of Purchases', 307–8.
85 Parsons, *Eleanor of Castile*, 53. A similar interest in the natural world is reflected in contemporaneous manuscripts commissioned by Eleanor's half-brother, Alfonso X, and King Frederick II of Sicily, both of whom kept well-stocked menageries.
86 Parsons, *Court and Household*, 16.
87 Sandler, *Gothic Manuscripts*, I, 24, 27 and II, 13–14 (no. 1).
88 Prestwich, *Edward I*, 128.
89 Dean, 'Cultural Relations in the Middle Ages'.
90 Established by a tenth-century Anglo-Saxon queen, Queen Ælfthryth, the convent was re-founded in 1177 by Mary's great-great-grandfather, Henry II, who brought nuns to live there from the prestigious Benedictine house of Fontevrault in northwest France.
91 Parsons, *Court and Household*, 11, n. 31.
92 Green, *Lives of the Princesses of England*, 421.
93 Dean, 'Cultural Relations in the Middle Ages', 562. Dean and Boulton, *Anglo-Norman Literature*, no. 70.
94 Parsons, 'Of Queens, Courts, and Books', 199 n. 55.
95 Parsons, 'Of Queens, Courts, and Books', 181.

CHAPTER SEVEN WORK

1 On the theme, see, for example, Alexander and Jones, 'Annunciation to the Shepherdess'.
2 Goldberg, 'Work', 857.
3 Alfonso X, *Cantigas de Santa María*, II, 131–2.
4 Brown, *World of the Luttrell Psalter*, 48.
5 Camille, *Mirror in Parchment*, 195–6.
6 Brown, *World of the Luttrell Psalter*, 48.
7 Camille, *Mirror in Parchment*, 301.
8 Henisch, *The Medieval Calendar Year*, 168.
9 Wright and Halliwell, *Reliquiae Antiquae*, II, 196–9.
10 Furnivall, *Hali Meidenhad*, cited by Amt, *Women's Lives in Medieval Europe*, 90–94.
11 Christine de Pizan, *Le livre des trois vertus*; trans. Christine de Pizan, *A Medieval Woman's Mirror of Honor*, cited by Amt, *Women's Lives in Medieval Europe*, 164–5.
12 Henisch, *The Medieval Calendar Year*, 76.
13 Henisch, *The Medieval Calendar Year*, 76.
14 Fiero, Pfeffer and Allain, *Three Medieval Views of Women*, 110–13.
15 Camille, *Mirror in Parchment*, 220.
16 Pernoud, *Joan of Arc*, 17. Witnesses mentioned that Joan had also cultivated the earth with her father ('*allant à la charrue*'), but whether this phrase refers to hoeing or ploughing is uncertain.
17 Gerald of Wales, *History and Topography of Ireland*, 73.
18 Booth, *Historical Library of Diodorus*, I, 119.
19 British Library, Harley MS 4375, Valerius Maximus, translated into French by Simon de Hesdin and Nicholas de Gonesse, *Les Fais et les Dis des Romains et de autres gens* (Part 2, Vol. 1). The work is not a translation in the modern sense and includes much material gleaned from other authors.
20 Brereton and Ferrier, *Le Ménagier de Paris*; English version adapted from the translation by Power, *Goodman of Paris*, by Amt, *Women's Lives in Medieval Europe*, 317–30, at 329.
21 Anderson and Zinsser, *A History of their Own*, I, 361.
22 Jewell, *Women in Late Medieval and Reformation Europe*, 68. See also Roff, '"Appropriate to Her Sex"?'.
23 Farmer, 'Merchant Women', 97.
24 Anderson and Zinsser, *A History of their Own*, I, 361.
25 Orme, *Medieval Schools*, 167.
26 Michael, 'English Illuminators'.
27 Power, *Medieval Women*, 57.
28 Bullock-Davies, *Menestrellorum Multitudo*, 137.
29 Jewell, *Women in Late Medieval and Reformation Europe*, 75.
30 Lespinasse and Bonnardot, *Le livre des métiers*; trans. Amt, *Women's Lives in Medieval Europe*, 197.
31 Anderson and Zinsser, *A History of their Own*, I, 372.
32 Jewell, *Women in Late Medieval and Reformation Europe*, 67.
33 Kittell, 'Flanders', 294.
34 Kittell, 'Flanders', 294. See also Kittell and Suydam, *The Texture of Society*.
35 Kittell, 'Flanders', 294.
36 Bening's 'eldest daughter, Livinia, became court painter to Edward VI of England, and another daughter became a dealer in paintings, miniatures, parchment, and silk.' http://www.getty.edu/art/gettyguide/artMakerDetails?maker=355.
37 Jewell, *Women in Late Medieval and Reformation Europe*, 67.
38 Alfonso X, *Cantigas de Santa María*, I, 104–8.
39 Barron, 'Bell-Founders', 105–6.
40 Rouse and Rouse, *Manuscripts and their Makers*, I, 235 60.
41 Rouse and Rouse, *Manuscripts and their Makers*, I, 235–60.
42 Rouse and Rouse, *Manuscripts and their Makers*, I, 244.
43 Martin, 'Exceptions and Assumptions', 20.
44 Rouse and Rouse, *Manuscripts and their Makers*, I, 237.
45 Neel, 'Dhuoda', 209.

FURTHER READING

Adams, Tracy. *The Life and Afterlife of Isabeau of Bavaria: Rethinking Theory*. Baltimore: Johns Hopkins University Press, 2010.

Albertus Magnus. *On Animals. A Medieval Summa Zoologica*, trans. Kenneth F. Kitchell, Jr. and Irven Michael Resnick, 2 vols. Baltimore and London: Johns Hopkins University Press, 1999.

Alexander, Jonathan J. G. and Paul Binski, eds. *Age of Chivalry: Art in Plantagenet England, 1200–1400*. London: Royal Academy of Arts in association with Weidenfeld and Nicolson, 1987.

Alexander, Jonathan J. G. and Leslie C. Jones. 'The Annunciation to the Shepherdess'. *Studies in Iconography* 24 (2003), 165–98.

Alfonso X, el Sabio. *Cantigas de Santa María*, 3 vols, ed. Walter Mettmann. Madrid: Editorial Castalia, 1986–9.

Allmand, Christopher. *The De Re Militari of Vegetius: The Reception, Transmission and Legacy of a Roman Text in the Middle Ages*. Cambridge: Cambridge University Press, 2011.

Amt, Emilie. *Women's Lives in Medieval Europe: A Sourcebook*. New York and London: Routledge, 1993.

Anderson, Bonnie S. and Judith P. Zinsser. *A History of their Own: Women in Europe from Prehistory to the Present*, 2 vols. Harmondsworth: Penguin, 1989–90.

Archambault, Paul J., trans. *A Monk's Confession: The Memoirs of Guibert of Nogent*. University Park: Pennsylvania State University Press, 1996.

Aucassin and Nicolette, and Other Tales, trans. Pauline Matarasso. Harmondsworth: Penguin, 1971.

Backhouse, Janet. *The Illuminated Page: Ten Centuries of Manuscript Painting in the British Library*. London: British Library, 1997.

Backhouse, Janet. 'The Psalter of Henry VI (London, BL, MS Cotton Dom. A XVII)'. In *The Illuminated Psalter: Studies in the Content, Purpose and Placement of its Images*, ed. F. O. Büttner, 329–36. Turnhout: Brepols, 2004.

Ballesteros Beretta, Antonio. *Alfonso X, el Sabio*. Barcelona: Espasa-Calpe, 1963; rpt (with index) Barcelona: El Albir, 1984.

Barratt, Alexandra, 'Small Latin? The Post-Conquest Learning of English Religious Women'. In *Anglo-Latin and its Heritage: Essays in Honor of A. G. Rigg on his 64th Birthday*, ed. Siân Echard and Gernot R. Wieland, 51–65. Turnhout, Brepols, 2001.

Barron, Caroline M. 'Johanna Hill (d. 1441) and Johanna Sturdy (d. *c.* 1460), Bell-Founders'. In *Medieval London Widows, 1300–1500*, ed. Caroline M. Barron and Anne F. Sutton, 99–111. London: Hambledon, 1994.

Barron, W. R. J. and Glyn S. Burgess, eds. *The Voyage of Saint Brendan: Representative Versions of the Legend in English Translation*. Exeter: University of Exeter Press, 2002, 65–102.

Beach, Alison I. *Women as Scribes: Book Production and Monastic Reform in Twelfth-Century Bavaria*. Cambridge Studies in Palaeography and Codicology, vol. 10. Cambridge: Cambridge University Press, 2004.

Bell, David. *What Nuns Read: Books and Libraries in Medieval English Nunneries*. Kalamazoo: Cistercian Publications, 1995.

Bell, Susan Groag. 'Medieval Women Book Owners: Arbiters of Lay Piety and Ambassadors of Culture'. *Signs: Journal of Women in Culture and Society* 7, 4 (1982), 742–68.

Benedeit. *The Anglo-Norman Voyage of Saint Brendan*, ed. Ian Short and Brian Merrilees. Manchester: Manchester University Press, 1979.

Bennett, Adelaide. 'Making Literate Lay Women Visible: Text and Image in French and Flemish Books of Hours, 1220–1320'. In *Thresholds of Medieval Visual Culture: Liminal Spaces*, ed. Elina Gertsman and Jill Stevenson, 125–58. Woodbridge: Boydell, 2012.

Bennett, Adelaide. 'Some Perspectives on Two French Horae in the Thirteenth Century'. In *Books of Hours Reconsidered*, ed. Sandra Hindman and James H. Marrow, 19–40. London and Turnhout: Harvey Miller, 2013.

Bepler, Jochen and Christian Heitzmann, eds. *The St Albans Psalter: Current Research and Perspectives*. Hildesheim: Georg Olms, 2013.

Bethlehem, Ulrike. *Guinevere, A Medieval Puzzle: Images of Arthur's Queen in the Medieval Literature of England and France*. Heidelberg: Universitätsverlag Winter, 2005.

Biller, P. P. A. 'Birth-Control in the West in the Thirteenth and Early Fourteenth Centuries'. *Past and Present* 94 (1982), 3–26.

Binski, Paul. 'Reflections on *La estoire de Seint Aedward le Rei*: Historiography and Kingship in Thirteenth-Century England'. *Journal of Medieval History* 16 (1990), 333–50.

Binski, Paul. *Westminster Abbey and the Plantagenets: Kingship and the Representation of Power, 1200–1400*. New Haven: Yale University Press, 1995.

Binski, Paul. *Medieval Death: Ritual and Representation*. Ithaca: Cornell University Press, 1996.

Binski, Paul. 'The Illumination and Patronage of the Douce Apocalypse'. *The Antiquaries Journal* 94 (2014), 127–34.

Blamires, Alcuin, ed. *Women Defamed and Defended: An Anthology of Medieval Texts*. Oxford: Clarendon Press, 1992.

Blamires, Alcuin and Gail C. Holian. *The 'Romance of the Rose' Illuminated: Manuscripts at the National Library of Wales, Aberystwyth*. Cardiff: University of Wales, 2002.

Blumenfeld-Kosinski, Renate. *Not of Woman Born: Representations of Caesarean Birth in Medieval and Renaissance Culture*. Ithaca and London: Cornell University Press, 1990.

Blumenfeld-Kosinski, Renate and Kevin Brownlee, eds. *The Selected Writings of Christine de Pizan: New Translations, Criticism*. New York and London: Norton, 1997.

Booth, George, trans. *The Historical Library of Diodorus the Sicilian: In Fifteen Books. To which are Added the Fragments of Diodorus, and Those Published by H. Valesius, I. Rhodomannus, and F. Ursinus*, 2 vols. London: W. M'Dowall, 1814.

Boswell, John Eastburn. '*Expositio* and *Oblatio*: The Abandonment of Children and the Ancient and Medieval Family'. *American Historical Review* 89 (1984), 10–33; rpt in *Medieval Families: Perspectives on Marriage, Household and Children*, ed. Carol Neel, 234–72. Toronto: University of Toronto Press, 2004.

Brantley, Jessica. 'Images of the Vernacular in the Taymouth Hours'. In *Decoration and Illustration in Medieval English Manuscripts*, English Manuscript Studies 1100–1700, vol. 10, ed. A. S. G. Edwards, 83–113. London: British Library, 2002.

Breeze, Andrew. 'The Girdle of Prato and its Rivals'. *Bulletin of the Board of Celtic Studies* 33 (1986), 95–100.

Brereton, Georgine E. and Janet M. Ferrier, eds. *Le Ménagier de Paris*. Oxford: Clarendon Press, 1981.

Brown, Michelle P. *The World of the Luttrell Psalter*. London: British Library, 2006.

Buchon, Jean Alexandre C., ed. *Les chroniques de sire Jean Froissart*, 3 vols. Paris: A. Desrez, 1835.

Bullock-Davies, Constance. *Menestrellorum Multitudo: Minstrels at a Royal Feast*. Cardiff: University of Wales Press, 1978.

Burgwinkle, William. 'The Marital and the Sexual'. In *The Cambridge Companion to Medieval French Literature*, ed. Simon Gaunt and Sarah Kay, 225–37. Cambridge: Cambridge University Press, 2008.

Busby, Keith. 'The Manuscripts of Marie de France'. In *A Companion to Marie de France*. Brill's Companions to the Christian Tradition, vol. 27, ed. Logan E. Whalen, 303–18. Leiden: Brill, 2011.

Byerly, B. F. and C. R. Byerly, eds. *Records of the Wardrobe and Household, 1285–1286*. London: HMSO, 1977.

Byerly, B. F. and C. R. Byerly, eds. *Records of the Wardrobe and Household, 1286–1289*. London: HMSO, 1986.

Caballero-Navas, Carmen. 'The Care of Women's Health and Beauty: An Experience Shared by Medieval Jewish and Christian Women'. *Journal of Medieval History* 34 (2008), 146–63.

Calendar of the Close Rolls of the Reign of Henry III, 1247–1251. London: HMSO, 1922.

Calendar of the Liberate Rolls Preserved in the Public Record Office, 1251–1260. London: HMSO, 1951.

Camille, Michael. *Image on the Edge: The Margins of Medieval Art*. London: Reaktion, 1992.

Camille, Michael. 'Manuscript Illumination and the Art of Copulation'. In *Constructing Medieval Sexuality*, ed. Karma Lochrie, Peggy McCracken and James A. Schultz, 58–90. Minneapolis: University of Minnesota Press, 1997.

Camille, Michael. *The Medieval Art of Love: Objects and Subjects of Desire*. New York: Harry N. Abrams, 1998.

Camille, Michael. *Mirror in Parchment: The Luttrell Psalter and the Making of Medieval England*. London: Reaktion, 1998.

Canadé Sautman, Francesca and Pamela Sheingorn, eds. *Same Sex Love and Desire Among Women in the Middle Ages*. New York: Palgrave Macmillan, 2001.

Careri, Maria, Christine Ruby and Ian Short. *Livres et écritures en français et en occitan au XIIe siècle*. Rome: Viella, 2011.
Carpenter, D. A. 'King Henry III and Saint Edward the Confessor: The Origins of the Cult'. *English Historical Review*, 122, 498 (2007), 865–91.
Cavanaugh, Susan H. 'Royal Books: King John to Richard II'. *The Library*, 6th series, 10 (1988), 304–16.
Caviness, Madeline H. *Visualizing Women in the Middle Ages: Sight, Spectacle, and Scopic Economy*. Philadelphia: University of Pennsylvania Press, 2001.
Chandler, Cullen J. 'Barcelona BC 569 and a Carolingian Programme on the Virtues'. *Early Medieval Europe* 18 (2010), 265–91.
Chibnall, Marjorie, ed. and trans. *The Ecclesiastical History of Ordericus Vitalis*, 6 vols. Oxford: Clarendon Press, 1969–80.
Chrétien de Troyes. *Lancelot, The Knight of the Cart*, trans. Burton Raffel with afterword by Joseph J. Duggan. New Haven: Yale University Press, 1997.
Christine de Pizan. *Le livre de la mutacion de Fortune*, ed. Suzanne Solente, 4 vols. Paris: Picard, 1959–66; rpt New York: Johnson Reprint, 1965.
Christine de Pisan. *The Treasure of the City of Ladies or The Book of the Three Virtues*, trans. Sarah Lawson. London: Penguin, 1985.
Christine de Pizan. *Le livre des trois vertus*, ed. Charity Cannon Willard. Paris: Honoré Champion, 1989.
Christine de Pizan. *A Medieval Woman's Mirror of Honor: The Treasury of the City of Ladies*, trans. Charity Cannon Willard, ed. Madeleine Pelner Cosman. New York and Tenafly, NJ: Persea Books and Bard Hall Press, 1989.
Christine de Pizan. *Le livre de l'advision Cristine*, ed. Christine Reno and Liliane Dulac. Études christiniennes, 4. Paris: Champion, 2001.
Christine de Pizan. *The Vision of Christine de Pizan*, trans. Glenda McLeod and Charity Cannon Willard. Woodbridge: Boydell and Brewer, 2005, rpt 2012.
Clanchy, Michael T. 'Learning to Read in the Middle Ages and the Role of Mothers'. In *Studies in the History of Reading*, ed. G. Brooks and A. K. Pugh, 33–9. Reading: Centre for the Teaching of Reading, University of Reading School of Education, with the United Kingdom Reading Association, 1984.
Clanchy, Michael T. *From Memory to Written Record: England 1066–1307*. Oxford: Blackwell, 1993, rpt 1999.
Clanchy, Michael T. 'Images of Ladies with Prayer Books: What do they Signify?' In *The Church and the Book*, ed. R. N. Swanson, 106–22. Woodbridge: Boydell, 2004.
Clanchy, Michael T. 'The ABC Primer: Was it in Latin or English?' In *Vernacularity in England and Wales, c. 1300–1550*, ed. Elizabeth Salter and Helen Wicker, 17–39. Turnhout: Brepols, 2011.
Clanchy, Michael T. 'Did Mothers Teach their Children to Read?' In *Motherhood, Religion, and Society in Medieval Europe, 400–1400: Essays Presented to Henrietta Leyser*, ed. Conrad Leyser and Lesley Smith, 129–54. Farnham: Ashgate, 2011.
Clark, Robert L. A. 'Jousting without a Lance: The Condemnation of Female Homoeroticism in the *Livre des manières*'. In *Same Sex Love and Desire Among Women in the Middle Ages*, ed. Francesca Canadé Sautman and Pamela Sheingorn, 143–77. New York: Palgrave, 2001.
Clark, Willene B. *A Medieval Book of Beasts: The Second-Family Bestiary*. Woodbridge: Boydell, 2006.
Clements, Jill Hamilton. 'The Construction of Queenship in the Illustrated *Estoire de Seint Aedward le Rei*'. *Gesta* 52, 1 (2013), 21–42.
Coldstream, Nicola. 'Eleanor of Castile and the New Jerusalem'. In *Image, Memory and Devotion: Liber Amicorum Paul Crossley*, ed. Zoë Opačić and Achim Timmermann, 225–30. Turnhout: Brepols, 2011.
Collins, Kristen, Peter Kidd and Nancy K. Turner. *The St. Albans Psalter: Painting and Prayer in Medieval England*. Los Angeles: J. Paul Getty Museum, 2013.
Connor, Carolyn Loessel. *Women of Byzantium*. New Haven: Yale University Press, 2004.
Costley, Clare L. 'David, Bathsheba, and the Penitential Psalms'. *Renaissance Quarterly* 57 (2004), 1235–77.
Cotter-Lynch, Margaret and Brad Herzog, eds. *Reading Memory and Identity in the Texts of Medieval European Holy Women*. New York: Palgrave Macmillan, 2012.
Crane, Susan. 'Anglo-Norman Cultures in England, 1066–1460'. In *The Cambridge History of Medieval English Literature*, ed. David Wallace, 35–60. Cambridge: Cambridge University Press, 1999.
Cyrus, Cynthia J. *The Scribes for Women's Convents in Late Medieval Germany*. Toronto: University of Toronto Press, 2009.
Davis, Norman, ed. *Paston Letters and Papers of the Fifteenth Century*, 2 vols. Oxford: Clarendon Press, 1971–6.
D'Avray, David. 'Marriage Ceremonies'. In *Women and Gender in Medieval Europe: An Encyclopedia*, ed. Margaret Schaus, 516–17. New York: Routledge, 2006.
Dean, Ruth J. 'Cultural Relations in the Middle Ages: Nicholas Trevet and Nicholas of Prato'. *Studies in Philology* 45, 4 (1948), 541–64.
Dean, Ruth J. and Maureen B. M. Boulton. *Anglo-Norman Literature: A Guide to Texts and Manuscripts*. Anglo-Norman Text Society, Occasional Publications Series 3. London: Anglo-Norman Text Society, 1999.
de Hamel, Christopher. *A History of Illuminated Manuscripts*, 2nd edn. London and New York: Phaidon, 1994, rpt. 2001.
Denholm-Young, Noel. *History and Heraldry, 1254 to 1320: A Study of the Historical Value of the Rolls of Arms*. Oxford: Clarendon Press, 1965.
Desmond, Marilynn. 'Christine de Pizan: gender, authorship and life-writing'. In *The Cambridge Companion to Medieval French Literature*, ed. Simon Gaunt and Sarah Kay, 123–35. Cambridge: Cambridge University Press, 2008.
Deyermond, Alan. 'Sexual Initiation in the Woman's-Voice Court Lyric'. In *Courtly Literature: Culture and Context; Selected Papers from the 5th Triennial Congress of the International Courtly Literature Society*, Dalfsen, The Netherlands, 9–16 August 1986, ed. Keith Busby and Erik Kooper, 125–58. Amsterdam: John Benjamins, 1990.
Donovan, Claire. *The de Brailes Hours: Shaping the Book of Hours in Thirteenth-Century Oxford*. London: British Library, 1991
Dronke, Peter. *Medieval Latin and the Rise of the European Love-Lyric*, 2 vols. Oxford: Clarendon Press, 1966.
Dronke, Peter. *Women Writers of the Middle Ages: A Critical Study of Texts from Perpetua (d. 203) to Marguerite Porete (d. 1310)*. Cambridge: Cambridge University Press, 1984, rpt 1996.
Duffy, Eamon. *The Stripping of the Altars: Traditional Religion in England, c. 1400–c. 1580*. New Haven: Yale University Press, 1992.
Duffy, Eamon. *Marking the Hours: English People and their Prayers 1240–1570*. New Haven: Yale University Press, 2006.
Eco, Umberto. *On Beauty: A History of a Western Idea*, trans. Alastair McEwen. London: Secker and Warburg, 2004.
Elsakkers, Marianne. 'In Pain You Shall Bear Children (Gen 3:16): Medieval Prayers for a Safe Delivery'. In *Women and Miracle Stories: A Multidisciplinary Exploration*, ed. Anne-Marie Korte, 179–209. Leiden: Brill, 2001.
The Etymologies of Isidore of Seville, ed. and trans. Stephen A. Barney, W. J. Lewis, J. A. Beach and Oliver Berghof. Cambridge: Cambridge University Press, 2006.
Farmer, David Hugh. 'Edward the Confessor'. In *The Oxford Dictionary of Saints*, 2nd edn. Oxford: Oxford University Press, 1987.
Farmer, Sharon. 'Merchant Women and the Administrative Glass Ceiling in Thirteenth-Century Paris'. In *Women and Wealth in Late Medieval Europe*, ed. Theresa Earenfight, 89–108. New York: Palgrave Macmillan, 2010.
Fasoli, Paolo. 'Body Language: Sex-manual Literature from Pietro Aretino's *Sixteen Positions* to Antonio Rocco's *Invitation to Sodomy*'. In *Sex Acts in Early Modern Italy: Practice, Performance, Perversion, Punishment*, ed. Allison M. Levy, 27–42. Farnham: Ashgate, 2010.
Fenster, Thelma S. and Mary Carpenter Erler, eds. *Poems of Cupid, God of Love*. Leiden: Brill, 1990.
Fery-Hue, Françoise. 'Le *Régime du corps* d'Aldebrandin de Sienne: tradition manuscrite et diffusion'. In *Santé, médecine et assistance au Moyen Âge*, Actes du 110e congrès national des sociétés savants, Montpellier, 1985, 113–34. Paris: C.T.H.S., 1987.
Fery-Hue, Françoise. 'Le *Régime du corps* d'Aldebrandin de Sienne: complément à la tradition manuscrite (suite)'. *Scriptorium* 58, 1 (2004), 99–108.
Field, Sean L. 'Marie of Saint-Pol and her Books'. *English Historical Review* 125 (2010), 255–78.
Fiero, Gloria K., Wendy Pfeffer and Mathé Allain, eds and trans. *Three Medieval Views of Women: 'La Contenance des Fames, 'Le Bien des Fames', 'Le Blasme des Fames'*. New Haven: Yale University Press, 1989.
Flanagan, Sabina. *Hildegard of Bingen, 1098–1179: A Visionary Life*. London and New York: Routledge, 1989, rpt 1990.
Flores, Nona C. '"Effigies Amicitiae . . . Veritas Inimicitiae": Antifeminism in the Iconography of the Woman-Headed Serpent in Medieval and Renaissance Art and Literature.' In *Animals in the Middle Ages: A Book of Essays*, ed. Nona C. Flores, 167–95. New York: Garland, 1996.
Forbes-Leith, William, trans. *The Life of St Margaret, Queen of Scotland by Turgot, Bishop of St Andrews*. Edinburgh: William Paterson, 1884.

Foster, Tara. 'Clemence of Barking: reshaping the legend of Saint Catherine of Alexandria.' *Women's Writing* 12 (2005), 13–27.

Fresco, Karen and Anne D. Hedeman, ed. *Collections in Context: The Organization of Knowledge and Community in Europe*. Columbus: Ohio State University Press, 2011.

Friedman, Joan Isobel. 'MS Cotton Claudius B.I.: A Middle English Edition of St Bridget of Sweden's *Liber Celestis*.' In *Prophets Abroad: The Reception of Continental Holy Women in Late-Medieval England*, ed. Rosalynn Voaden, 91–114. Woodbridge: Boydell and Brewer, 1996.

Furnivall, F. J., ed. *Hali Meidenhad: An Alliterative Homily of the Thirteenth Century*. London: Early English Text Society, 1922; rpt New York: Greenwood Press, 1969.

Gameson, Richard. 'The Gospels of Margaret of Scotland and the Literacy of an Eleventh-Century Queen'. In *Women and the Book: Assessing the Visual Evidence*, ed. Jane H. M. Taylor and Lesley Smith, 148–71. London: British Library, 1997.

Gee, Loveday Lewes. *Women, Art and Patronage from Henry III to Edward III: 1216–1377*. Woodbridge: Boydell, 2002.

Gee, Loveday Lewes. 'Patterns of Patronage: Female Initiatives and Artistic Enterprises in England in the 13th and 14th Centuries'. In *Reassessing the Roles of Women as 'Makers' of Medieval Art and Architecture*, 2 vols, ed. Therese Martin, II, 565–631. Leiden: Brill, 2012.

Geffrei Gaimar. *Estoire des Engleis* (*History of the English*), ed. and trans. Ian Short. Oxford: Oxford University Press, 2009.

Gerald of Wales. *The History and Topography of Ireland*, trans. John J. O'Meara. Harmondsworth: Penguin, 1951, rpt 1982.

Girart d'Amiens. *Escanor: Roman arthurien en vers de la fin du XIIIe siècle*, ed. Richard Trachsler, 2 vols. Geneva: Droz, 1994.

Goldberg, P. J. P. 'Work'. In *Women and Gender in Medieval Europe: An Encyclopedia*, ed. Margaret Schaus, 856–9. London and New York: Routledge, 2006.

Gonzalo de Berceo. *Milagros de Nuestra Señora*, ed. Vicente Beltrán, 3rd edn. Barcelona: Planeta, 1990.

Gonzalo de Berceo. *Miracles of Our Lady*, trans. Richard Terry Mount and Annette Grant Cash. Lexington: University Press of Kentucky, 1997.

Goodall, John A. 'Heraldry in the Decoration of English Medieval Manuscripts'. *Antiquaries Journal* 77 (1997), 179–220.

Goodich, M. 'Bartholomaeus Anglicus on Child-Rearing'. *History of Childhood Quarterly* 3 (1975), 75–84.

Gottlieb, Beatrice. 'The Meaning of Clandestine Marriages'. In *Family and Sexuality in French History*, ed. Robert Wheaton and Tamara K. Hareven, 49–83. Philadelphia: University of Pennsylvania Press, 1980.

Green, D. H. *Women Readers in the Middle Ages*. Cambridge: Cambridge University Press, 2007.

Green, Mary Anne Everett. *Lives of the Princesses of England from the Norman Conquest*, vol. II. London: Henry Colburn, 1850.

Green, Monica. 'Women's Medical Practice and Health Care in Medieval Europe'. In *Sisters and Workers in the Middle Ages*, ed. Judith M. Bennett et al., 39–78. Chicago: University of Chicago Press, 1989.

Green, Monica, ed. and trans. *The 'Trotula': A Medieval Compendium of Women's Medicine*. Philadelphia: University of Pennsylvania Press, 2001.

Green, Monica. *Making Women's Medicine: The Rise of Male Authority in Pre-Modern Gynaecology*. Oxford: Oxford University Press, 2008.

Grössinger, Christa. *Picturing Women in Late Medieval and Renaissance Art*. Manchester: Manchester University Press, 1997.

Guillaume de Lorris and Jean de Meun. *The Romance of the Rose*, trans. Charles Dahlberg. Princeton: Princeton University Press, 1995.

Guillaume de Lorris and Jean de Meun. *The Romance of the Rose*, trans. Harry W. Robbins, ed. Charles W. Dunn. Syracuse: Syracuse University Press, 2002.

Gussenhoven, Frances. 'The Serpent with a Matron's Face: Medieval Iconography of Satan in the Garden of Eden'. *European Medieval Drama* 4 (2000), 207–30.

Hamburger, Jeffrey F. 'Review of *Image on the Edge: The Margins of Medieval Art* by Michael Camille'. *The Art Bulletin* 75, 2 (1993), 319–27.

Hamburger, Jeffrey F. *Nuns as Artists: The Visual Culture of a Medieval Convent*. Berkeley and Los Angeles: University of California Press, 1997.

Hamburger, Jeffrey F. 'Another Perspective: The Book of Hours in Germany'. In *Books of Hours Reconsidered*, ed. Sandra Hindman and James H. Marrow, 97–152. London and Turnhout: Harvey Miller, 2013.

Hamilton, Bernard. 'Eleanor of Castile and the Crusading Movement'. *Mediterranean Historical Review* 10 (1995), 92–103.

Harris-Stoertz, Fiona. 'Pregnancy and Childbirth in Twelfth- and Thirteenth-Century French and English Law'. *Journal of the History of Sexuality* 21, 2 (May 2012), 263–81.

Harvey, Barbara. 'The Monks of Westminster and the Old Lady Chapel'. In *Westminster Abbey: The Lady Chapel of Henry VII*, ed. Tim Tatton-Brown and Edward Mortimer, 5–31. Woodbridge: Boydell, 2003.

Henderson, George. 'Bede and the Visual Arts'. In *Studies in English Bible Illustration*, I, 46–75. London: Pindar, 1985.

Henderson, John. *Piety and Charity in Late Medieval Florence*. Oxford: Oxford University Press, 1994.

Henisch, Bridget Ann. *The Medieval Calendar Year*. University Park: Pennsylvania State University Press, 1999.

Herrad of Lansberg. *Hortus deliciarum*, ed. and trans. Aristide D. Caratzas. New Rochelle: Caratzas Brothers, 1977.

Herrad of Lansberg. *Hortus deliciarum*, ed. Rosalie Green. London: Warburg Institute, 1979.

Higgitt, John. *The Murthly Hours: Devotion, Literacy and Luxury in Paris, England and the Gaelic West*. London: British Library, 2000.

Hildebert of Lavardin. *Carmina minora*, ed. A. B. Scott. Leipzig: Teubner, 1969.

Hinde, H., ed. *Vita S. Margaretae Scotorum Reginae* in *Symeonis Dunelmensis Opera et Collectanea* I. Surtees Society 51 (1868), 234–54.

Hodgson, Natasha R. *Women, Crusading and the Holy Land in Historical Narrative*. Woodbridge: Boydell, 2007.

Howell, Margaret. *Eleanor of Provence: Queenship in Thirteenth-Century England*. Oxford: Blackwell, 1998, rpt 2001.

Hult, David F. 'The *Roman de la Rose*, Christine de Pizan, and the *querelle des femmes*'. In *The Cambridge Companion to Medieval Women's Writing*, ed. Carolyn Dinshaw and David Wallace, 184–94. Cambridge: Cambridge University Press, 2003.

Huneycutt, Lois L. 'The Idea of the Perfect Princess: The Life of St. Margaret in the Reign of Matilda II (1100–1118)'. *Anglo-Norman Studies* 12 (1989), 81–97.

Huneycutt, Lois L. '"Proclaiming her dignity abroad": The Literary and Artistic Network of Matilda of Scotland, Queen of England 1100–1118'. In *The Cultural Patronage of Medieval Women*, ed. June Hall McCash, 155–71. Athens: University of Georgia Press, 1996.

Huneycutt, Lois L. *Matilda of Scotland: A Study in Medieval Queenship*. Woodbridge: Boydell, 2003.

Jackson, Deirdre. 'Saint and Simulacra: Images of the Virgin in the *Cantigas de Santa Maria* of Alfonso X of Castile (1252–1284)'. Unpublished PhD thesis, Courtauld Institute of Art, University of London, 2002.

Jackson, Deirdre. *Marvellous to Behold: Miracles in Medieval Manuscripts*. London: British Library, 2007.

Jacobus de Voragine. *The Golden Legend: Readings on the Saints*, 2 vols, trans. William Granger Ryan. Princeton: Princeton University Press, 1993.

Jacquart, Danielle and Claude Thomasset. *Sexuality and Medicine in the Middle Ages*, trans. Matthew Adamson. Cambridge: Polity Press, 1988.

Jaeger, C. Stephen. *Ennobling Love: In Search of a Lost Sensibility*. Philadelphia: University of Pennsylvania Press, 1999.

Jewell, Helen M. *Women in Late Medieval and Reformation Europe 1200–1550*. New York: Palgrave Macmillan, 2007.

John of Howden. *Rossignos*, ed. Glynn Hesketh. London: Anglo-Norman Text Society, 2006.

Joinville. *Vie de Saint Louis*, ed. and trans. Jacques Monfrin. Paris: Garnier, 1995.

Joinville and Villehardouin. *Chronicles of the Crusades*, trans. M. R. B. Shaw. Harmondsworth: Penguin, 1963.

Karras, Ruth Mazo. *Sexuality in Medieval Europe: Doing Unto Others*. 2nd edn. New York and London: Routledge, 2012.

Kauffmann, C. M. 'British Library, Lansdowne Ms. 383: the Shaftesbury Psalter?' In *New Offerings, Ancient Treasures; Studies in Medieval Art for George Henderson*, ed. Paul Binski and William Noel, 256–79. Stroud: Sutton, 2001.

Kennedy, Elspeth. 'The Scribe as Editor'. In *Mélanges de langue et de littérature du moyen âge et de la renaissance offerts à Jean Frappier*, 2 vols, I, 523–31. Geneva: Droz, 1970.

Kersey, Shirley Nelson. *Classics in the Education of Girls and Women*. Metuchen, NJ and London: Scarecrow Press, 1981.

Kinch, Ashby. *Imago Mortis: Mediating Images of Death in Late Medieval Culture*. Leiden: Brill, 2013.

Kinoshita, Sharon and Peggy McCracken. *Marie de France: A Critical Companion*. Woodbridge: D. S. Brewer, 2012.

Kittell, Ellen E. and Mary Suydam, eds. *The Texture of Society: Medieval Women in the Southern Low Countries*. New York and Basingstoke: Palgrave Macmillan, 2004.

Kittell, Ellen E. 'Flanders'. In *Women and Gender in Medieval Europe: An Encyclopedia*, ed. Margaret Schaus, 294–5. New York: Routledge, 2006.

Kjellman, Hilding, ed. *La vie seint Edmund le rei, poème anglo-normand du XIIe siècle*. Göteborg: Wettergren and Kerbor, 1935.

Kline, Daniel T. 'Girls and Boys: Adolescentia: Courtship and Marriage'. In *Women and Gender in Medieval Europe: An Encyclopedia*, ed. Margaret Schaus, 325–7. New York: Routledge, 2006.

König, Eberhard et al. *Das Berliner Stundenbuch der Maria von Burgund und Kaiser Maximilians*. Lachen am Zürichsee: Coron, 1998.

Kralik, Christine. 'Death is Not the End: The Encounter of the Three Living and the Three Dead in the Berlin Hours of Mary of Burgundy and Maximilian I'. In *The Ends of the Body: Identity and Community in Medieval Culture*, ed. Jill Ross and Suzanne Conklin Akbari, 62–85. Toronto: University of Toronto Press, 2013.

Kren, Thomas. 'Looking at Louis XII's Bathsheba'. In *A Masterpiece Reconstructed, The Hours of Louis XII*, ed. Thomas Kren with Mark Evans, 43–61. Los Angeles and London: Getty Publications and British Library, 2005.

Kren, Thomas. 'Bathsheba Imagery in French Books of Hours made for Women, c.1470–1500'. In *The Medieval Book: Glosses from Friends and Colleagues of Christopher de Hamel*, ed. James H. Marrow, Richard A. Linenthal and William Noel, 169–82. Houton: Hes & De Graaf, 2010.

Kren, Thomas and Scot McKendrick, eds. *Illuminating the Renaissance: The Triumph of Flemish Manuscript Painting in Europe*. London and Los Angeles: Royal Academy of Arts and J. Paul Getty Museum, 2003.

Krinsky, Carol Herselle. 'A View of the Palazzo Medici and the Church of San Lorenzo'. *Journal of the Society of Architectural Historians* 28, 2 (1969), 133–5.

Krueger, Roberta L. 'Introduction'. In *The Cambridge Companion to Medieval Romance*, ed. Roberta L. Krueger, 1–9. Cambridge: Cambridge University Press, 2000.

Krueger, Roberta L. 'Questions of Gender in Old French Courtly Romance'. In *The Cambridge Companion to Medieval Romance*, ed. Roberta L. Krueger, 132–49. Cambridge: Cambridge University Press, 2000.

Krueger, Roberta L. 'Marie de France'. In *The Cambridge Companion to Medieval Women's Writing*, ed. Carolyn Dinshaw and David Wallace, 172–83. Cambridge: Cambridge University Press, 2003.

Krug, Rebecca. 'The Fifteen Oes'. In *Cultures of Piety: Medieval English Devotional Literature in Translation*, ed. Anne Clark Bartlett and Thomas Howard Bestul, 107–17. Ithaca: Cornell University Press, 1999.

Kulp-Hill, Kathleen, trans. *Songs of Holy Mary of Alfonso X, The Wise: A Translation of the Cantigas de Santa Maria*. Tempe: Arizona Center for Medieval and Renaissance Studies, 2000.

Kumler, Aden. *Translating Truth: Ambitious Images and Religious Knowledge in Late Medieval France and England*. New Haven: Yale University Press, 2011.

Labande, Edmond-René. *Guibert de Nogent: Autobiographie*. Paris: Les Belles Lettres, 1981.

Laborderie, Olivier de. 'The First Manuals of English History: Two Late Thirteenth-Century Genealogical Rolls of the Kings of England in the Royal Collection'. eBLJ (2014), Article 4.

Landouzy, Louis and Roger Pepin, eds. *Le régime du corps de maître Aldebrandin de Siénne: texte français du XIIIe siecle*. Paris: Honoré Champion, 1911.

Larrington, Carolyne. *Women and Writing in Medieval Europe: A Sourcebook*. London and New York: Routledge, 1995.

Larson, Wendy R. 'Who is the Master of this Narrative? Maternal Patronage of the Cult of St Margaret'. In *Gendering the Master Narrative: Women and Power in the Middle Ages*, ed. Mary C. Erler and Maryanne Kowaleski, 94–104. Ithaca and London: Cornell University Press, 2003.

Lawrence, C.H., trans. and ed. *The Life of St Edmund by Matthew Paris*. Stroud: Alan Sutton, 1996.

Legge, Mary Dominica. 'John Pecham's *Jerarchie*'. *Medium Aevum* 11 (1942), 77–84.

Legge, Mary Dominica. *Anglo-Norman Literature and its Background*. Oxford: Clarendon Press, 1963.

Lekai, Louis Julius. *The Cistercians: Ideals and Reality*. Kent: Kent State University Press, 1977.

Lespinasse, René de and François Bonnardot, eds. *Le livre des métiers d' Étienne Boiteau, XIIIe siècle*. Paris: Imprimerie nationale, 1879; rpt Geneva: Slatkine Reprints, 1980.

Lewis, Gertrud Jaron. *By Women, for Women, about Women: The Sister-Books of Fourteenth-Century Germany*. Toronto: Pontifical Institute of Mediaeval Studies, 1996.

Lewis, Suzanne. *The Art of Matthew Paris in the* Chronica Majora. Berkeley and Los Angeles: University of California Press, 1987.

Leyser, Conrad and Lesley Smith, eds. *Motherhood, Religion, and Society in Medieval Europe, 400–1400: Essays Presented to Henrietta Leyser*. Farnham: Ashgate, 2011.

Leyser, Henrietta. *Medieval Women: A Social History of Women in England, 450–1500*. London: Phoenix, 1996.

Lowden, John. *The Making of the Bibles moralisées*, 2 vols, I. *The Manuscripts*, II. *The Book of Ruth*. University Park: Pennsylvania State University Press, 2000.

Lowden, John. 'The Apocalypse in the Early-Thirteenth-Century Bibles Moralisées: A Re-Assessment'. In *Prophecy, Apocalypse and the Day of Doom, Proceedings of the 2000 Harlaxton Symposium*, Harlaxton Medieval Studies, 12, ed. Nigel Morgan, 195–217. Donington: Shaun Tyas, 2004.

Lowden, John. *Treasures Known and Unknown in the British Library*, virtual exhibition (http://www.bl.uk/catalogues/illuminatedmanuscripts/TourKnownA.asp) based on a keynote address given at a British Library conference, 'Treasures Known and Unknown', 2–3 July 2007.

Lowden, John. 'The Holkham Bible Picture Book and the Bible Moralisée'. In *The Medieval Book: Glosses from Friends and Colleagues of Christopher de Hamel*, ed. James H. Marrow, Richard A. Linenthal and William Noel, 75–83. Houton: Hes & De Graaf, 2010.

Luard, H. R., ed. *Matthei Parisiensis Chronica Majora*. 7 vols. London: Rolls Series, 1872–83.

Lusignan, Serge. 'French Language in Contact with English: Social Context and Linguistic Change (mid-13th–14th centuries)'. In *Language and Culture in Medieval Britain: The French of England c. 1100–c. 1500*, ed. Jocelyn Wogan-Browne, 19–30. Woodbridge: York Medieval Press with Boydell, 2009.

Lysons, Samuel. 'Copy of a Roll of Purchases made for the Tournament of Windsor Park, in the sixth year of King Edward the First, preserved in the Record Office of the Tower'. *Archaeologia* 17 (1814), 297–310.

Mandach, André de. 'A Royal Wedding Present in the Making'. *Nottingham Medieval Studies* 18 (1974), 56–76.

Marie de France. *Les Lais de Marie de France*, ed. Jean Rychner. Paris: Champion, 1966.

Marie de France. *Fables*, ed. and trans. Harriet Spiegel. Toronto: University of Toronto Press, 1987.

Marie de France. *Saint Patrick's Purgatory*. Medieval and Renaissance Texts and Studies, 94, trans. Michael J. Curley. Binghamton, NY: Center for Medieval and Renaissance Studies, 1993.

Marie de France. *L'espurgatoire seint Patriz*, ed. Yolande de Pontfarcy. Louvain: Peeters, 1995.

Marrow, James H. *Pictorial Invention in Netherlandish Manuscript Illumination of the Late Middle Ages: The Play of Illusion and Meaning*. Paris and Leuven: Peeters, 2005.

Martin, Therese, ed. *Reassessing the Roles of Women as 'Makers' of Medieval Art and Architecture*, 2 vols. Leiden: Brill, 2012.

Martin, Therese. 'Exceptions and Assumptions: Women in Medieval Art History'. In *Reassessing the Roles of Women as 'Makers' of Medieval Art and Architecture*, 2 vols, ed. Therese Martin, I, 1–33. Leiden: Brill, 2012.

Martínez Díez, Gonzalo. *Fernando III, 1217–1252*. Reyes de Castilla y León 1. Palencia: Editorial La Olmeda for the Diputación Provincial de Palencia, 1993.

Mattelaer, Johan J. 'The Phallus Tree: A Medieval and Renaissance Phenomenon'. *Journal of Sexual Medicine* 7, 2 (2010), 846–51.

Matthew Paris. *La Estoire de seint Aedward le rei*, ed. Kathryn Young Wallace. ANTS 41. London: Anglo-Norman Text Society, 1983.

Matthew Paris. *The History of St Edward the King*, trans. Thelma S. Fenster and Jocelyn Wogan-Browne. The French of England Translation Series 1. Medieval and Renaissance Texts and Studies 341. Tempe: Arizona Center for Medieval and Renaissance Studies, 2008.

McCash, June Hall, ed. *The Cultural Patronage of Medieval Women*. Athens: University of Georgia Press, 1996.

McDonnell, Ernest W. *The Beguines and Beghards in Medieval Culture: With Special Emphasis on the Belgian Scene*. New York: Octagon Books, 1969.

McKendrick, Scot, John Lowden and Kathleen Doyle, eds. *Royal Manuscripts: The Genius of Illumination*. London: British Library, 2011.

McKitterick, David et al. *The Trinity Apocalypse*. London: British Library, 2005.

McNamara, Jo Ann and John E. Halborg, trans. *The Rule of Donatus of Besançon*, 2nd edn. Toronto: Peregrina, 1993.

McNamara, Martin. 'The Psalms in the Irish Church'. In *The Bible as Book: The Manuscript Tradition*, ed. John L. Sharpe III and Kimberley van Kampen, 89–103. London: British Library, 1998.

Meale, Carol M. 'Literacy and Reading: Vernacular'. In *Women and Gender in Medieval Europe: An Encyclopedia*, ed. Margaret Schaus, 471–3. London and New York: Routledge, 2006.

Mews, Constant J. *Abelard and Heloise*. Oxford: Oxford University Press, 2005.

Michael, M. A. 'English Illuminators *c.* 1190–1450: A Survey from Documentary Sources'. In *English Manuscript Studies 1100–1700*, vol. 4, ed. Peter Beal and Jeremy Griffiths, 62–113. London and Toronto: British Library and University of Toronto Press, 1993.

Monroe, Elizabeth. 'Dangerous Passages and Spiritual Redemption in the *Hortus Deliciarum*'. In *Push Me, Pull You: Imaginative and Emotional Interaction in Late Medieval and Renaissance Art*, 2 vols, ed. Sarah Blick and Laura D. Gelfand, I, 39–74. Leiden: Brill, 2011.

Montaiglon, M. Anatole de, ed. *Le livre du chevalier de La Tour Landry pour l'enseignement de ses filles, publié d'après les manuscrits de Paris et de Londres*. Paris: Jannet, 1854; rpt Millwood: Kraus, 1982.

Morgan, Nigel J. *Early Gothic Manuscripts 1190–1250 (I)*. A Survey of Manuscripts Illuminated in the British Isles 4. London: Harvey Miller, 1982.

Morgan, Nigel J. *Early Gothic Manuscripts 1250–1285 (II). A Survey of Manuscripts Illuminated in the British Isles* 4. London: Harvey Miller, 1988.

Morgan, Nigel J. 'Patrons and their Devotions in the Historiated Initials and the Full-Page Miniatures of 13th-Century English Psalters'. In *The Illuminated Psalter: Studies in the Content, Purpose and Placement of its Images*, ed. F. O. Büttner, 309–22. London: Harvey Miller, 2004.

Morgan, Nigel J. *The Douce Apocalypse: Picturing the End of the World in the Middle Ages*. Oxford: Bodleian Library, 2006.

Morgan, Nigel J. 'English Books of Hours, *c.* 1240–*c.* 1480'. In *Books of Hours Reconsidered*, ed. Sandra Hindman and James H. Marrow, 65–95. London and Turnhout: Harvey Miller, 2013.

Morgan, Nigel J. and Rodney M. Thomson, eds. *The Cambridge History of the Book in Britain, Volume 2: 1100–1400*. Cambridge: Cambridge University Press, 2008.

Muratova, Xénia. 'The Decorated Manuscripts of the Bestiary of Phillipe de Thaon (the MS 3466 from the Royal Library in Copenhagen and the MS 249 in the Merton College Library, Oxford) and the Problem of the Illustrations of the Medieval Poetical Bestiary'. In *Third International Beast Epic, Fable and Fabliau Colloquium, Munster 1979: Proceedings*, ed. Jan Goossens and Timothy Sodmann, 217–46. Cologne: Böhlau, 1981.

Musson, Anthony. 'Images of Marriage: A Comparison of Law, Custom and Practice in Medieval Europe'. In *Regional Variations in Matrimonial Law and Custom in Europe, 1150–1600*, ed. Mia Korpiola, 117–46. Leiden: Brill, 2011.

Naughton, Joan. 'A Minimally-intrusive Presence: Portraits in Illustrations for Prayers to the Virgin'. In *Medieval Texts and Images: Studies of Manuscripts from the Middle Ages*, ed. Margaret M. Manion and Bernard J. Muir, 111–26. Chur: Harwood Academic, 1991.

Neel, Carol, trans. *The Handbook for William: A Carolingian Woman's Counsel for Her Son*. Lincoln: University of Nebraska Press, 1991.

Neel, Carol. 'Dhuoda'. In *Women and Gender in Medieval Europe: An Encyclopedia*, ed. Margaret Schaus, 209–10. London and New York: Routledge, 2006.

Noonan, John T. *Contraception: A History of its Treatment by the Catholic Theologians and Canonists*. Cambridge, MA: Harvard University Press, 1965.

Oakes, Catherine. *Ora pro nobis: The Virgin as Intercessor in Medieval Art and Devotion*. London: Harvey Miller, 2008.

O'Callaghan, Joseph F. *Alfonso X and the Cantigas de Santa Maria: A Poetic Biography*. Leiden: Brill, 1998.

O'Donnell, Thomas, Matthew Townend and Elizabeth M. Tyler, 'European literature and eleventh-century England'. In *The Cambridge History of Early Medieval English Literature*, ed. Clare A. Lees, 607–36. Cambridge: Cambridge University Press, 2012.

Oliver, Judith H. 'A Primer of Thirteenth-Century German Convent Life: The Psalter as Office and Mass Book (London, BL, MS Add 60629)'. In *The Illuminated Psalter: Studies in the Content, Purpose and Placement of its Images*, ed. F. O. Büttner, 259–70. Turnhout: Brepols, 2004.

Oliver, Judith H. '*Te Matrem Laudamus*: The Many Roles of Mary in Liège Psalter-Hours'. In *The Cambridge Illuminations: The Conference Papers*, ed. Stella Panayotova, 159–72. London and Turnhout: Harvey Miller, 2007.

Orme, Nicholas. *From Childhood to Chivalry: The Education of the English Kings and Aristocracy 1066–1530*. London and New York: Methuen, 1984.

Orme, Nicholas. *Medieval Children*. New Haven and London: Yale University Press, 2001.

Orme, Nicholas. *Medieval Schools: From Roman Britain to Renaissance England*. New Haven and London: Yale University Press, 2006.

Parsons, John Carmi. *The Court and Household of Eleanor of Castile in 1290: An Edition of British Library Additional Manuscript 35294*. Toronto: Pontifical Institute of Mediaeval Studies, 1977.

Parsons, John Carmi. *Eleanor of Castile: Queen and Society in Thirteenth-Century England*. Basingstoke: Macmillan, 1995.

Parsons, John Carmi. 'Of Queens, Courts, and Books: Reflections on the Literary Patronage of Thirteenth-Century Plantagenet Queens.' In *The Cultural Patronage of Medieval Women*, ed. June Hall McCash, 175–201. Athens: University of Georgia Press, 1996.

Payer, Pierre J. *Sex and the New Medieval Literature of Confession, 1150–1300*. Toronto: Pontifical Institute of Mediaeval Studies, 2009.

Pernoud, Régine. *Joan of Arc By Herself and Her Witnesses*, trans. Edward Hyams. London: Macdonald, 1964; rpt Lanham: Rowman & Littlefield, 1994.

Philippe de Thaon. *Comput (MS BL Cotton Nero A V)*, Anglo-Norman Text Society, Plain Series 2, ed. Ian Short. London: Anglo-Norman Text Society, 1984.

Power, Eileen. *The Goodman of Paris*. London: George Routledge & Sons, 1928.

Power, Eileen (published posthumously). *Medieval Women*, ed. Michael Moïssey Postan. Cambridge: Cambridge University Press, 2012.

Prestwich, Michael. *Edward I*, 2nd edn. Berkeley and Los Angeles: University of California Press and London: Methuen, 1988.

Radice, Betty, trans. *The Letters of Abelard and Heloise*. London: Penguin, 1974.

Randall, Lilian M. C. *Images in the Margins of Gothic Manuscripts*. Berkeley and Los Angeles: University of California Press, 1966.

Reinburg, Virginia. *French Books of Hours: Making an Archive of Prayer, c. 1400–1600*. Cambridge: Cambridge University Press, 2012.

Reinburg, Virginia. 'An Archive of Prayer: The Book of Hours in Manuscript and Print'. In *Manuscripta Illuminata: Approaches to Understanding Medieval and Renaissance Manuscripts*, ed. Colum Hourihane, 221–39. University Park: Pennsylvania State University Press, 2014.

Reno, Christine. 'Christine de Pizan's *Enseignemens moraux*: Good Advice for Several Generations'. (2005), http://www.pizan.lib.ed.ac.uk/morauxnov05.pdf.

Rieger, Angelica. 'Was Bieiris de Romans Lesbian? Women's Relations with Each Other in the World of the Troubadours'. In *The Voice of the Trobairitz: Perspectives on the Women Troubadours*, ed. William D. Paden, 73–94. Philadelphia: University of Pennsylvania Press, 1989.

Rigg, A. G. *Gawain on Marriage: The textual tradition of the 'De coniuge non ducenda'*. Toronto: Pontifical Institute of Mediaeval Studies, 1986.

Robert de Blois, son oeuvre didactique et narrative. Étude linguistique et littéraire, suivie d'une édition critique de l'Enseignement des Princes et du Chastoiement des Dames, ed. John Fox. Paris: Nizet, 1950.

Robertson, Duncan, 'Writing in the Textual Community: Clemence of Barking's Life of St Catherine'. *French Forum* 21 (1996), 5–28.

Roff, Shelley E. '"Appropriate to Her Sex"? Women's Participation on the Construction Site in Medieval and Early Modern Europe.' In *Women and Wealth in Late Medieval Europe*, ed. Theresa Earenfight, 109–34. New York: Palgrave Macmillan, 2010.

Ross, Sarah Gwyneth. *The Birth of Feminism: Woman as Intellect in Renaissance Italy and England*. Cambridge, MA: Harvard University Press, 2009.

Rouse, Richard H. and Mary A. Rouse, *Manuscripts and their Makers: Commercial Book Producers in Medieval Paris, 1200–1500*, 2 vols. London: Harvey Miller, 2000.

Roy, Maurice, ed. *Oeuvres poétiques de Christine de Pisan*, 3 vols. Paris: Firmin Didot, 1886–96.

Rubin, Miri. *Mother of God: A History of the Virgin Mary*. New Haven: Yale University Press, 2009.

Rudy, Kathryn M. 'An Illustrated Mid-Fifteenth-Century Primer for a Flemish Girl: British Library, Harley MS 3828'. *Journal of the Warburg and Courtauld Institutes* 69 (2006), 51–94.

Rudy, Kathryn M. 'Children and Domestic Interiors in the Miniatures by the Master of Catherine of Cleves'. In *From the Hand of the Master: The Hours of Catherine of Cleeves*, ed. Anne Margreet W. As-Vijvers, trans. Kathryn M. Rudy, 62–78. Antwerp: Ludion, 2009.

Rupp, Leila J. *Sapphistries: A Global History of Love Between Women*. New York and London: New York University Press, 2009.
Rushforth, Rebecca. *St. Margaret of Scotland's Gospel-Book: The Favourite Book of an Eleventh-Century Queen of Scots* Oxford: Bodleian Library, 2007.
Russell, Delbert W. 'The Cultural Context of the French Prose *remaniement* of the Life of Edward the Confessor by a Nun of Barking Abbey'. In *Language and Culture in Medieval Britain: The French of England c. 1100–c. 1500*, ed. Jocelyn Wogan-Browne, 290–302. Woodbridge: York Medieval Press, 2009.
Russell, Delbert W. '"Sun num n'i vult dire a ore": Identity Matters at Barking Abbey'. In *Barking Abbey and Medieval Literary Culture: Authorship and Authority in a Female Community*, ed. Jennifer N. Brown and Donna Alfano Bussell, 117–34. Woodbridge: York Medieval Press with Boydell, 2012.
Samples, Susann. 'Guinevere: A Re-Appraisal'. In *Lancelot and Guinevere: A Casebook*, ed. Lori J. Walters, 219–28. New York: Routledge, 1996.
Sand, Alexa. 'The Fairest of them all: Reflections on some Fourteenth-Century Mirrors'. In *Push Me, Pull You: Imaginative and Emotional Interaction in Late Medieval and Renaissance Art*, 2 vols, ed. Sarah Blick and Laura D. Gelfand, I, 529–59. Leiden: Brill, 2011.
Sand, Alexa. *Vision, Devotion, and Self-Representation in Late Medieval Art*. Cambridge: Cambridge University Press, 2014.
Sandler, Lucy Freeman. *The Psalter of Robert de Lisle in the British Library*. London: Harvey Miller, 1983.
Sandler, Lucy Freeman. *Gothic Manuscripts 1285–1385. A Survey of Manuscripts Illuminated in the British Isles* 5. 2 Vols. London: Harvey Miller, 1986.
Sandler, Lucy Freeman. *Omne Bonum: A Fourteenth-Century Encyclopedia of Universal Knowledge*, British Library, MSS Royal 6 EVI–6 EVII. 2 Vols. London: Harvey Miller, 1996.
Scase, Wendy. 'St Anne and the Education of the Virgin: Literary and Artistic Traditions and their Implications'. In *England in the Fourteenth Century: Proceedings of the 1991 Harlaxton Symposium*, ed. N. Rogers, 81–96. Stamford: Paul Watkins, 1993.
Schaus, Margaret, ed. *Women and Gender in Medieval Europe: An Encyclopedia*. London and New York: Routledge, 2006.
Scheepsma, Wybren. '"For herby I hope to rouse some piety": Books of Sisters from Convents and Sister-Houses associated with the *Devotio Moderna* in the Low Countries'. In *Women, the Book and the Godly: Selected Proceedings of the St Hilda's Conference, 1993*, vol. I, ed. Lesley Smith and Jane H. M. Taylor, 27–40. Woodbridge: Brewer, 1995.
Schmitt, Francis S., ed. *S. Anselmi Cantuariensis archiepiscopi opera omnia*, 6 vols. Stuttgart: Bad Canstatt, 1946–61, rpt Fromann 1968.
Schulze-Busacker, Elizabeth. 'Christine de Pizan, *Les Enseignements moraux*'. In *Plaist vos oïr bone cançon vaillant? Mélanges offerts a François Suard*, ed. Dominique Boutet et al., 831–44. Lille: Université Charles-de-Gaulle, n.d.
Sciacca, Christine. *Building the Medieval World*. Los Angeles: J. Paul Getty Museum and London: British Library, 2010.
Scot, Margaret. *Medieval Dress and Fashion*. London: British Library, 2007.
Scott, Kathleen L. *Later Gothic Manuscripts 1390–1490*, A Survey of Manuscripts Illuminated in the British Isles, 6. 2 Vols. London: Harvey Miller, 1996.
Scott-Stokes, Charity. *Women's Books of Hours in Medieval England: Selected Texts Translated from Latin, Anglo-Norman French and Middle English*. Woodbridge: D.S. Brewer, 2006.
Sellevold, Berit J. 'Child Burials and Children's Status in Medieval Norway'. In *Youth and Age in the Medieval North*, ed. Shannon Lewis-Simpson, 57–71. Leiden: Brill, 2008.
Shahar, Shulamith. *The Fourth Estate: A History of Women in the Middle Ages*, 2nd rev. edn. trans. Chaya Galai, New York and London: Routledge, 2003.
Sheingorn, Pamela. '"The Wise Mother": The Image of St. Anne Teaching the Virgin Mary'. *Gesta* 32, 1 (1993), 69–80.
Short, Ian. 'Denis Piramus and the Truth of Marie's *Lais*'. *Cultura Neolatina* 67 (2007), 319–40.
Simons, Walter. *Cities of Ladies: Beguine Communities in the Medieval Low Countries, 1200–1565*. Philadelphia: University of Pennsylvania Press, 2001.
Smith, Kathryn A. *Art, Identity and Devotion in Fourteenth-Century England: Three Women and their Books of Hours*. London: British Library, 2003.
Smith, Kathryn A. *The Taymouth Hours: Stories and the Construction of the Self in Late Medieval England*. London: British Library, 2012.
Smith, Susan L. *The Power of Women: A Topos in Medieval Art and Literature*. Philadelphia: University of Pennsylvania Press, 1995.
Södergård, Östen, ed. *La Vie d'Edouard le confesseur, poème anglo-normand du XIIe siècle*. Uppsala: Almquist and Wiksells, 1948.
Stahl, Harvey. 'Bathsheba and the Kings: The Beatus Initial in the Psalter of Saint Louis (Paris, BNF, ms. lat. 10525)'. In *The Illuminated Psalter: Studies in the Content, Purpose and Placement of its Images*, ed. F. O. Büttner (London: Harvey Miller, 2004), 427–34.
Stahl, Harvey. *Picturing Kingship: History and Painting in the Psalter of Saint Louis*. University Park: Pennsylvania State University Press, 2008.
Stanton, Anne Rudloff. 'Turning the Pages: Marginal Narratives and Devotional Practice in Gothic Prayerbooks'. In *Push Me, Pull You: Imaginative and Emotional Interaction in Late Medieval and Renaissance Art*, 2 vols, ed. Sarah Blick and Laura D. Gelfand, I, 75–121. Leiden: Brill, 2011.
Stanton, Anne Rudloff. 'Design, Devotion, and Durability in Gothic Prayerbooks'. In *Manuscripta Illuminata: Approaches to Understanding Medieval and Renaissance Manuscripts*, ed. Colum Hourihane, 87–107. University Park: Pennsylvania State University Press, 2014.
Stejskal, Karel. 'Die wundertätigen Bilder und Grabmäler in Böhmen zur Zeit der Luxemburger'. In *King John of Luxembourg (1296–1346) and the Art of His Era*. Proceedings of the International Conference, Prague, 16–20 September 1996, ed. Klara Benesovskà, 270–77. Prague: KLP-Koniasch Latin Press, 1998.
Stones, Alison. 'Illustrating Lancelot and Guinevere'. In *Lancelot and Guinevere: A Casebook*, ed. Lori J. Walters, 125–57. New York: Routledge, 2002.
Stones, Alison. *Gothic Manuscripts, 1260–1320 (I)*. A Survey of Manuscripts Illuminated in France. 2 Vols. London: Harvey Miller, 2013.
Stones, Alison. *Gothic Manuscripts, c. 1260–1320 (II)*. A Survey of Manuscripts Illuminated in France. 2 Vols. London: Harvey Miller, 2014.
Stuard, Susan Mosher. 'Dowry and Other Marriage Gifts'. In *Women and Gender in Medieval Europe: An Encyclopedia*, ed. Margaret Schaus, 229–31. London and New York: Routledge, 2006.
Sutton, Anne F. and Livia Visser-Fuchs. 'The Cult of Angels in Late Fifteenth-Century England: An Hours of the Guardian Angel Presented to Queen Elizabeth Woodville'. In *Women and the Book: Assessing the Visual Evidence*, ed. Jane H. M. Taylor and Lesley Smith, 230–65. London: British Library, 1997.
Taglia, Karen. 'Delivering a Christian Identity: Midwives in Northern French Synodal Legislation, *c.* 1200–1500'. In *Religion and Medicine in the Middle Ages*, ed. Peter Biller and Joseph Ziegler, 77–90. York: York Medieval Press, 2001.
Talbot, C. H., ed. and trans. *The Life of Christina of Markyate: A Twelfth-Century Recluse*. Oxford Medieval Texts. Oxford: Clarendon Press, 1959; rev. by Samuel Fanous and Henrietta Leyser. Oxford: Oxford University Press, 2008.
Taylor, Andrew. *Textual Situations: Three Medieval Manuscripts and Their Readers*. Philadelphia: University of Pennsylvania Press, 2002.
Taylor, Andrew. 'The French Self-Presentation of an English Mastiff: John Talbot's Book of Chivalry'. In *Language and Culture in Medieval Britain: The French of England, c. 1100–c. 1500*, ed. Jocelyn Wogan-Browne et al., 444–56. Woodbridge: Boydell, 2009.
Thiebaux, Marcelle, ed. and trans. *Dhuoda: Handbook for Her Warrior Son*, Cambridge Medieval Classics 8. Cambridge: Cambridge University Press, 1998.
Thomasset, Claude. 'The Nature of Women'. In *A History of Women in the West: II. Silences of the Middle Ages*, ed. Christiane Klapisch-Zuber, 43–69. Cambridge, MA: Belknap Press, 1992.
Thomson, Rodney M. 'Monastic and Cathedral Book Production'. In *The Cambridge History of the Book in Britain, Volume 2: 1100–1400*, ed. Nigel Morgan and Rodney M. Thomson, 136–67. Cambridge: Cambridge University Press, 2008.
Thorpe, Lewis. 'Mastre Richard, a Thirteenth-century Translator of the "De re militari" of Vegetius'. *Scriptorium* 6 (1952), 39–50.
Thorpe, Lewis. 'Mastre Richard at the Skirmish of Kenilworth?'. *Scriptorium* 7 (1953), 120–21.
Tristram, E.W. and Monica Bardswell. *English Medieval Wall Painting: The Thirteenth Century*. 2 Vols. Oxford: Oxford University Press, 1950.
Udry, Susan. 'Robert de Blois and Geoffroy de la Tour Landry on Feminine Beauty: Two Late Medieval French Conduct Books for Women'. *Essays in Medieval Studies* 19 (2002), 90–102.
Underhill, Frances A. 'Elizabeth de Burgh: Connoisseur and Patron'. In *The Cultural Patronage of Medieval Women*, ed. June Hall McCash, 266–87. Athens: University of Georgia Press, 1996.
Vallet de Viriville, Auguste. *La bibliothèque d'Isabeau de Bavière, femme de Charles VI, roi de France. Suivi de la notice d'un livre d'heures qui parait*

avoir appartenu à cette princesse. Paris: J. Techener, 1858.
van Buren, Anne. *Illuminating Fashion: Dress in the Art of Medieval France and the Netherlands, 1325–1515*, ed. Roger S. Wieck. New York: Morgan Library and Museum, 2011.
Varty, Kenneth, ed. *Christine de Pisan's Ballades, Rondeaux and Virelais: An Anthology*. Leicester: Leicester University Press, 1965.
Vincent, Nicholas. 'The Great Lost Library of England's Medieval Kings'. In *1000 Years of Royal Books and Manuscripts*, ed. Kathleen Doyle and Scot McKendrick, 73–112. London: British Library, 2013.
Walberg, Emmanuel, ed. *Le Bestiaire de Philippe de Thaün*. Lund: H. J. Möller, 1900.
Walker-Meikle, Kathleen. *Medieval Dogs*. London: British Library, 2013.
Walters, Barbara R., Vincent Corrigan and Peter T. Ricketts, eds. *The Feast of Corpus Christi*. University Park: Pennsylvania State University Press, 2006.
Walters, Barbara R. 'The Feast and its Founder'. In *The Feast of Corpus Christi*, ed. Barbara R. Walters, Vincent Corrigan and Peter T. Ricketts, 3–54. University Park: Pennsylvania State University Press, 2006.
Walters, Barbara R. 'Introduction to Mosan Psalters'. In *The Feast of Corpus Christi*, ed. Barbara R. Walters, Vincent Corrigan and Peter T. Ricketts, 429–44. University Park: Pennsylvania State University Press, 2006.
Walters, Lori J., ed. *Lancelot and Guinevere: A Casebook*. New York: Routledge, 2002.
Ward, Jennifer C. *Women of the English Nobility and Gentry, 1066–1500*. Manchester: Manchester University Press, 1995.
Ward, Jennifer C., ed. *Elizabeth de Burgh, Lady of Clare (1295–1360): household and other records*. Woodbridge: Boydell, 2014.
Weston, L. M. C. 'Women's Medicine, Women's Magic: The Old English Metrical Childbirth Charms'. *Modern Philology* 92 (1995), 279–93.
Whalen, Logan E. 'The Prologues and the Epilogues of Marie de France'. In *A Companion to Marie de France*, Brill's Companions to the Christian Tradition, vol. 2, ed. Logan E. Whalen, 1–30. Leiden: Brill, 2011.
Whalen, Logan E., ed. *A Companion to Marie de France*, Brill's Companions to the Christian Tradition, vol. 2. Leiden: Brill, 2011.
Whatley, Laura Julinda. 'Romance, Crusade, and the Orient in King Henry III of England's Royal Chambers'. *Viator* 44, 3 (2013), 175–98.
Wheeler, Bonnie and John C. Parsons, eds. *Eleanor of Aquitaine: Lord and Lady*. New York: Palgrave Macmillan, 2002.
Wieck, Roger S. *Time Sanctified: The Book of Hours in Medieval Art and Life*. New York: George Braziller, 1988.
Wieck, Roger S. 'Bibliophilic Jealousy and the Manuscript Patronage of Jean, duc de Berry'. In *The Limbourg Brothers: Nijmegen Masters at the French Court, 1400–1416*, ed. R. Dückers and P. Roelofs, 121–34. Ghent: Ludion, 2005.
Wiesner-Hanks, Merry E. *Women and Gender in Early Modern Europe*, 3rd edn. Cambridge: Cambridge University Press, 2008, rpt 2011.
Willard, Charity Cannon. *Christine de Pizan: Her Life and Works*. New York: Persea, 1984.
Willey, Russ. *London Gazetteer*. Edinburgh: Chambers, 2006.
William of Malmesbury. *Gesta regum Anglorum*, ed. and trans. R. A. B. Mynors, completed by R. M. Thomson and M. Winterbottom, 2 vols. Oxford: Clarendon Press, 1998–1999.
Wilson, Stephen. *The Magical Universe: Everyday Ritual and Magic in Pre-Modern Europe*. London: Hambledon, 2000.
Winstead, Karen A., ed. and trans. *Chaste Passions: Medieval English Virgin Martyr Legends*. Ithaca and London: Cornell University Press, 2000.
Wogan-Browne, Jocelyn and Glyn S. Burgess, trans. *Virgin Lives and Holy Deaths: Two Exemplary Biographies for Anglo-Norman Women*. London: Everyman, 1996.
Wolfthal, Diane. 'The Sexuality of the Medieval Comb'. In *Thresholds of Medieval Visual Culture: Liminal Spaces*, ed. Elina Gertsman and Jill Stevenson, 176–94. Woodbridge: Boydell, 2012.
Wolfthal, Diane. 'Sin or Sexual Pleasure? A Little-Known Bather in a Flemish Book of Hours'. In *The Meanings of Nudity in Medieval Art*, ed. Sherry C. M. Lindquist, 279–97. Farnham: Ashgate, 2012.
Woolgar, C. M. *The Great Household in Late Medieval England*. New Haven: Yale University Press, 1999.
Wright, Thomas, ed. *Popular Treatises on Science Written During the Middle Ages in Anglo-Saxon, Anglo-Norman, and English*. London: Historical Society of Science, 1841.
Wright, Thomas and James Orchard Halliwell, eds. *Reliquiae Antiquae: scraps from ancient manuscripts, illustrating chiefly early English literature and the English language*, 2 vols. London: John Russell Smith, 1845.
Wrightson, Kellinde, ed. *Fourteenth Century Icelandic Verse on the Virgin Mary*. London: Viking Society for Northern Research, University College London, 2001.
Zimbalist, Barbara. 'Imitating the Imagined: Clemence of Barking's *Life of St. Catherine*'. In *Reading, Memory and Identity in the Texts of Medieval European Holy Women*, ed. Margaret Cotter-Lynch and Brad Herzog, 105–34. New York: Palgrave Macmillan, 2012.

INDEX OF MANUSCRIPTS

Figures in italics refer to pages with illustrations

INDEX

Figures in italics refer to pages with illustrations